INJUSTICE

GODS AMONG US: YEAR TWO

VOLUME 1

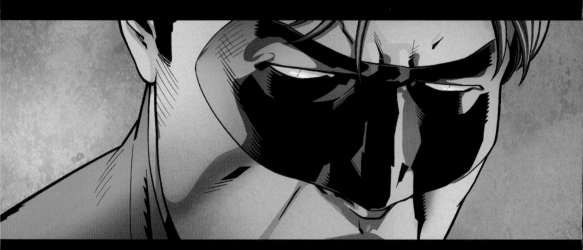

David Lopez & Santi Casas of Ikari Studio
Cover Artists

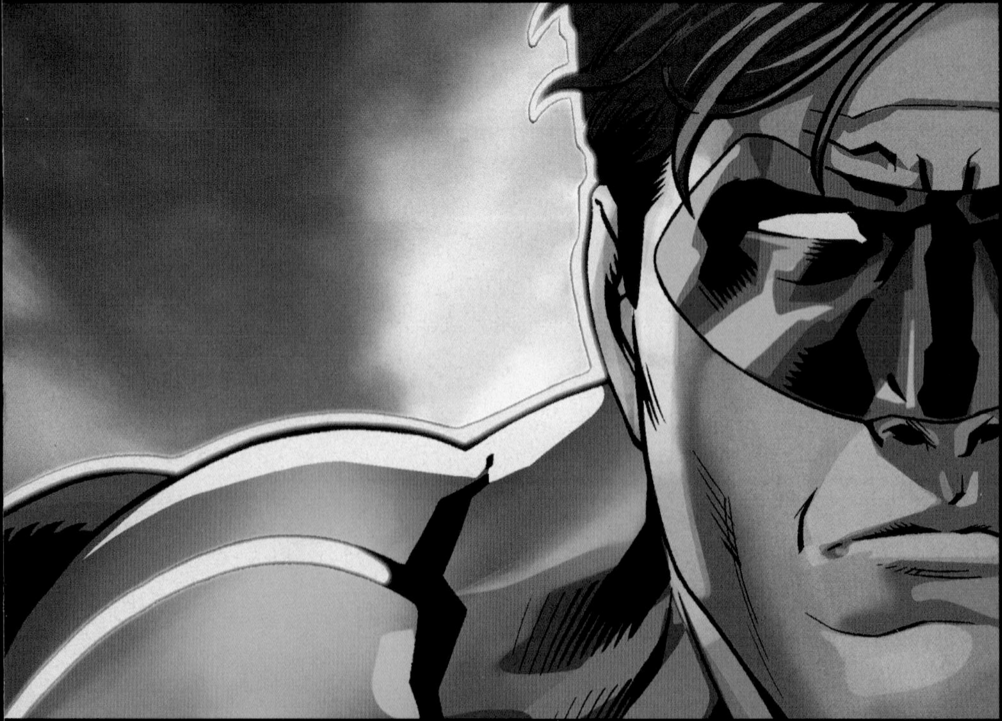

STICE

U S: YEAR TWO

VOLUME 1

Jim Chadwick Editor – Original Series
Aniz Ansari Assistant Editor – Original Series
Rachel Pinnelas Editor
Robbin Brosterman Design Director – Books
Louis Prandi Publication Design

Hank Kanalz Senior VP – Vertigo & Integrated Publishing

Diane Nelson President
Dan DiDio and Jim Lee Co-Publishers
Geoff Johns Chief Creative Officer
Amit Desai Senior VP – Marketing & Franchise Management
Amy Genkins Senior VP – Business & Legal Affairs
Nairi Gardiner Senior VP – Finance
Jeff Boison VP – Publishing Planning
Mark Chiarello VP – Art Direction & Design
John Cunningham VP – Marketing
Terri Cunningham VP – Editorial Administration
Larry Ganem VP – Talent Relations & Services
Alison Gill Senior VP – Manufacturing & Operations
Jay Kogan VP – Business & Legal Affairs, Publishing
Jack Mahan VP – Business Affairs, Talent
Nick Napolitano VP – Manufacturing Administration
Sue Pohja VP – Book Sales
Fred Ruiz VP – Manufacturing Operations
Courtney Simmons Senior VP – Publicity
Bob Wayne Senior VP – Sales

Library of Congress Cataloging-in-Publication Data

Taylor, Tom, 1978- author.
  Injustice : Gods Among Us Year 2 Volume 1 / Tom Taylor, Mike S. Miller
    pages cm
ISBN 978-1-4012-5340-0 (Paperback)
  1. Graphic novels. I. Miller, Mike S., illustrator. II. Derenick, Tom,
illustrator. III. Title. IV. Title: Gods Among Us Year 2 Volume 1.
  PN6727.T293158 2014
  741.5'973—dc23
                              2014011937

THE STORY SO FAR

When the Joker ditches Gotham and heads for Metropolis, Superman and Lois Lane are the victims of his most sinister plot to date. The aftermath unleashes an atomic explosion that destroys the City of Tomorrow, and with it, Lois Lane and their unborn child. Mad with grief, the Man of Steel does the unthinkable and murders the Joker in cold blood as Batman looks on in horror. When Superman is willing to commit atrocities, who can possibly stand against him?

Superman begins a campaign to end violence the world over, involving himself in civil wars and international conflict. Batman warns that this level of intervention is a slippery slope towards a police state, but the Justice League sides with Clark. After a tense conflict with Aquaman over who holds authority over the oceans, some members question their actions and, like Batman, feel that they're overstepping their bounds.

As their peacekeeping efforts increase, the Justice League ends up at war with their own government, who attempt to use Jonathan and Martha Kent as leverage against the Man of Steel. When the League starts taking the inmates at Arkham to somewhere more secure, a terrible accident takes the life of Nightwing. A broken Bruce Wayne tries to cope with the death with the help of Catwoman, and the two work toward a solution to the increasingly oppressive activities of Superman.

The Justice League finds one unlikely survivor of the Metropolis massacre, Lex Luthor, safe within his fallout shelter, and he joins their efforts to save the planet. But Superman is again forced to escalate what he is willing to do to protect Earth when an invasion from Apokolips led by Kalibak overtakes Earth. Vaporizing the oncoming forces from space leads to widespread celebration of Superman, despite the carnage.

But Batman is still plotting against his old friend. When it's revealed that Batman has been in league with Martian Manhunter to spy on the Justice League, Superman responds by outing Bruce Wayne as Batman. Bruce then retaliates by knocking out power to the Watchtower, sending it hurtling to Earth from orbit. The resulting conflict leads to the death of Martian Manhunter at the hands of Superman.

Batman and his resistance team try for one last-ditch effort to get their hands on a Kryptonite-powered pill that grants super powers to give them a weapon in the fight against Superman. They succeed, but at the cost of Green Arrow and Captain Atom, and Bruce is badly injured in his fight with Clark. Superman and the remaining Justice League members then swear before the U.N. to defend Earth not only from themselves, but also from Batman and his allies.

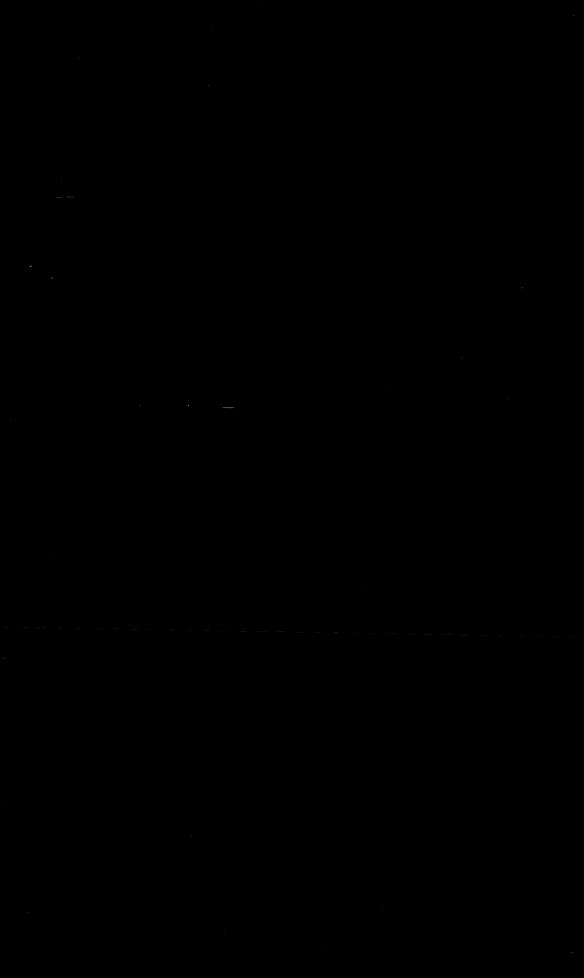

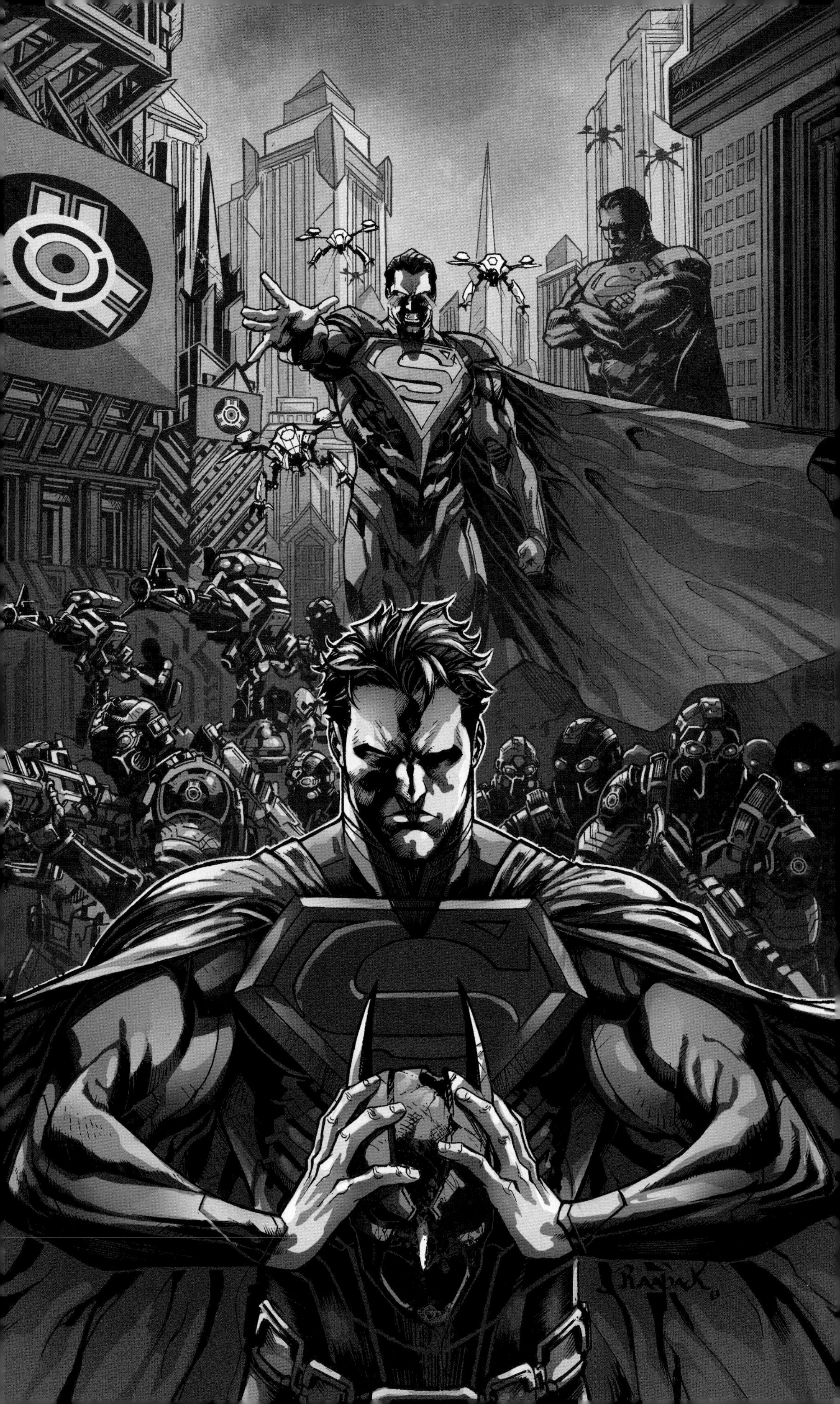

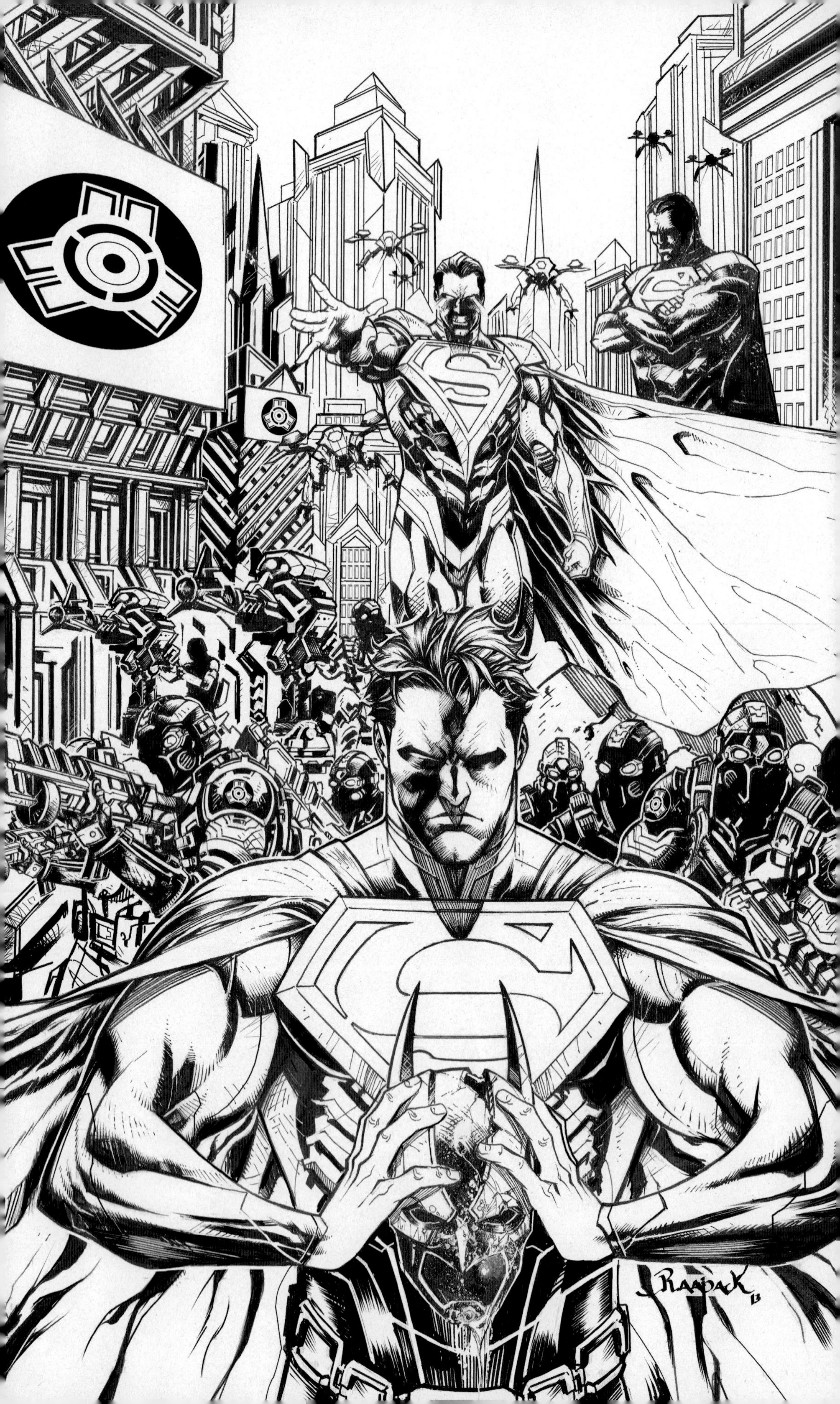

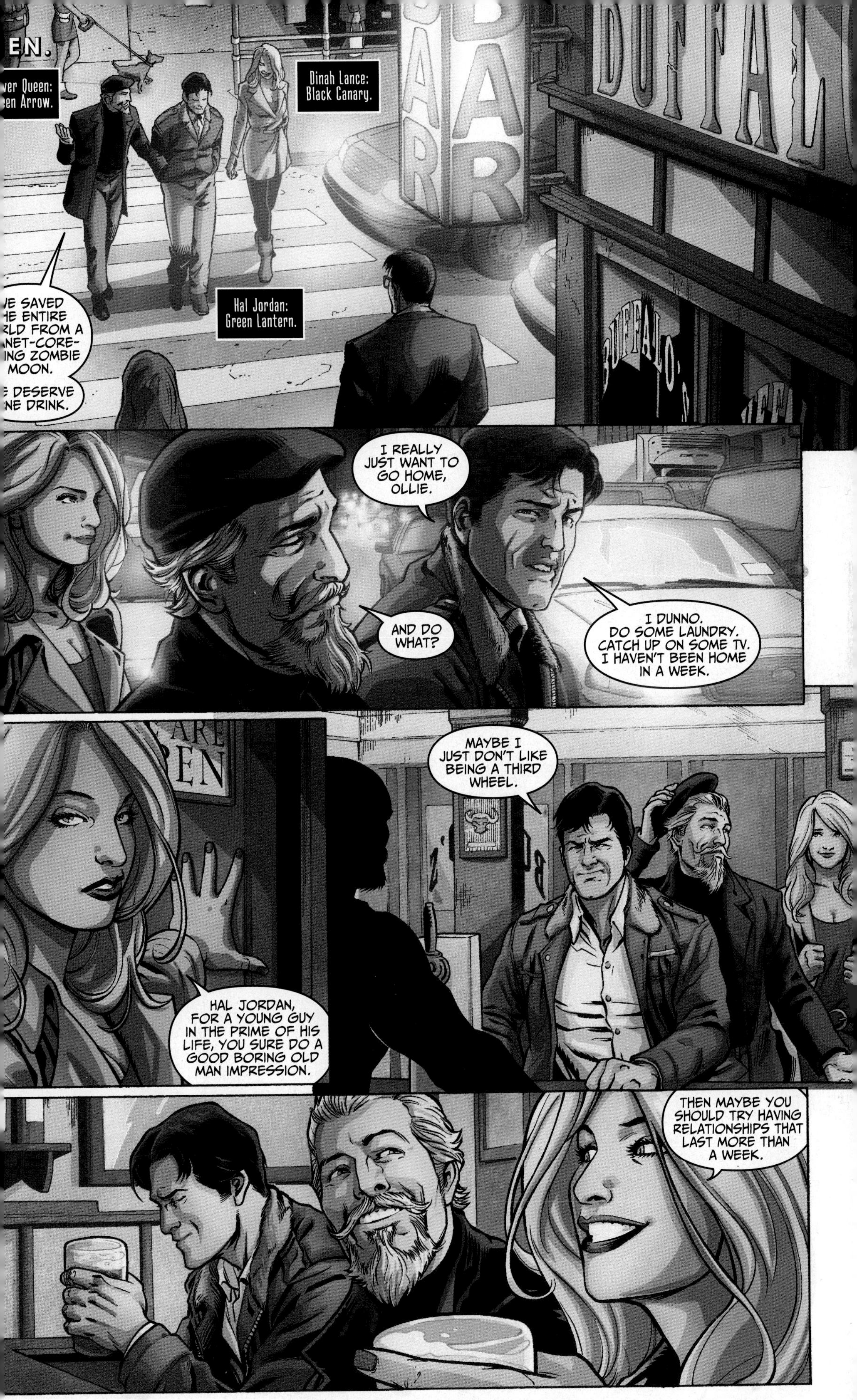
EN.
ver Queen:
en Arrow.
Dinah Lance:
Black Canary.
Hal Jordan:
Green Lantern.
WE SAVED HE ENTIRE RLD FROM A ANET-CORE-ING ZOMBIE MOON.
E DESERVE NE DRINK.
BAR
BUFFAL
BUFFALO'S
I REALLY JUST WANT TO GO HOME, OLLIE.
AND DO WHAT?
I DUNNO. DO SOME LAUNDRY. CATCH UP ON SOME TV. I HAVEN'T BEEN HOME IN A WEEK.
MAYBE I JUST DON'T LIKE BEING A THIRD WHEEL.
HAL JORDAN, FOR A YOUNG GUY IN THE PRIME OF HIS LIFE, YOU SURE DO A GOOD BORING OLD MAN IMPRESSION.
THEN MAYBE YOU SHOULD TRY HAVING RELATIONSHIPS THAT LAST MORE THAN A WEEK.

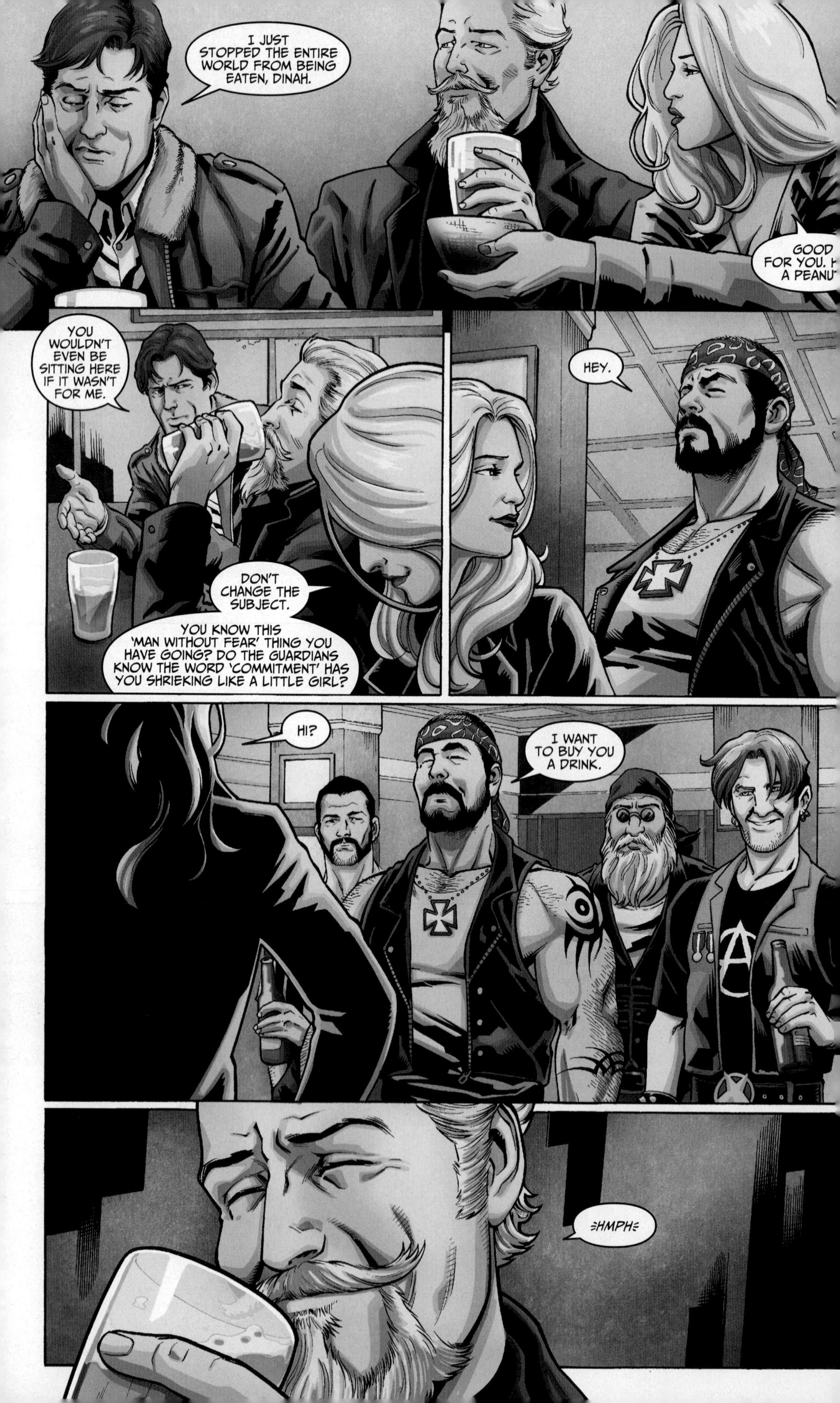
I JUST STOPPED THE ENTIRE WORLD FROM BEING EATEN, DINAH.
GOOD FOR YOU. H A PEANU
YOU WOULDN'T EVEN BE SITTING HERE IF IT WASN'T FOR ME.
DON'T CHANGE THE SUBJECT.
YOU KNOW THIS 'MAN WITHOUT FEAR' THING YOU HAVE GOING? DO THE GUARDIANS KNOW THE WORD 'COMMITMENT' HAS YOU SHRIEKING LIKE A LITTLE GIRL?
HEY.
HI?
I WANT TO BUY YOU A DRINK.
HMPH

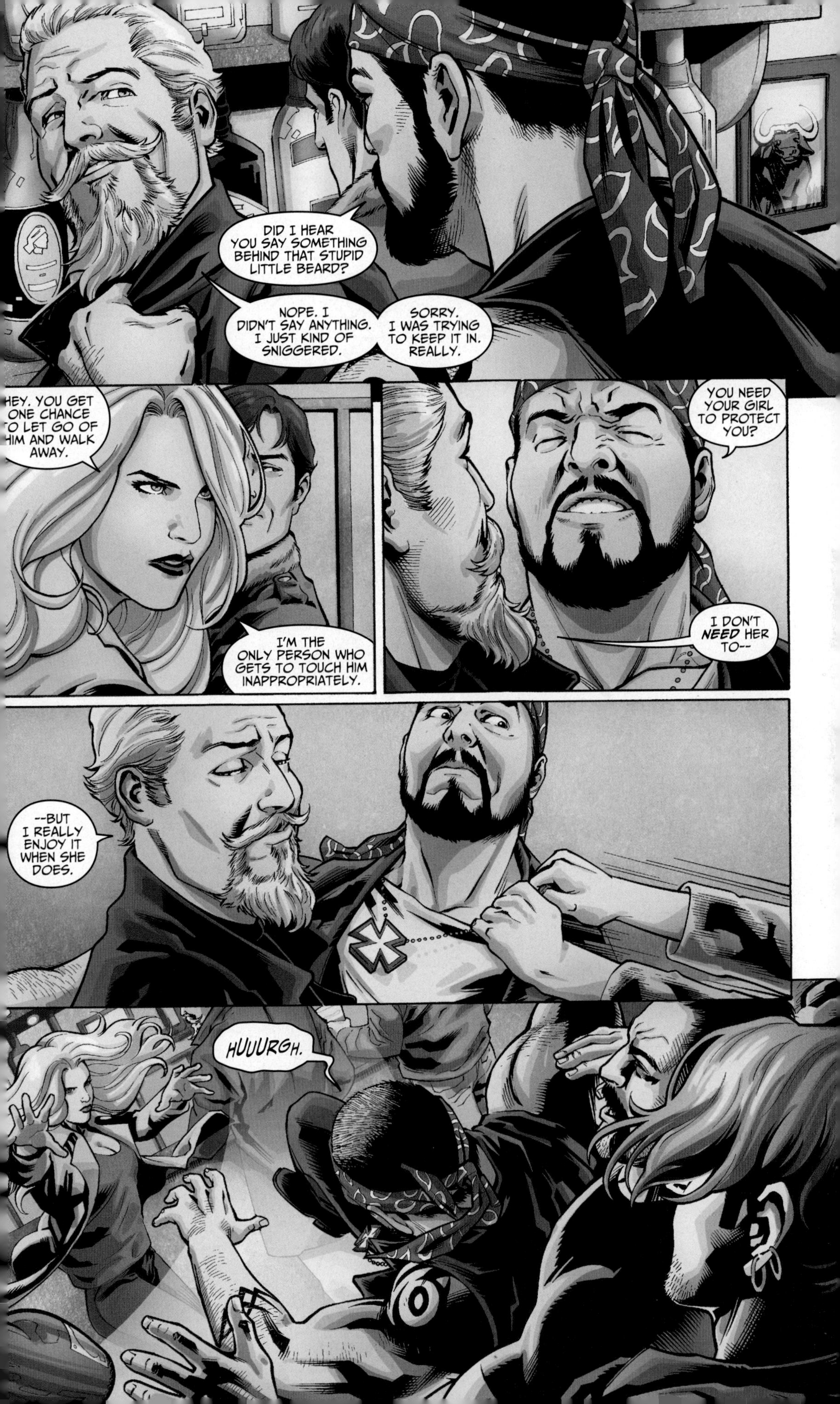

DID I HEAR YOU SAY SOMETHING BEHIND THAT STUPID LITTLE BEARD?
NOPE. I DIDN'T SAY ANYTHING. I JUST KIND OF SNIGGERED.
SORRY. I WAS TRYING TO KEEP IT IN. REALLY.
HEY. YOU GET ONE CHANCE TO LET GO OF HIM AND WALK AWAY.
I'M THE ONLY PERSON WHO GETS TO TOUCH HIM INAPPROPRIATELY.
YOU NEED YOUR GIRL TO PROTECT YOU?
I DON'T NEED HER TO--
--BUT I REALLY ENJOY IT WHEN SHE DOES.
HUUURGH.

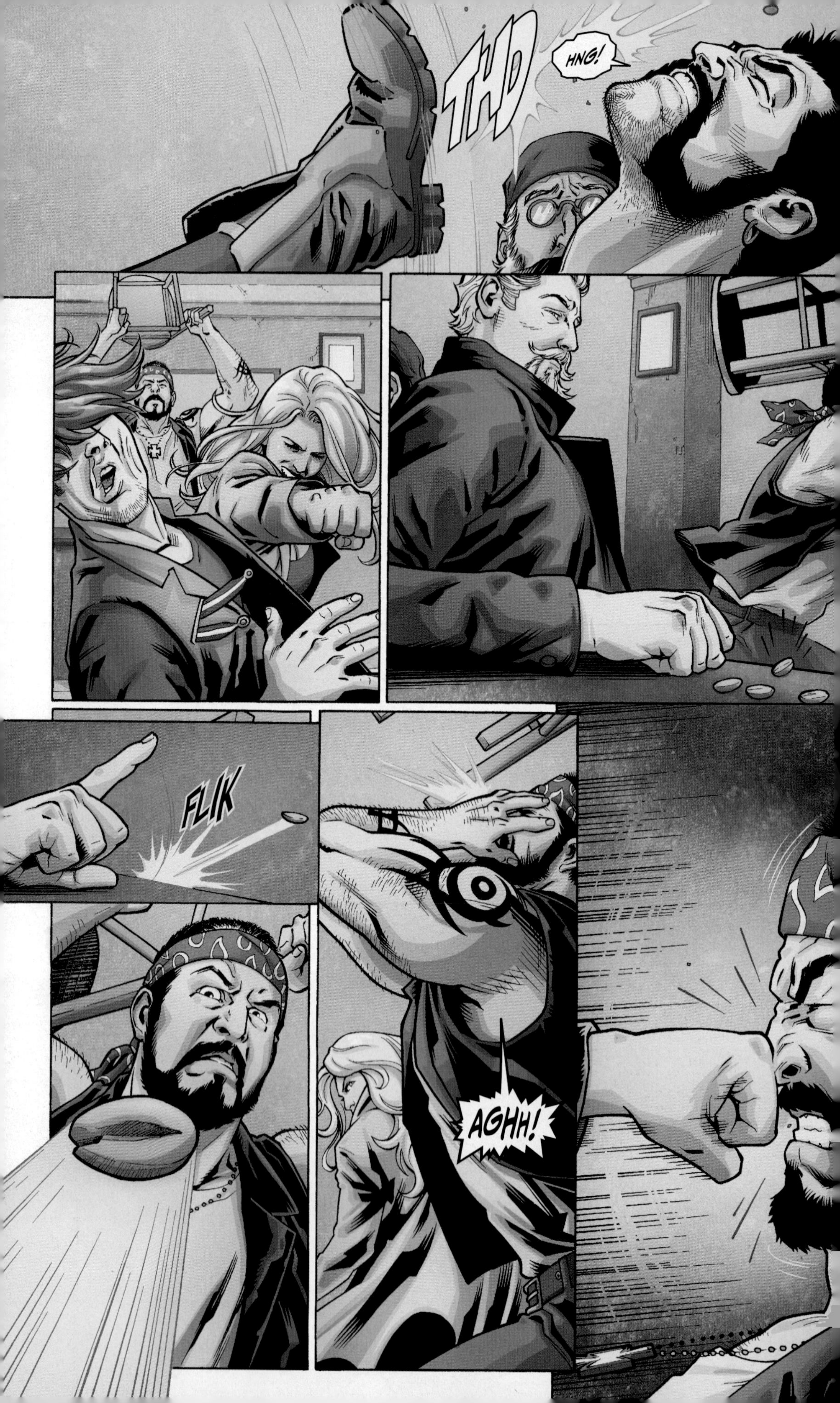
THD
HNG!
FLIK
AGHH!

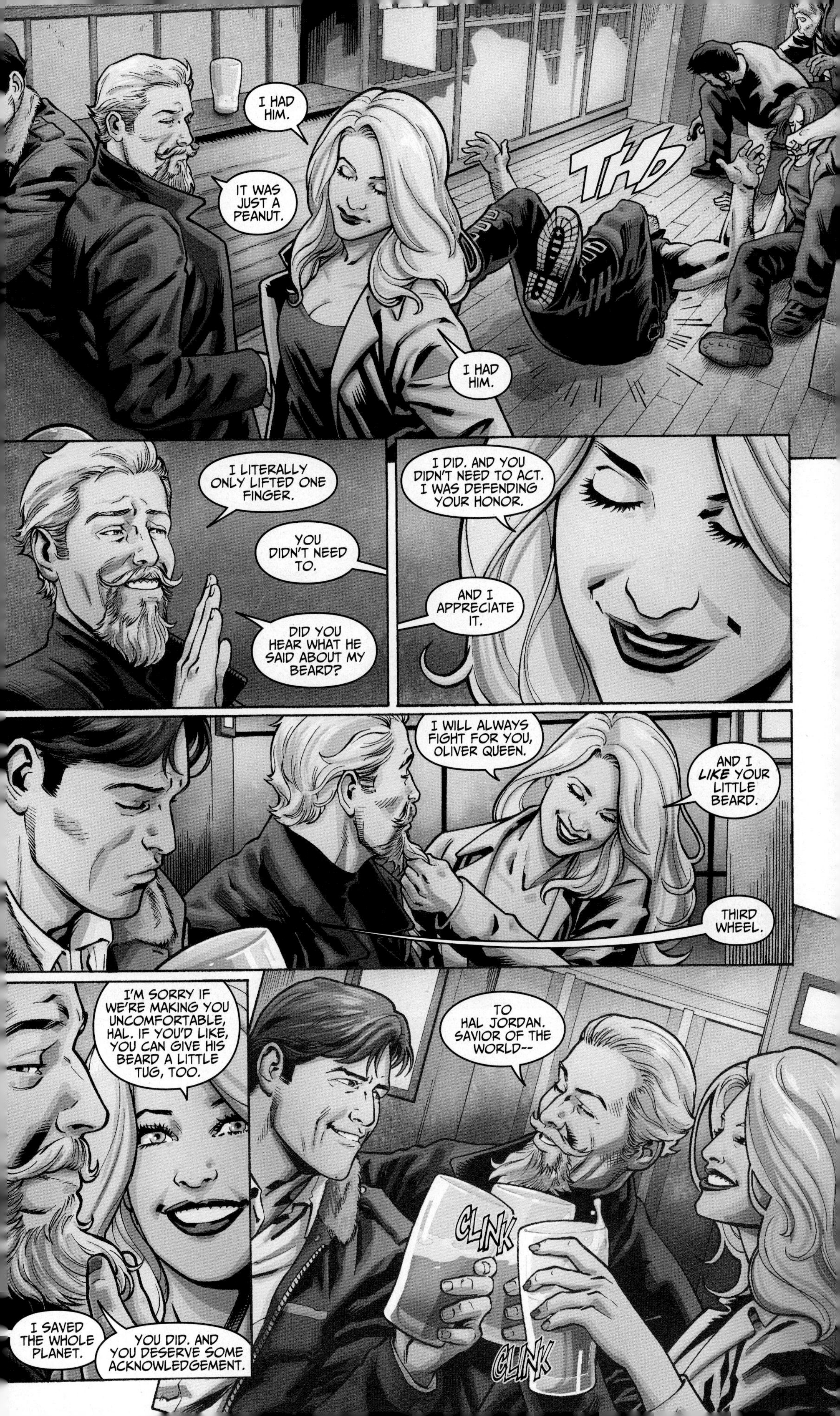
I HAD HIM.
IT WAS JUST A PEANUT.
THD
I HAD HIM.
I LITERALLY ONLY LIFTED ONE FINGER.
YOU DIDN'T NEED TO.
DID YOU HEAR WHAT HE SAID ABOUT MY BEARD?
I DID. AND YOU DIDN'T NEED TO ACT. I WAS DEFENDING YOUR HONOR.
AND I APPRECIATE IT.
I WILL ALWAYS FIGHT FOR YOU, OLIVER QUEEN.
AND I *LIKE* YOUR LITTLE BEARD.
THIRD WHEEL.
I'M SORRY IF WE'RE MAKING YOU UNCOMFORTABLE, HAL. IF YOU'D LIKE, YOU CAN GIVE HIS BEARD A LITTLE TUG, TOO.
TO HAL JORDAN. SAVIOR OF THE WORLD--
I SAVED THE WHOLE PLANET.
YOU DID. AND YOU DESERVE SOME ACKNOWLEDGEMENT.
CLINK
CLINK

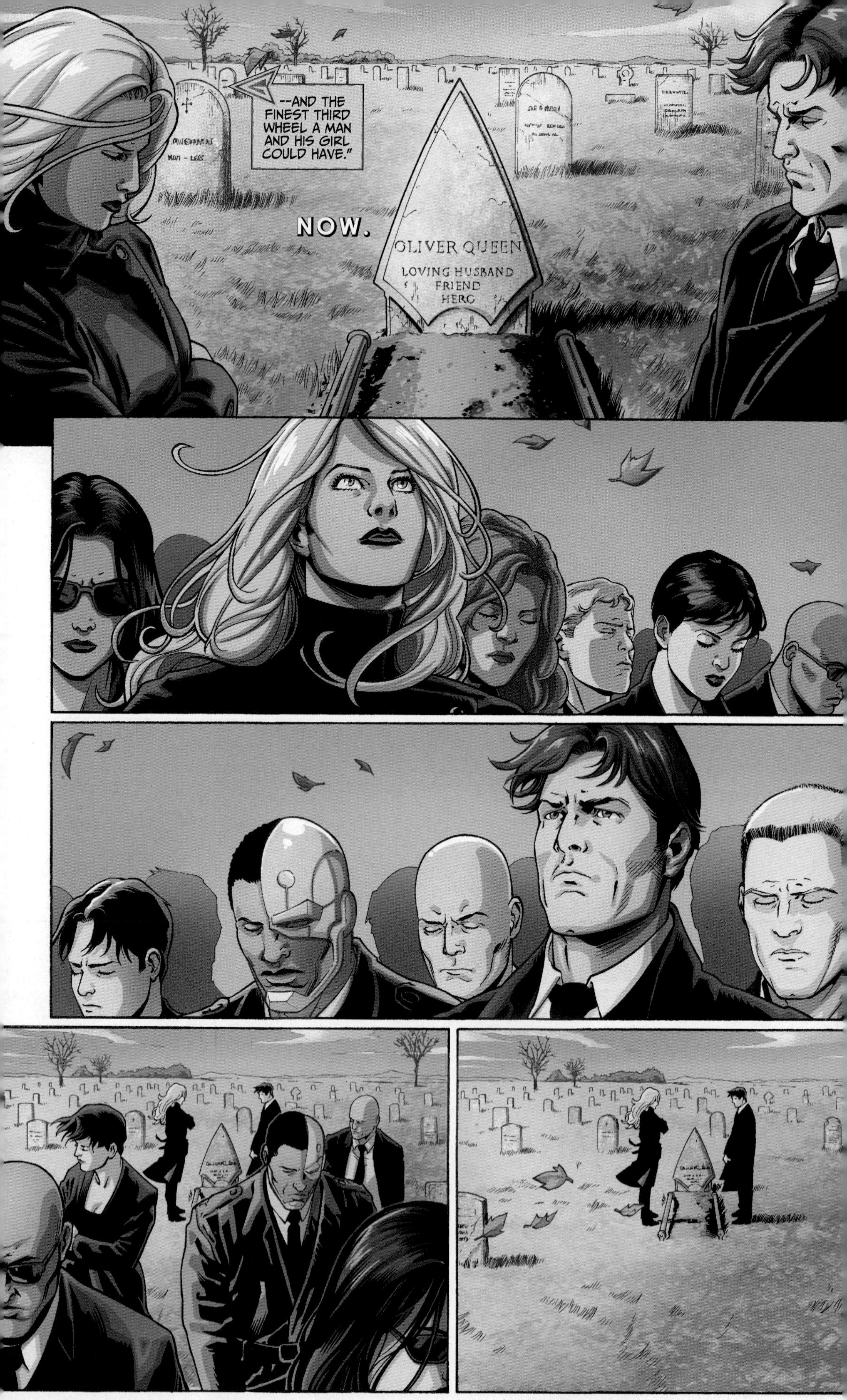
--AND THE FINEST THIRD WHEEL A MAN AND HIS GIRL COULD HAVE."
NOW.
OLIVER QUEEN
LOVING HUSBAND
FRIEND
HERO

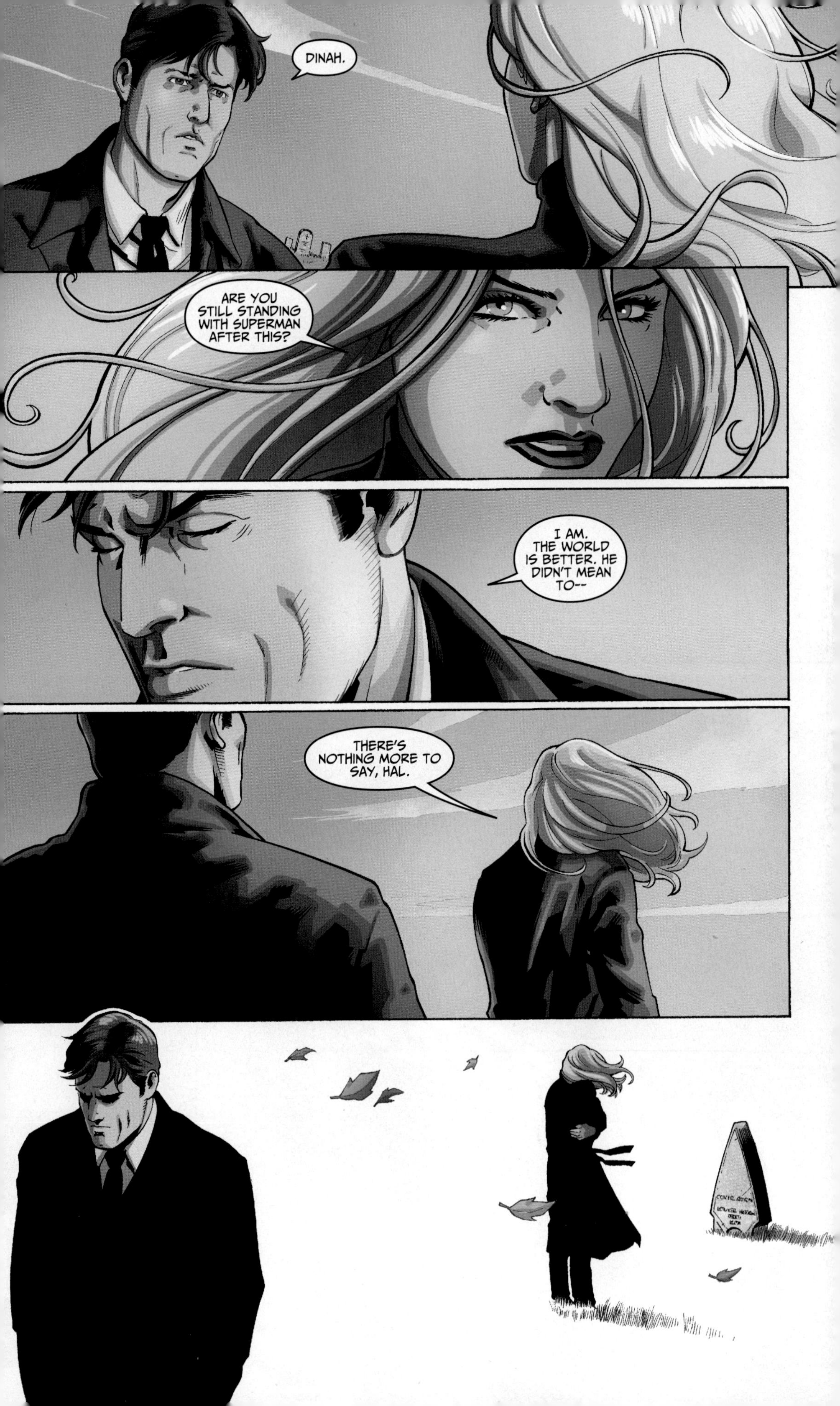
DINAH.
ARE YOU STILL STANDING WITH SUPERMAN AFTER THIS?
I AM. THE WORLD IS BETTER. HE DIDN'T MEAN TO--
THERE'S NOTHING MORE TO SAY, HAL.

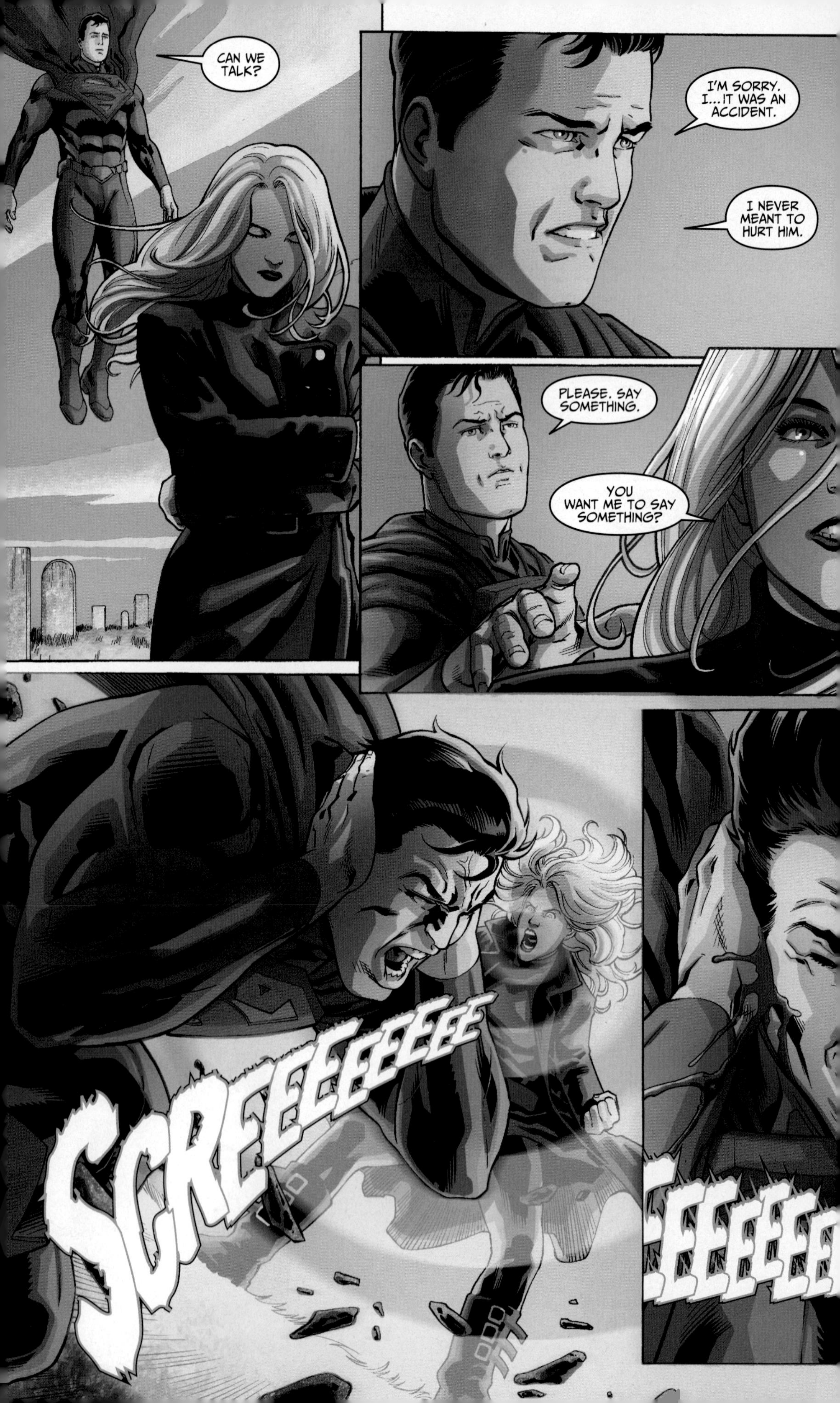
CAN WE TALK?
I'M SORRY. I...IT WAS AN ACCIDENT.
I NEVER MEANT TO HURT HIM.
PLEASE. SAY SOMETHING.
YOU WANT ME TO SAY SOMETHING?
SCREEEEEEEEE
EEEEEEEE

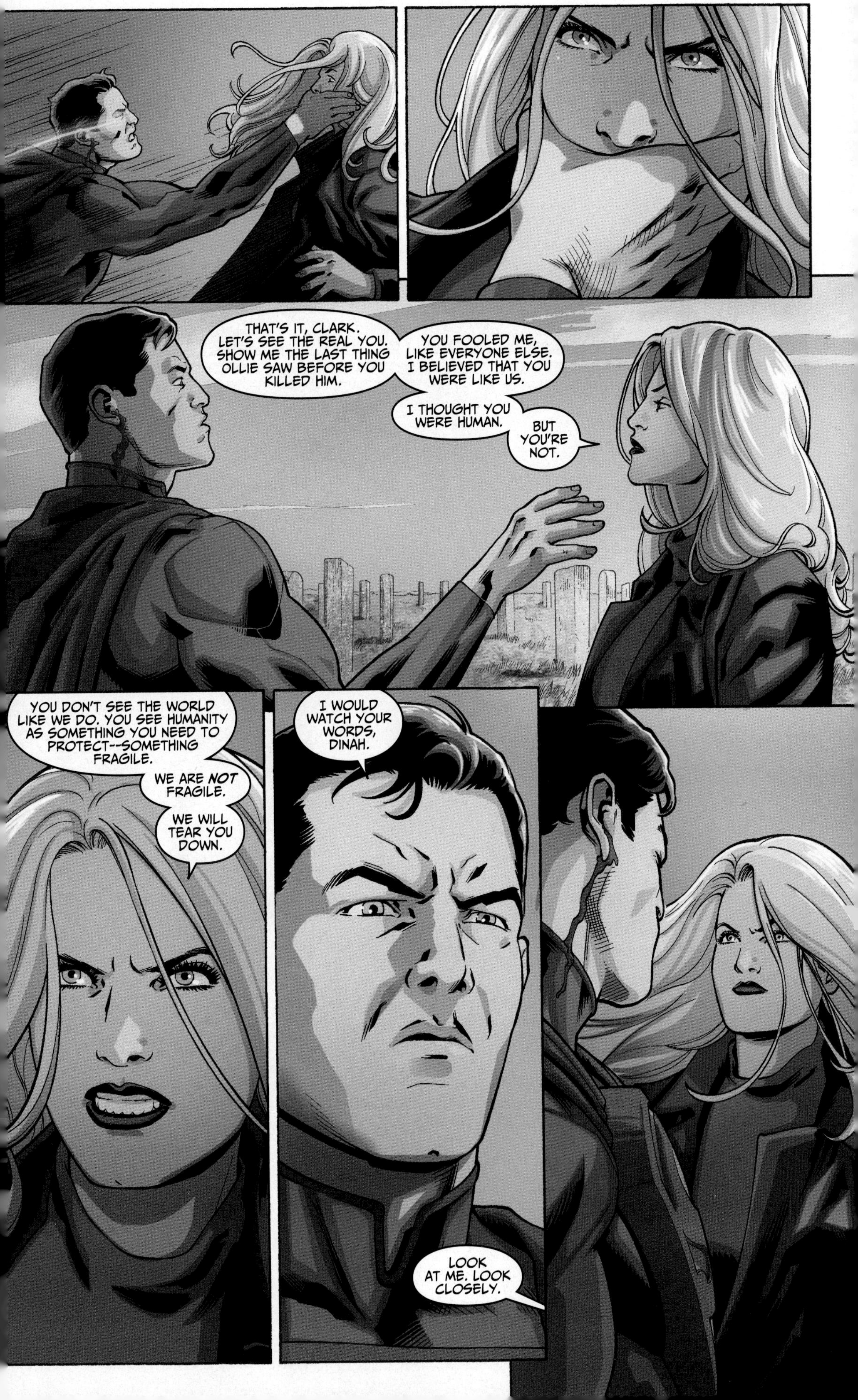
THAT'S IT, CLARK. LET'S SEE THE REAL YOU. SHOW ME THE LAST THING OLLIE SAW BEFORE YOU KILLED HIM.
YOU FOOLED ME, LIKE EVERYONE ELSE. I BELIEVED THAT YOU WERE LIKE US.
I THOUGHT YOU WERE HUMAN.
BUT YOU'RE NOT.
YOU DON'T SEE THE WORLD LIKE WE DO. YOU SEE HUMANITY AS SOMETHING YOU NEED TO PROTECT--SOMETHING FRAGILE.
WE ARE *NOT* FRAGILE.
WE WILL TEAR YOU DOWN.
I WOULD WATCH YOUR WORDS, DINAH.
LOOK AT ME. LOOK CLOSELY.

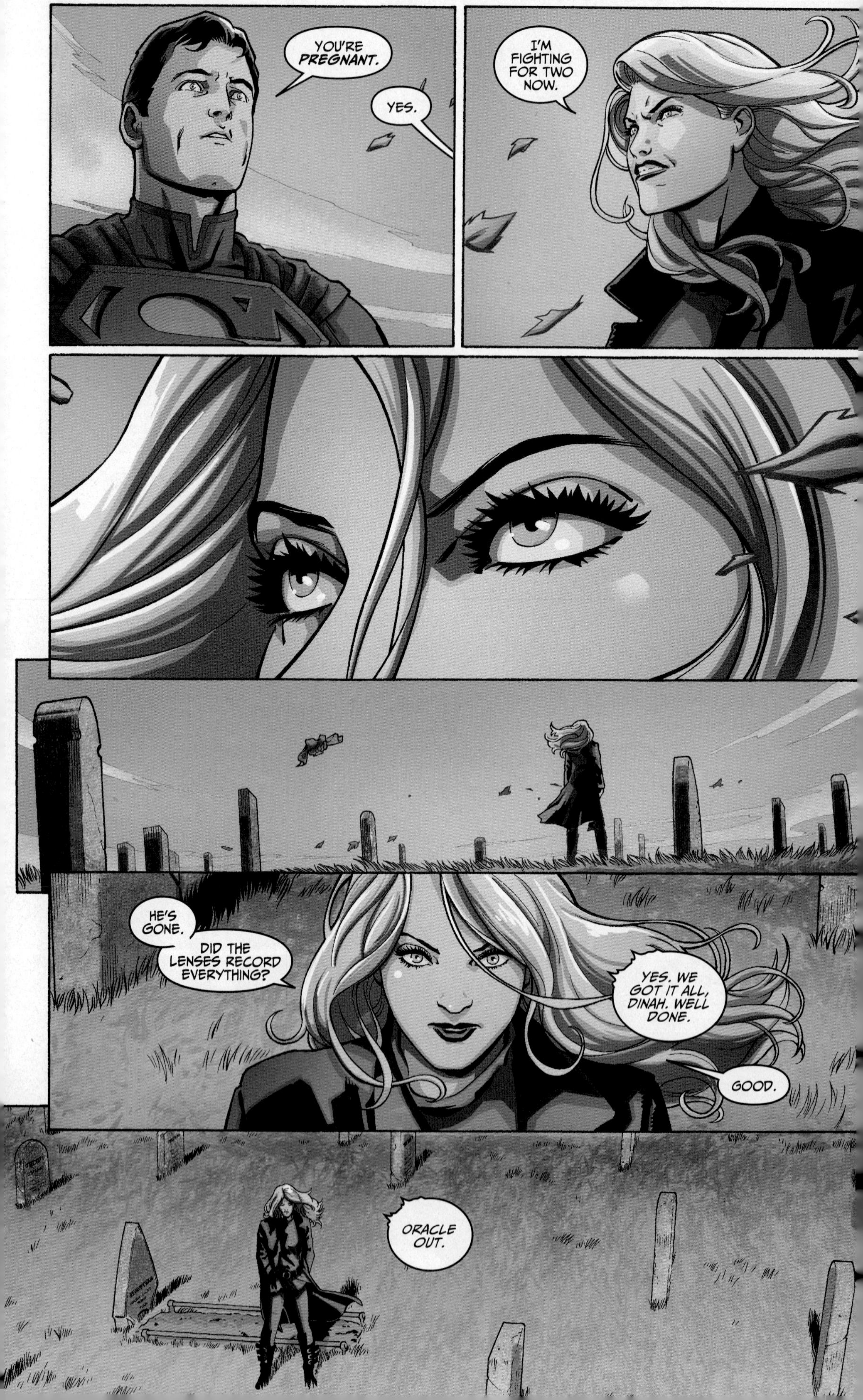
YOU'RE PREGNANT.
YES.
I'M FIGHTING FOR TWO NOW.
HE'S GONE.
DID THE LENSES RECORD EVERYTHING?
YES. WE GOT IT ALL, DINAH. WELL DONE.
GOOD.
ORACLE OUT.

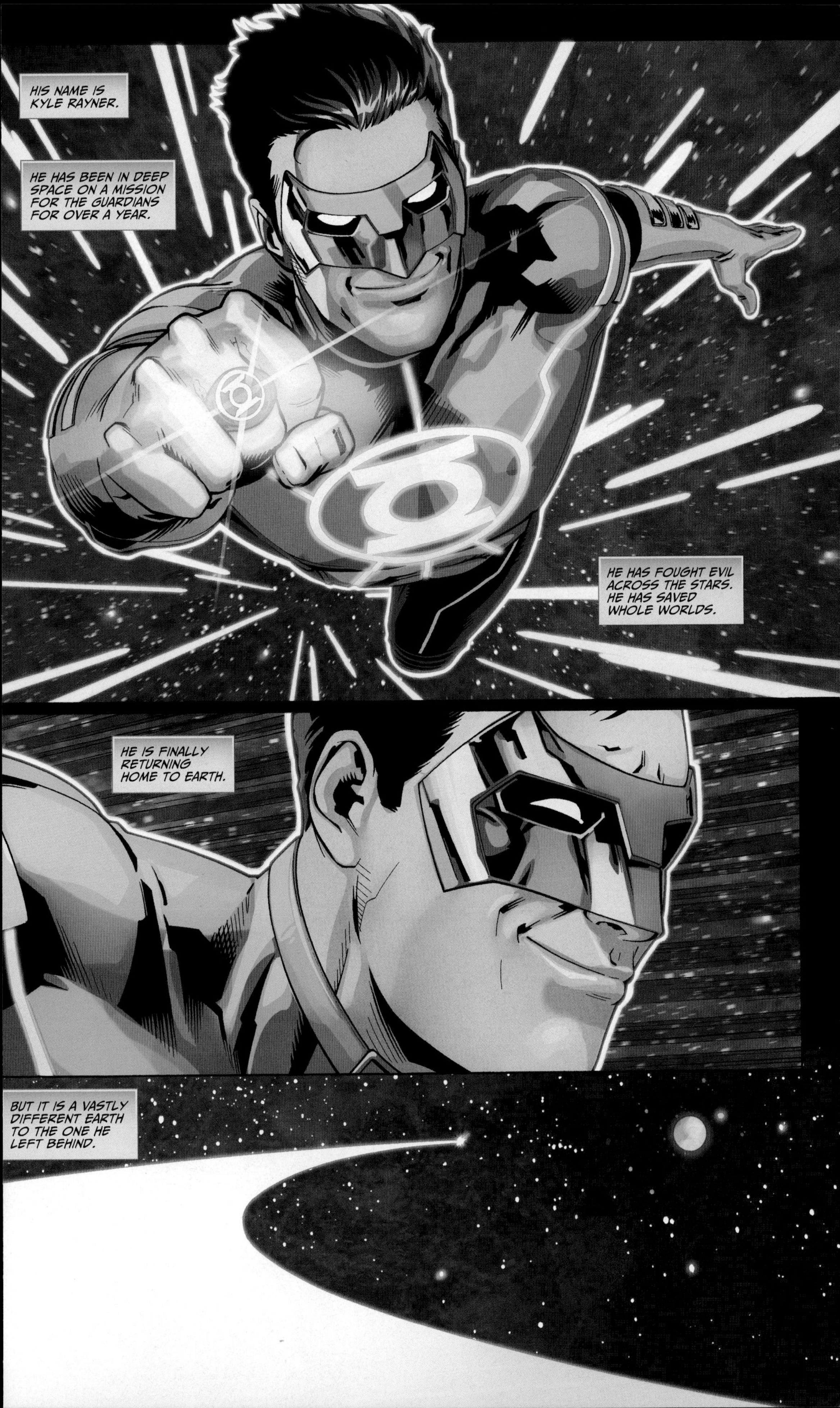
HIS NAME IS KYLE RAYNER.
HE HAS BEEN IN DEEP SPACE ON A MISSION FOR THE GUARDIANS FOR OVER A YEAR.
HE HAS FOUGHT EVIL ACROSS THE STARS. HE HAS SAVED WHOLE WORLDS.
HE IS FINALLY RETURNING HOME TO EARTH.
BUT IT IS A VASTLY DIFFERENT EARTH TO THE ONE HE LEFT BEHIND.

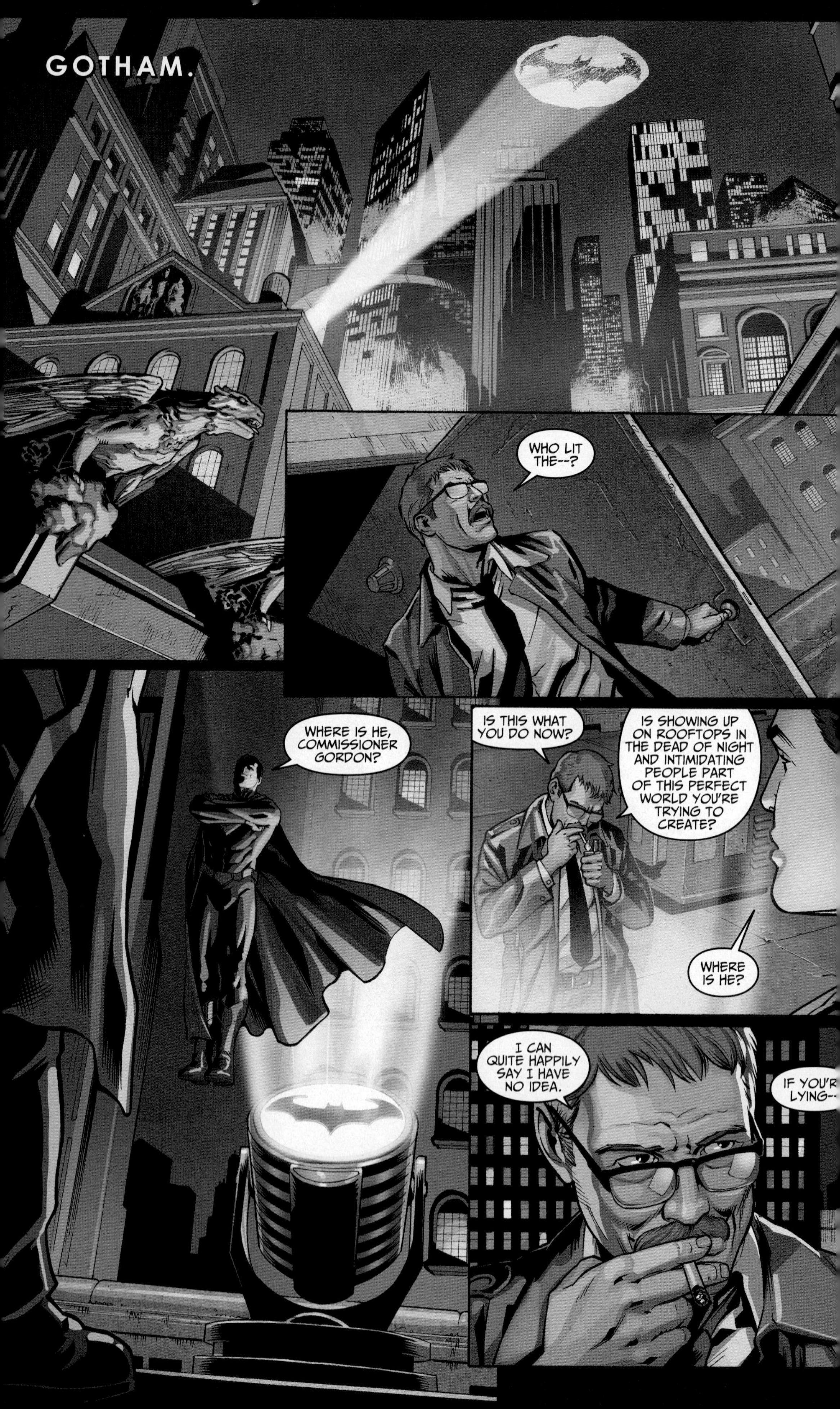
GOTHAM.
WHO LIT THE--?
WHERE IS HE, COMMISSIONER GORDON?
IS THIS WHAT YOU DO NOW?
IS SHOWING UP ON ROOFTOPS IN THE DEAD OF NIGHT AND INTIMIDATING PEOPLE PART OF THIS PERFECT WORLD YOU'RE TRYING TO CREATE?
WHERE IS HE?
I CAN QUITE HAPPILY SAY I HAVE NO IDEA.
IF YOU'R LYING--

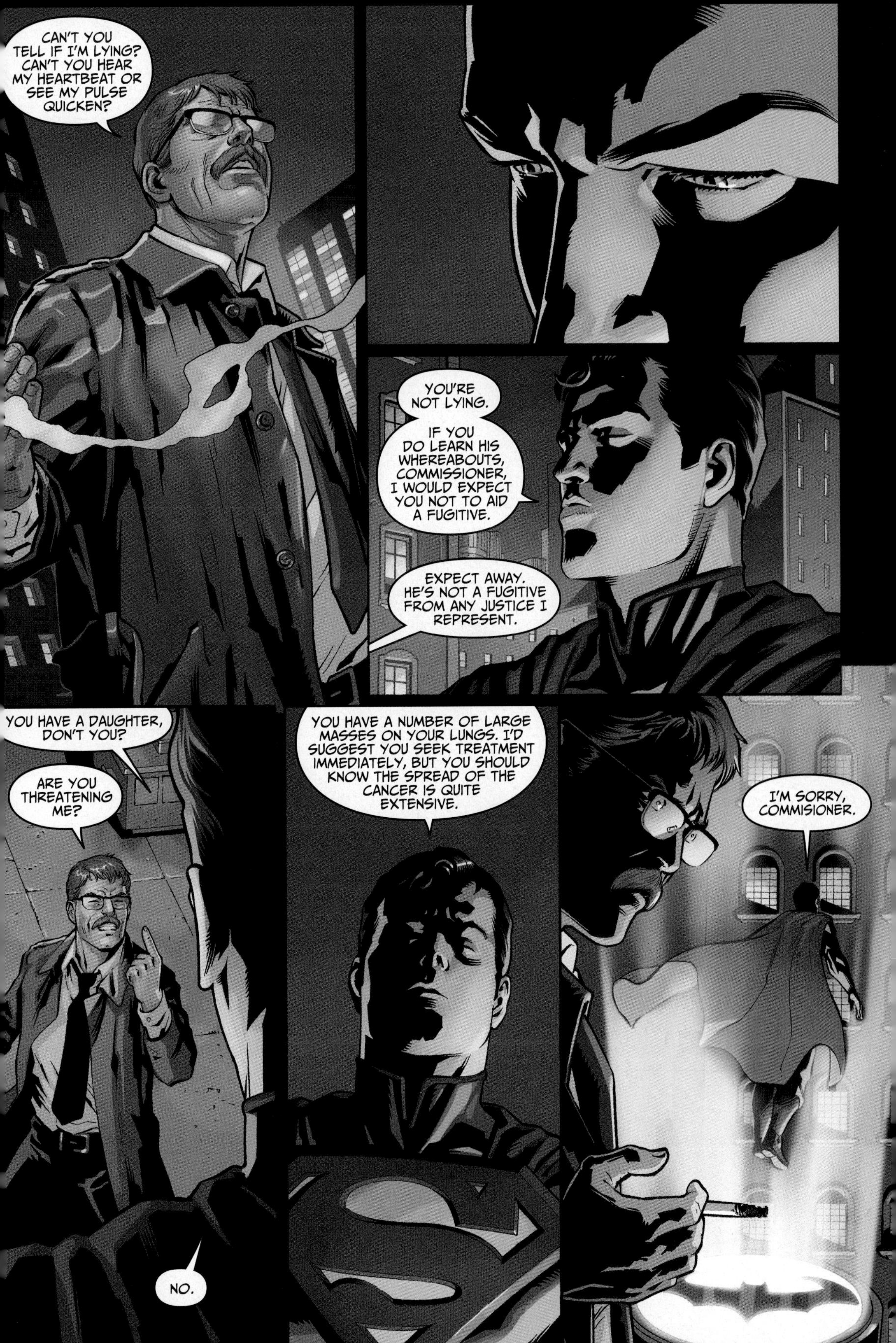
CAN'T YOU TELL IF I'M LYING? CAN'T YOU HEAR MY HEARTBEAT OR SEE MY PULSE QUICKEN?
YOU'RE NOT LYING.
IF YOU DO LEARN HIS WHEREABOUTS, COMMISSIONER, I WOULD EXPECT YOU NOT TO AID A FUGITIVE.
EXPECT AWAY. HE'S NOT A FUGITIVE FROM ANY JUSTICE I REPRESENT.
YOU HAVE A DAUGHTER, DON'T YOU?
ARE YOU THREATENING ME?
NO.
YOU HAVE A NUMBER OF LARGE MASSES ON YOUR LUNGS. I'D SUGGEST YOU SEEK TREATMENT IMMEDIATELY, BUT YOU SHOULD KNOW THE SPREAD OF THE CANCER IS QUITE EXTENSIVE.
I'M SORRY, COMMISIONER.

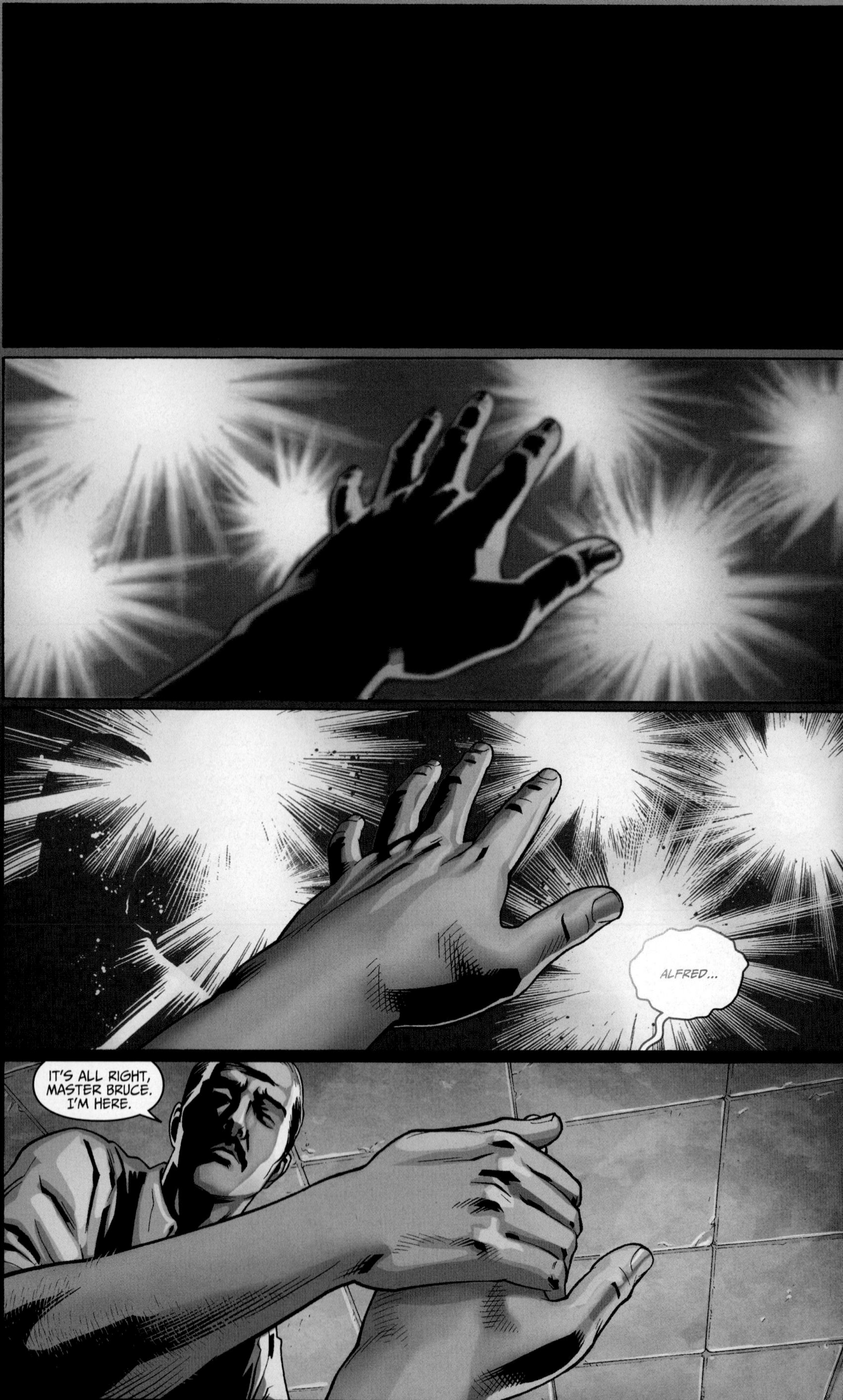
ALFRED...
IT'S ALL RIGHT, MASTER BRUCE. I'M HERE.

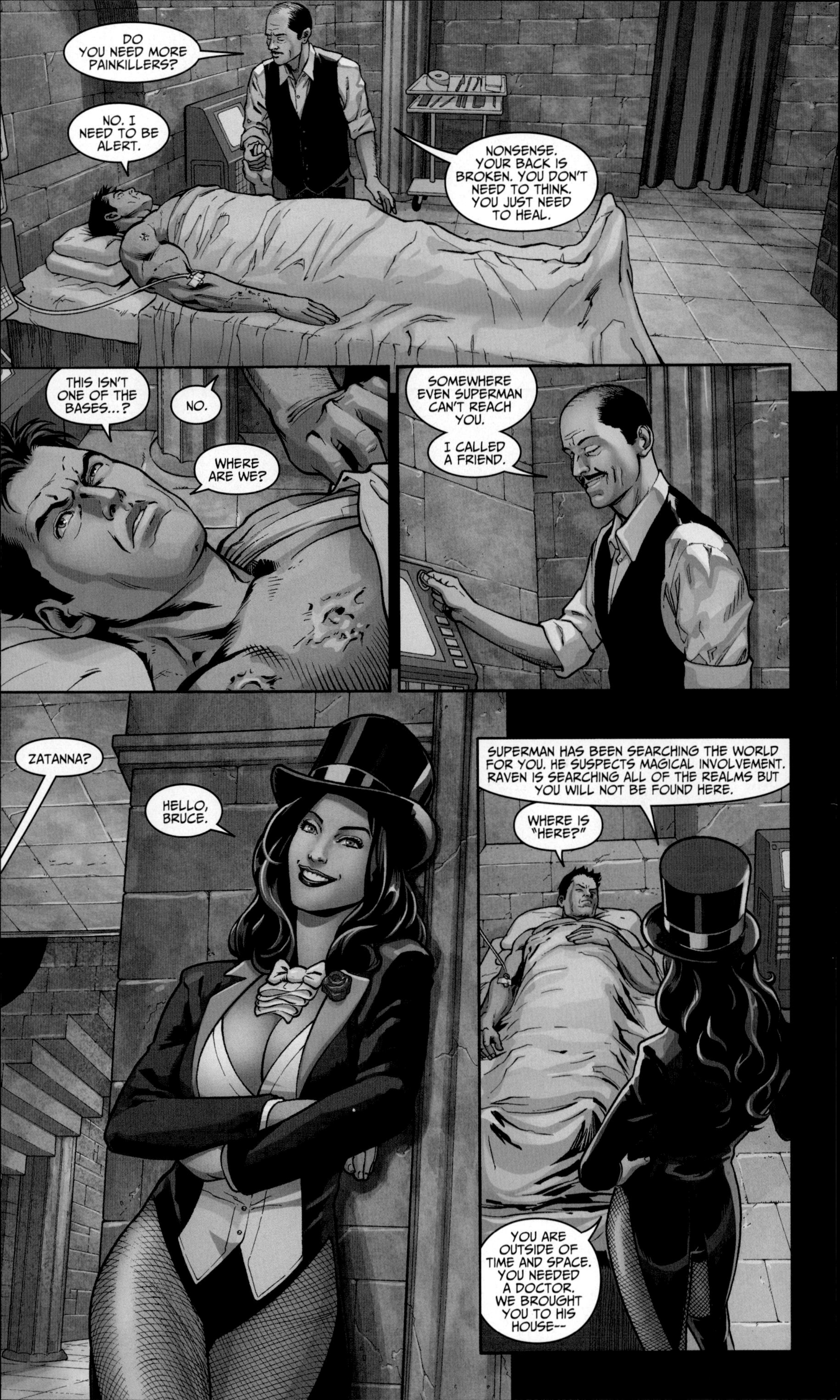
DO YOU NEED MORE PAINKILLERS?
NO. I NEED TO BE ALERT.
NONSENSE. YOUR BACK IS BROKEN. YOU DON'T NEED TO THINK. YOU JUST NEED TO HEAL.
THIS ISN'T ONE OF THE BASES...?
NO.
WHERE ARE WE?
SOMEWHERE EVEN SUPERMAN CAN'T REACH YOU.
I CALLED A FRIEND.
ZATANNA?
HELLO, BRUCE.
SUPERMAN HAS BEEN SEARCHING THE WORLD FOR YOU. HE SUSPECTS MAGICAL INVOLVEMENT. RAVEN IS SEARCHING ALL OF THE REALMS BUT YOU WILL NOT BE FOUND HERE.
WHERE IS "HERE?"
YOU ARE OUTSIDE OF TIME AND SPACE. YOU NEEDED A DOCTOR. WE BROUGHT YOU TO HIS HOUSE--

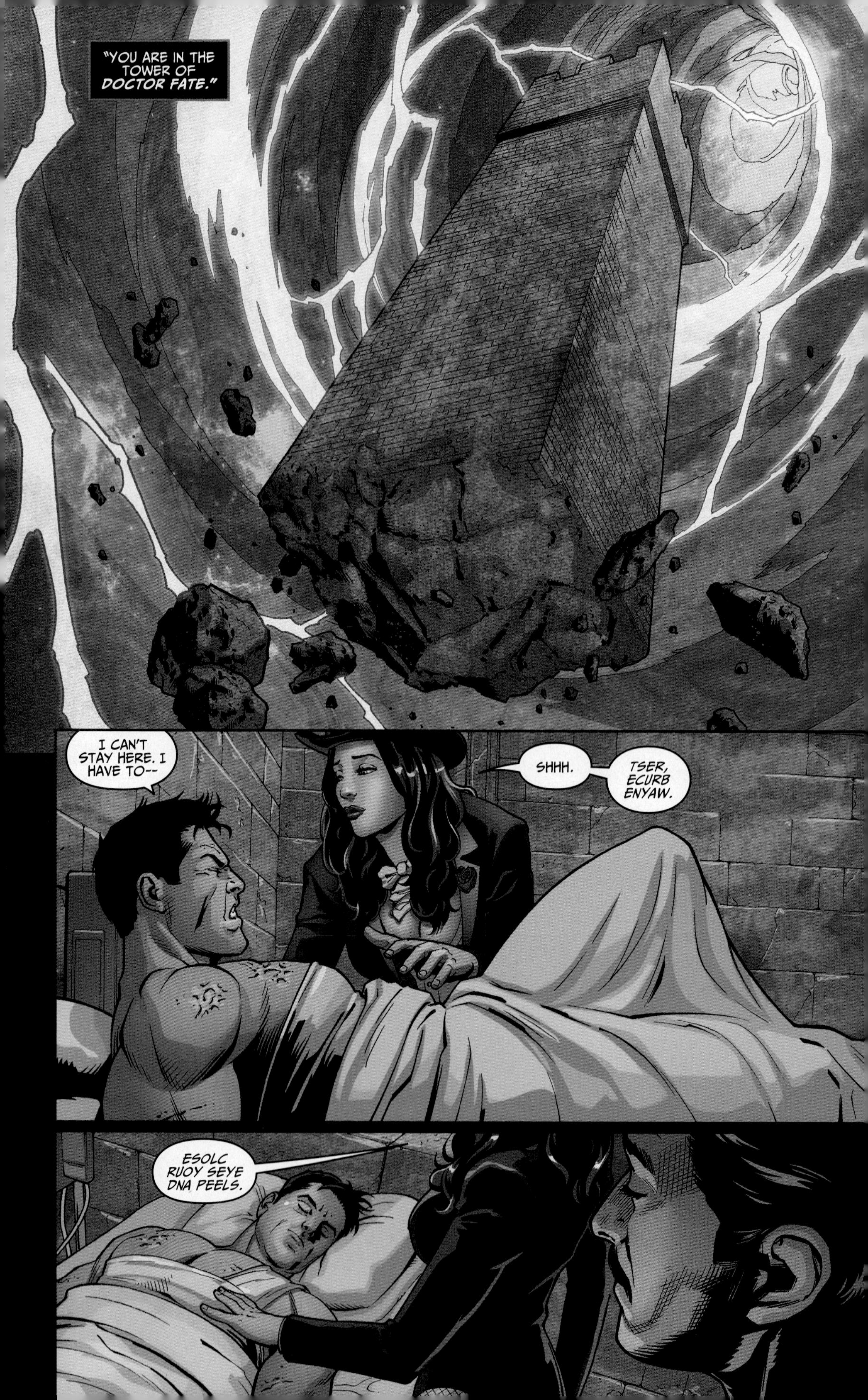
"YOU ARE IN THE TOWER OF DOCTOR FATE."
I CAN'T STAY HERE. I HAVE TO--
SHHH.
TSER, ECURB ENYAW.
ESOLC RUOY SEYE DNA PEELS.

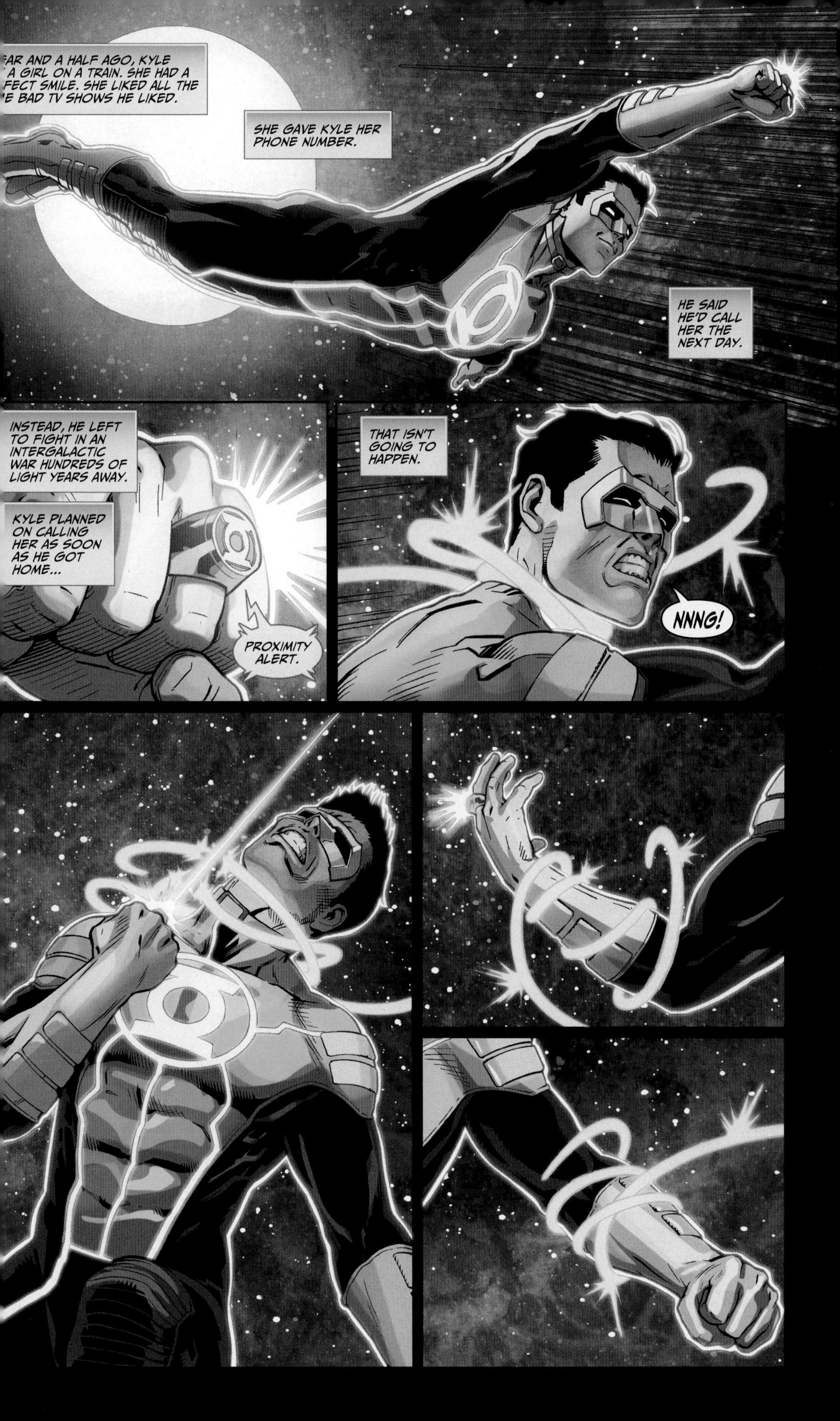
FAR AND A HALF AGO, KYLE A GIRL ON A TRAIN. SHE HAD A FECT SMILE. SHE LIKED ALL THE E BAD TV SHOWS HE LIKED.
SHE GAVE KYLE HER PHONE NUMBER.
HE SAID HE'D CALL HER THE NEXT DAY.
INSTEAD, HE LEFT TO FIGHT IN AN INTERGALACTIC WAR HUNDREDS OF LIGHT YEARS AWAY.
KYLE PLANNED ON CALLING HER AS SOON AS HE GOT HOME...
PROXIMITY ALERT.
THAT ISN'T GOING TO HAPPEN.
NNNG!

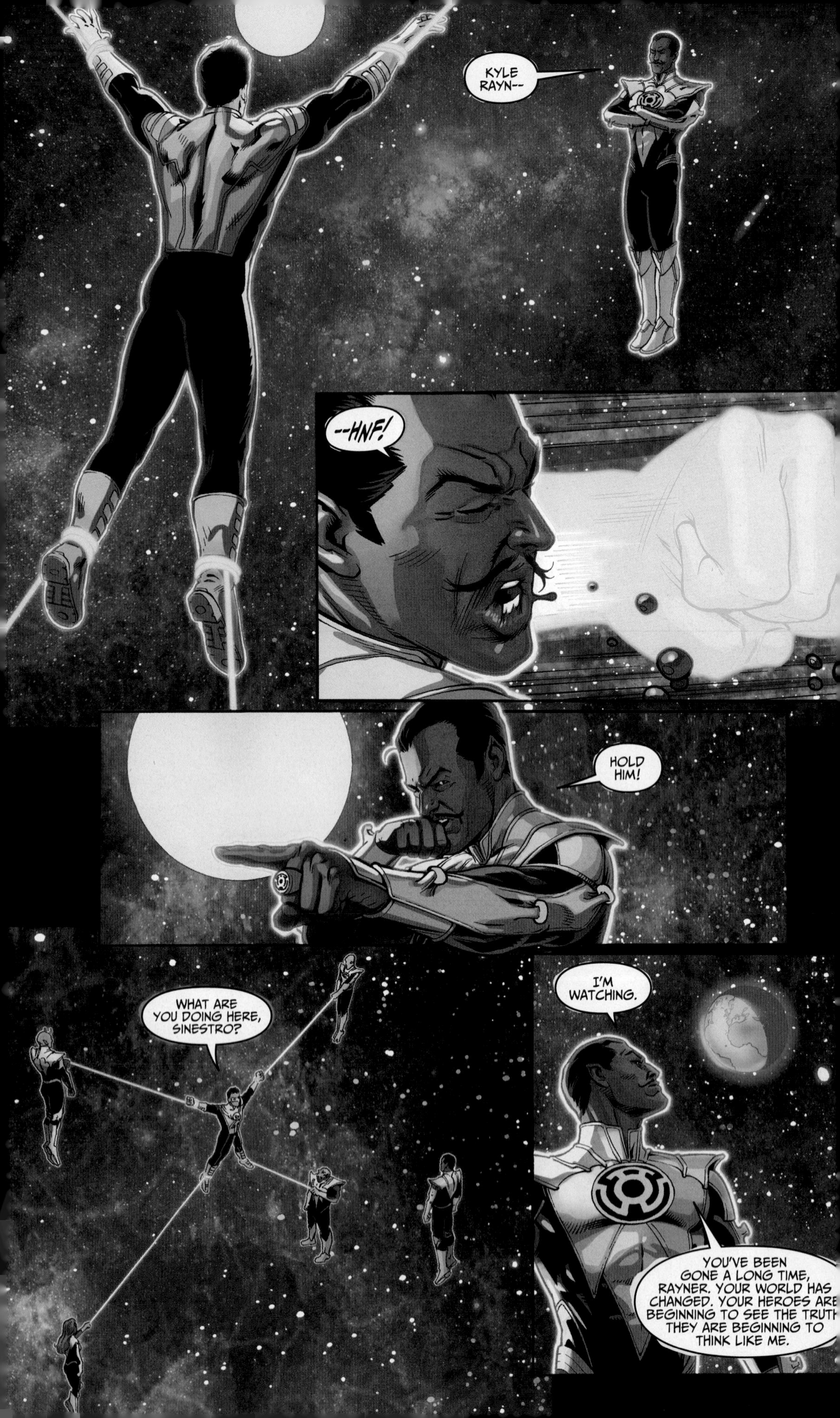
KYLE RAYN--
--HNF!
HOLD HIM!
WHAT ARE YOU DOING HERE, SINESTRO?
I'M WATCHING.
YOU'VE BEEN GONE A LONG TIME, RAYNER. YOUR WORLD HAS CHANGED. YOUR HEROES ARE BEGINNING TO SEE THE TRUTH. THEY ARE BEGINNING TO THINK LIKE ME.

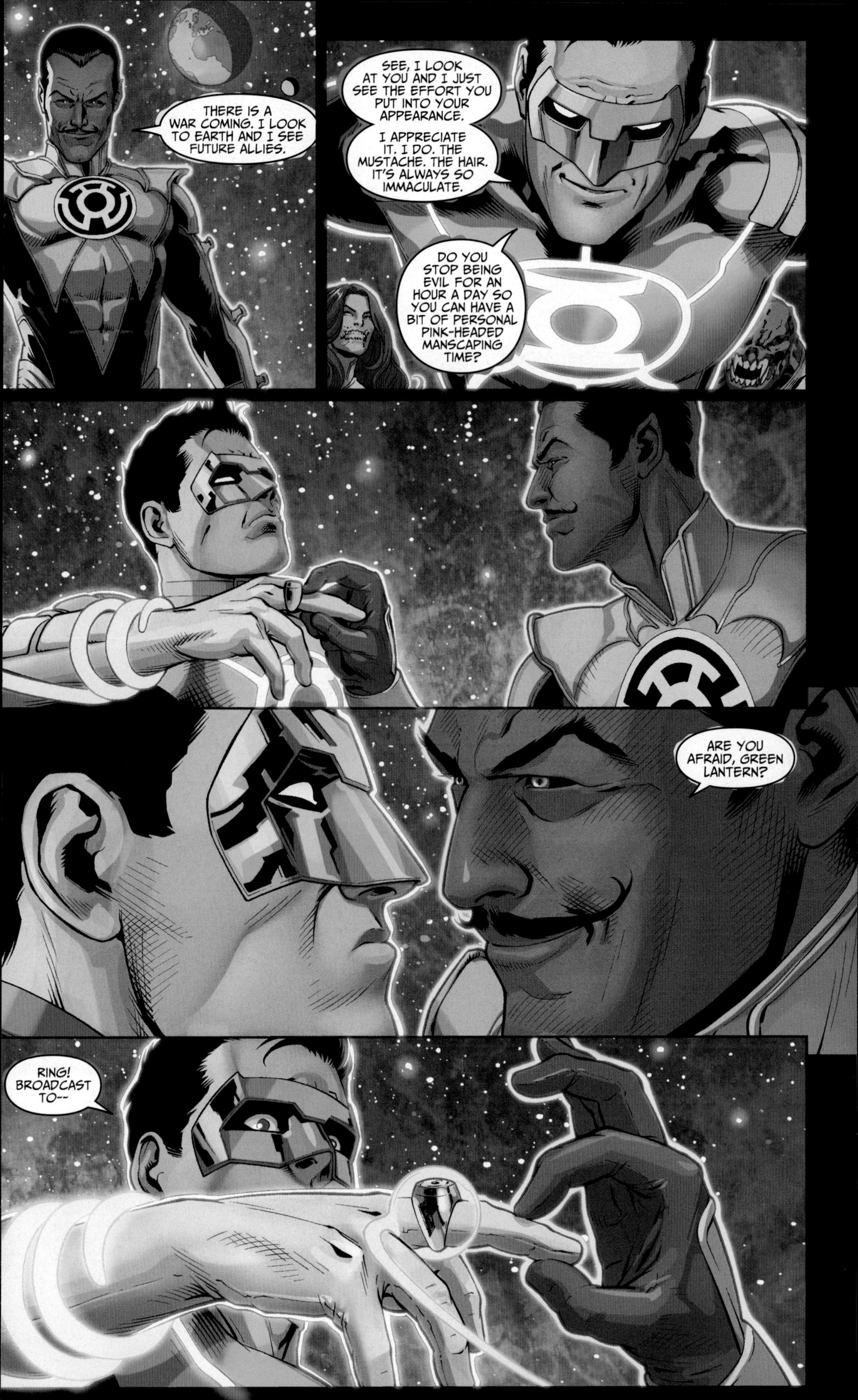
THERE IS A WAR COMING. I LOOK TO EARTH AND I SEE FUTURE ALLIES.
SEE, I LOOK AT YOU AND I JUST SEE THE EFFORT YOU PUT INTO YOUR APPEARANCE.
I APPRECIATE IT. I DO. THE MUSTACHE. THE HAIR. IT'S ALWAYS SO IMMACULATE.
DO YOU STOP BEING EVIL FOR AN HOUR A DAY SO YOU CAN HAVE A BIT OF PERSONAL PINK-HEADED MANSCAPING TIME?
ARE YOU AFRAID, GREEN LANTERN?
RING! BROADCAST TO--

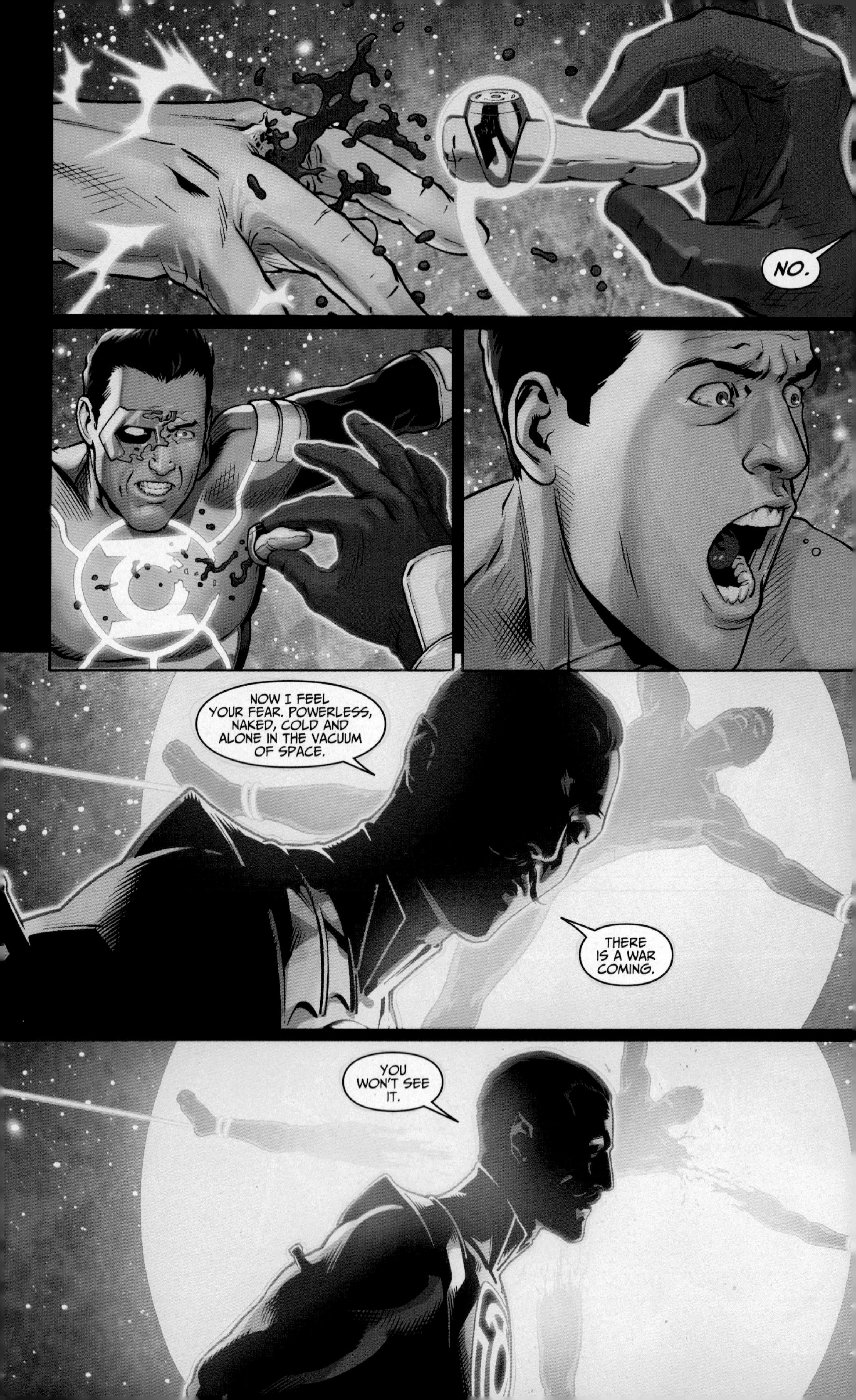
NO.
NOW I FEEL YOUR FEAR. POWERLESS, NAKED, COLD AND ALONE IN THE VACUUM OF SPACE.
THERE IS A WAR COMING.
YOU WON'T SEE IT.

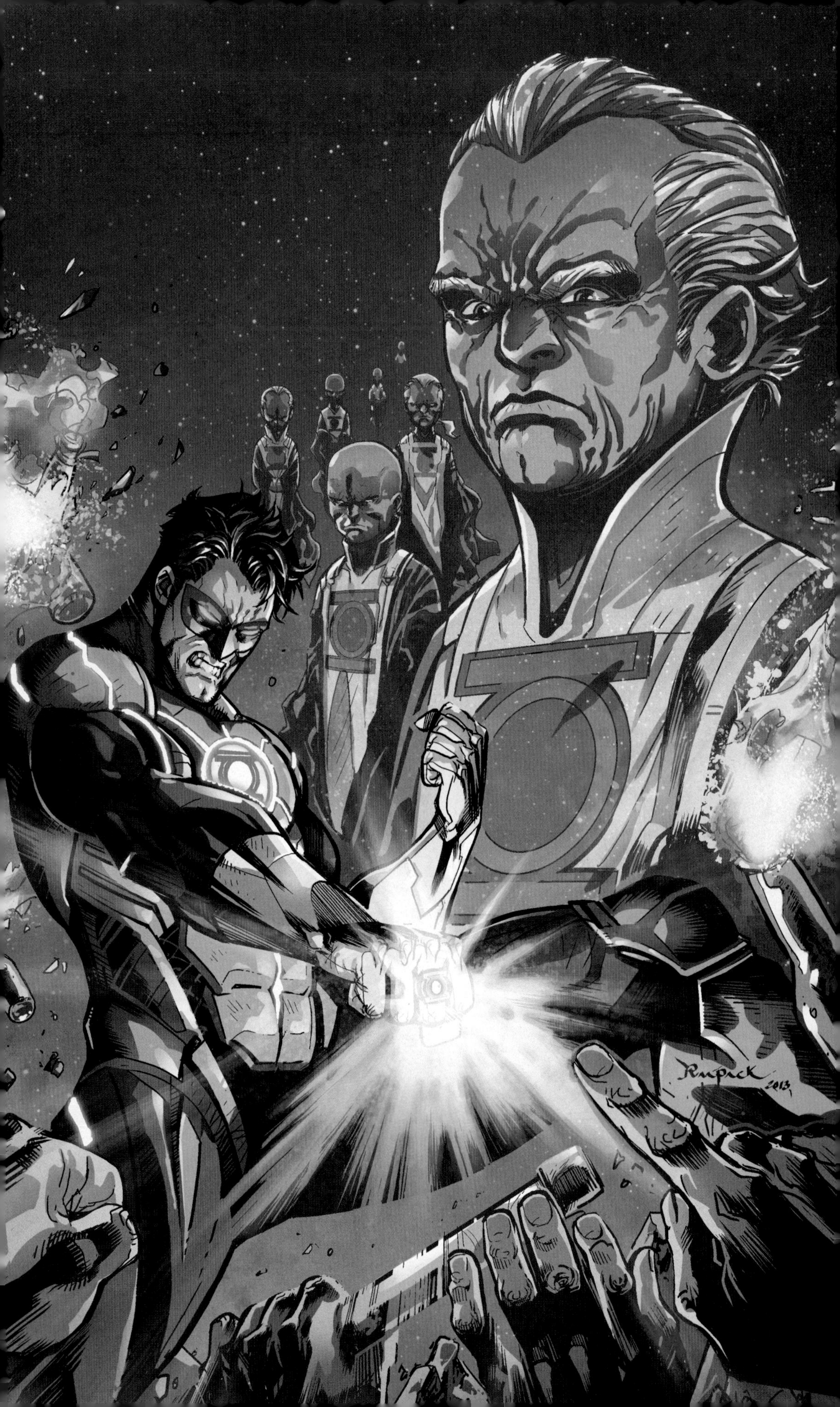

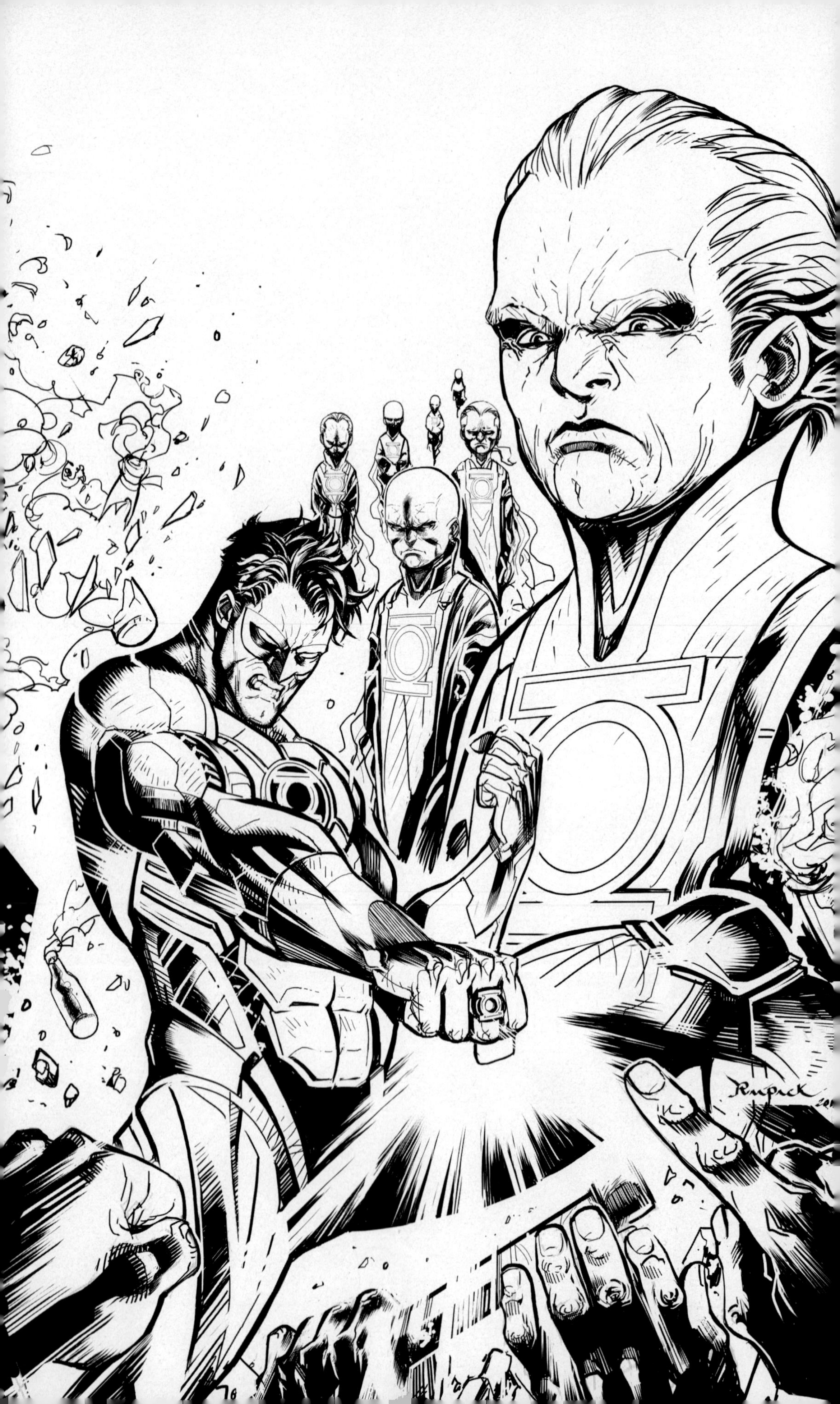

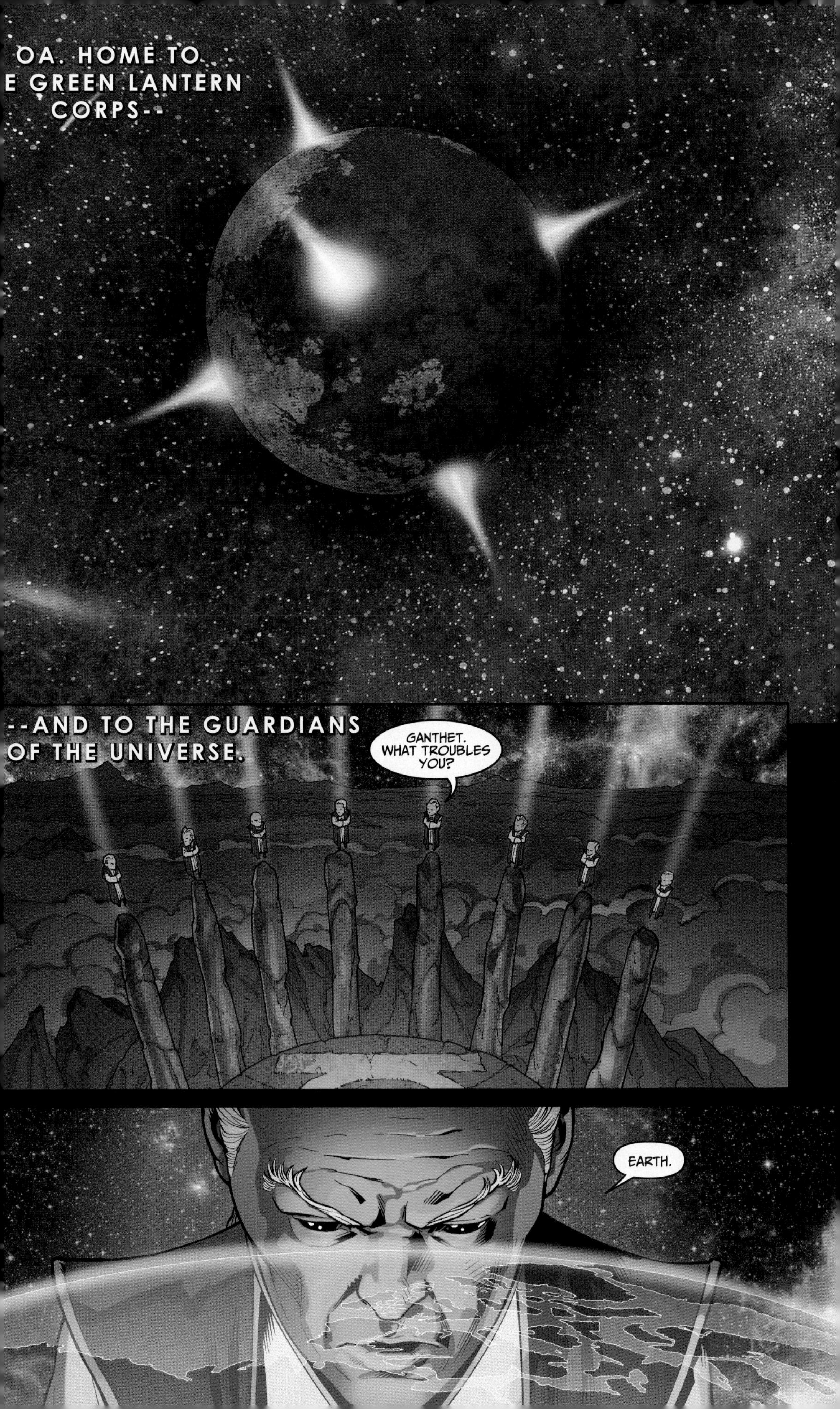
OA. HOME TO
E GREEN LANTERN
CORPS--
--AND TO THE GUARDIANS
OF THE UNIVERSE.
GANTHET. WHAT TROUBLES YOU?
EARTH.

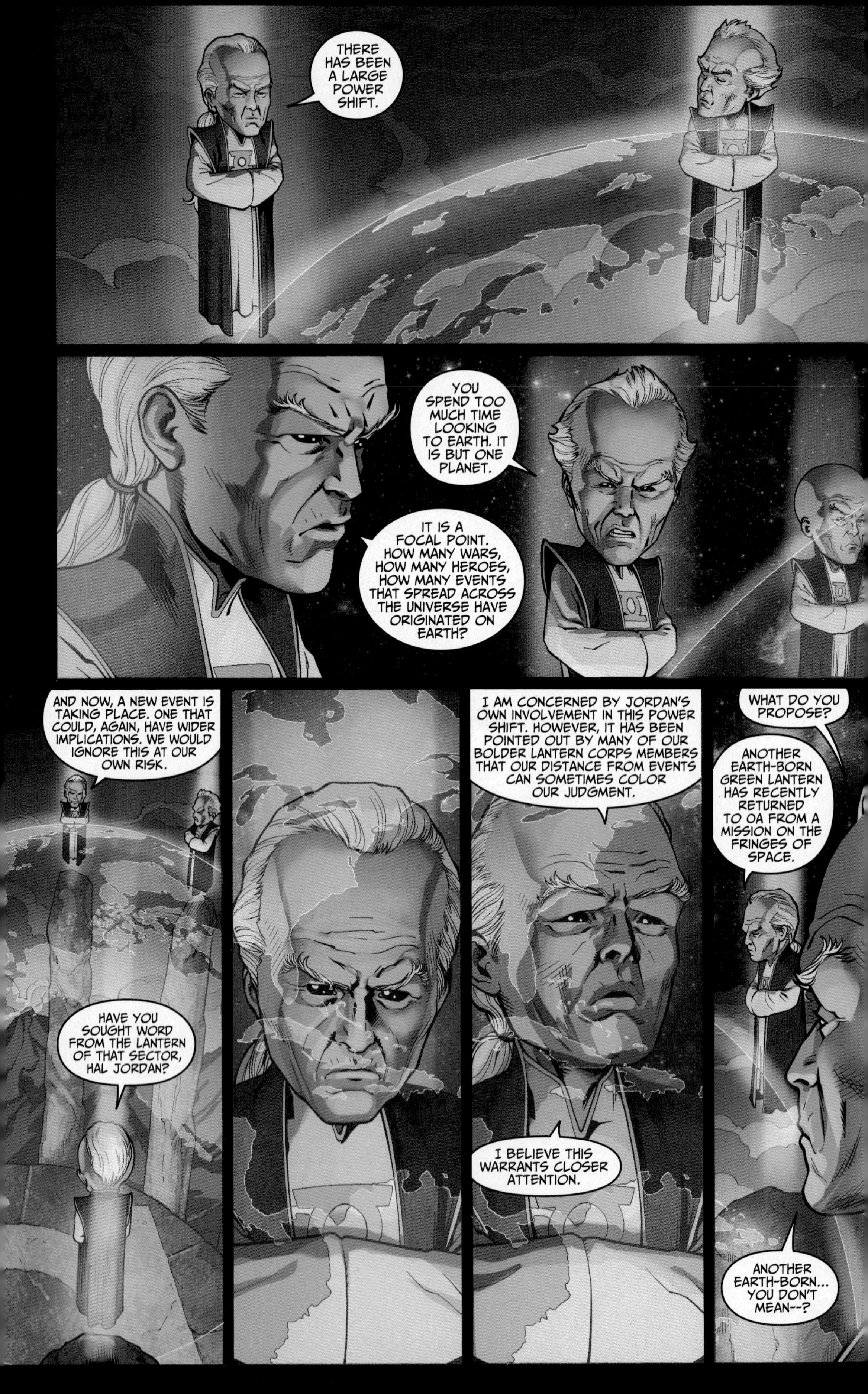
THERE HAS BEEN A LARGE POWER SHIFT.
YOU SPEND TOO MUCH TIME LOOKING TO EARTH. IT IS BUT ONE PLANET.
IT IS A FOCAL POINT. HOW MANY WARS, HOW MANY HEROES, HOW MANY EVENTS THAT SPREAD ACROSS THE UNIVERSE HAVE ORIGINATED ON EARTH?
AND NOW, A NEW EVENT IS TAKING PLACE. ONE THAT COULD, AGAIN, HAVE WIDER IMPLICATIONS. WE WOULD IGNORE THIS AT OUR OWN RISK.
HAVE YOU SOUGHT WORD FROM THE LANTERN OF THAT SECTOR, HAL JORDAN?
I AM CONCERNED BY JORDAN'S OWN INVOLVEMENT IN THIS POWER SHIFT. HOWEVER, IT HAS BEEN POINTED OUT BY MANY OF OUR BOLDER LANTERN CORPS MEMBERS THAT OUR DISTANCE FROM EVENTS CAN SOMETIMES COLOR OUR JUDGMENT.
I BELIEVE THIS WARRANTS CLOSER ATTENTION.
WHAT DO YOU PROPOSE?
ANOTHER EARTH-BORN GREEN LANTERN HAS RECENTLY RETURNED TO OA FROM A MISSION ON THE FRINGES OF SPACE.
ANOTHER EARTH-BORN... YOU DON'T MEAN--?

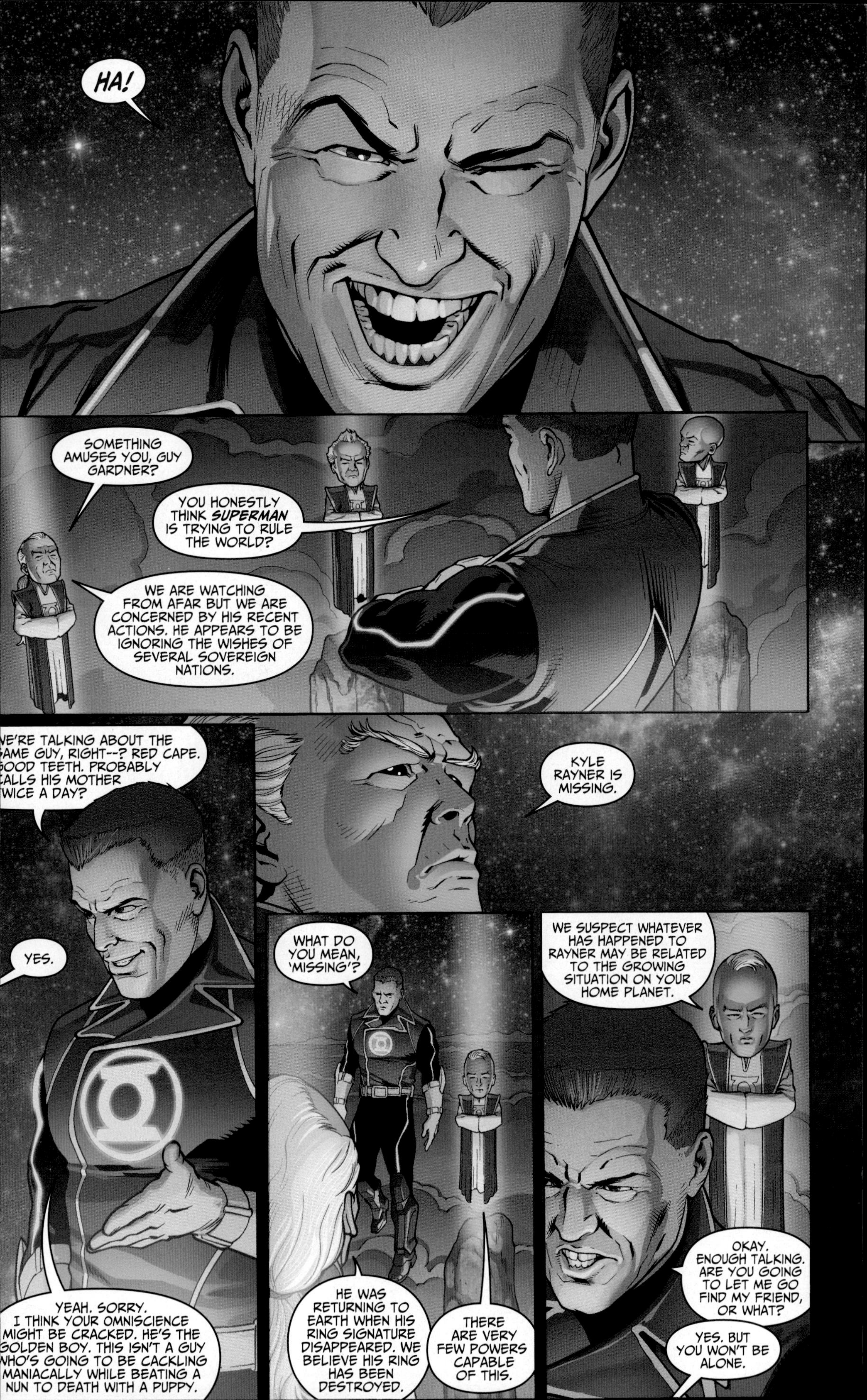
HA!
SOMETHING AMUSES YOU, GUY GARDNER?
YOU HONESTLY THINK SUPERMAN IS TRYING TO RULE THE WORLD?
WE ARE WATCHING FROM AFAR BUT WE ARE CONCERNED BY HIS RECENT ACTIONS. HE APPEARS TO BE IGNORING THE WISHES OF SEVERAL SOVEREIGN NATIONS.
E'RE TALKING ABOUT THE AME GUY, RIGHT--? RED CAPE. OOD TEETH. PROBABLY ALLS HIS MOTHER WICE A DAY?
YES.
YEAH. SORRY. I THINK YOUR OMNISCIENCE MIGHT BE CRACKED. HE'S THE OLDEN BOY. THIS ISN'T A GUY HO'S GOING TO BE CACKLING MANIACALLY WHILE BEATING A NUN TO DEATH WITH A PUPPY.
KYLE RAYNER IS MISSING.
WHAT DO YOU MEAN, 'MISSING'?
HE WAS RETURNING TO EARTH WHEN HIS RING SIGNATURE DISAPPEARED. WE BELIEVE HIS RING HAS BEEN DESTROYED.
THERE ARE VERY FEW POWERS CAPABLE OF THIS.
WE SUSPECT WHATEVER HAS HAPPENED TO RAYNER MAY BE RELATED TO THE GROWING SITUATION ON YOUR HOME PLANET.
OKAY. ENOUGH TALKING. ARE YOU GOING TO LET ME GO FIND MY FRIEND, OR WHAT?
YES. BUT YOU WON'T BE ALONE.

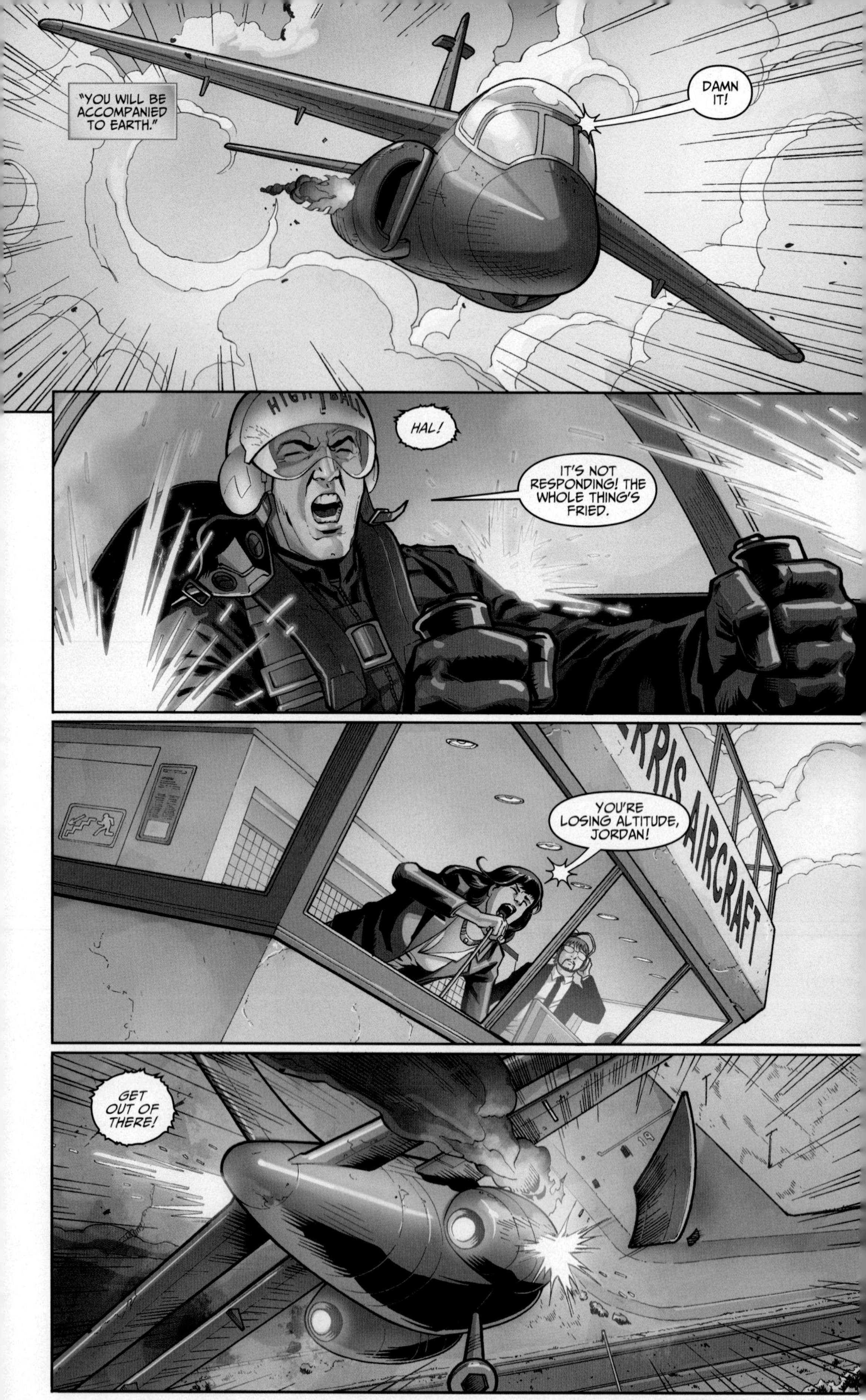

"YOU WILL BE ACCOMPANIED TO EARTH."
DAMN IT!
HAL!
IT'S NOT RESPONDING! THE WHOLE THING'S FRIED.
YOU'RE LOSING ALTITUDE, JORDAN!
GET OUT OF THERE!

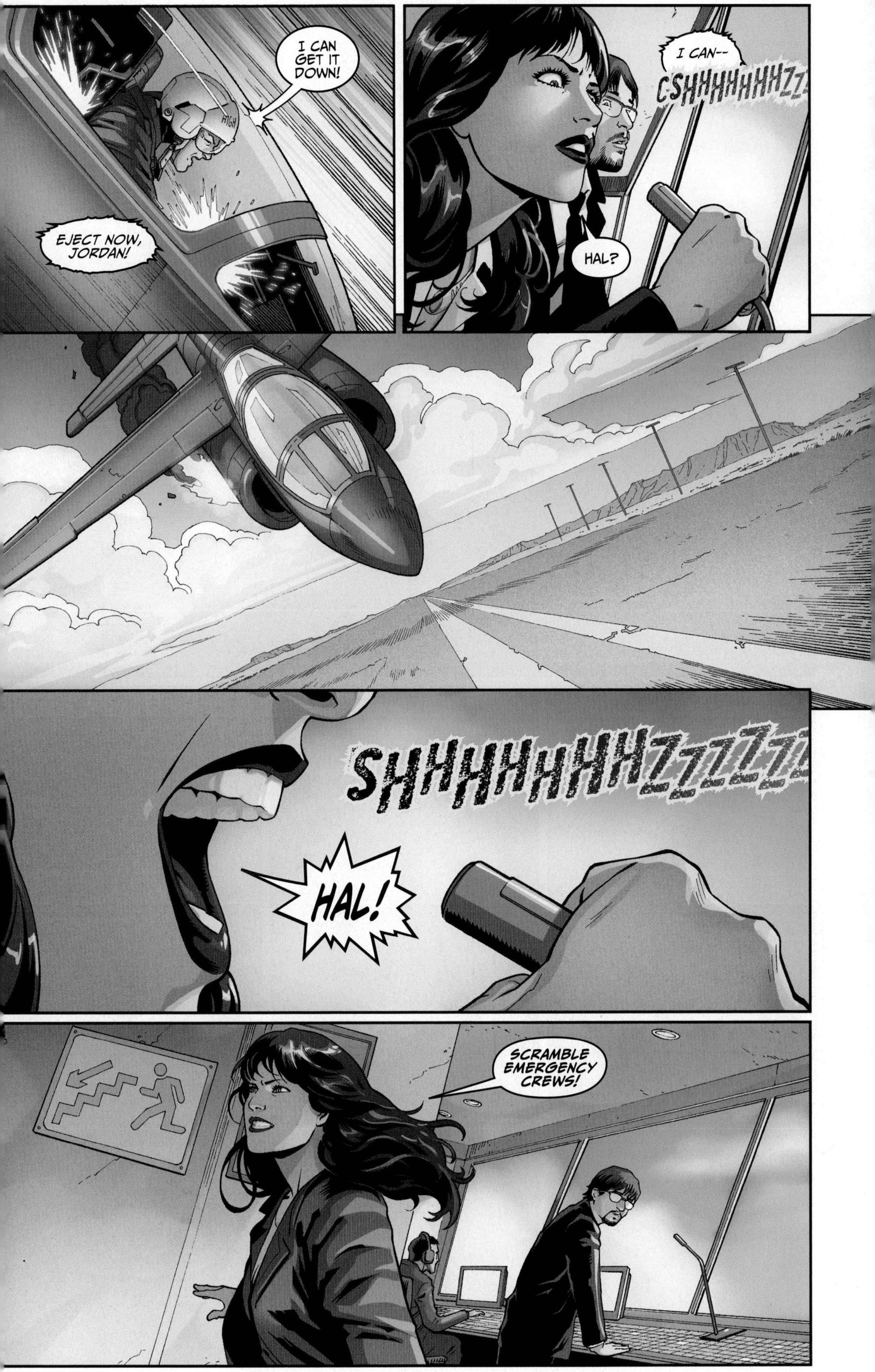

I CAN GET IT DOWN!
EJECT NOW, JORDAN!
I CAN--
CSHHHHHHHZZZ
HAL?
SHHHHHHHHZZZZZ
HAL!
SCRAMBLE EMERGENCY CREWS!

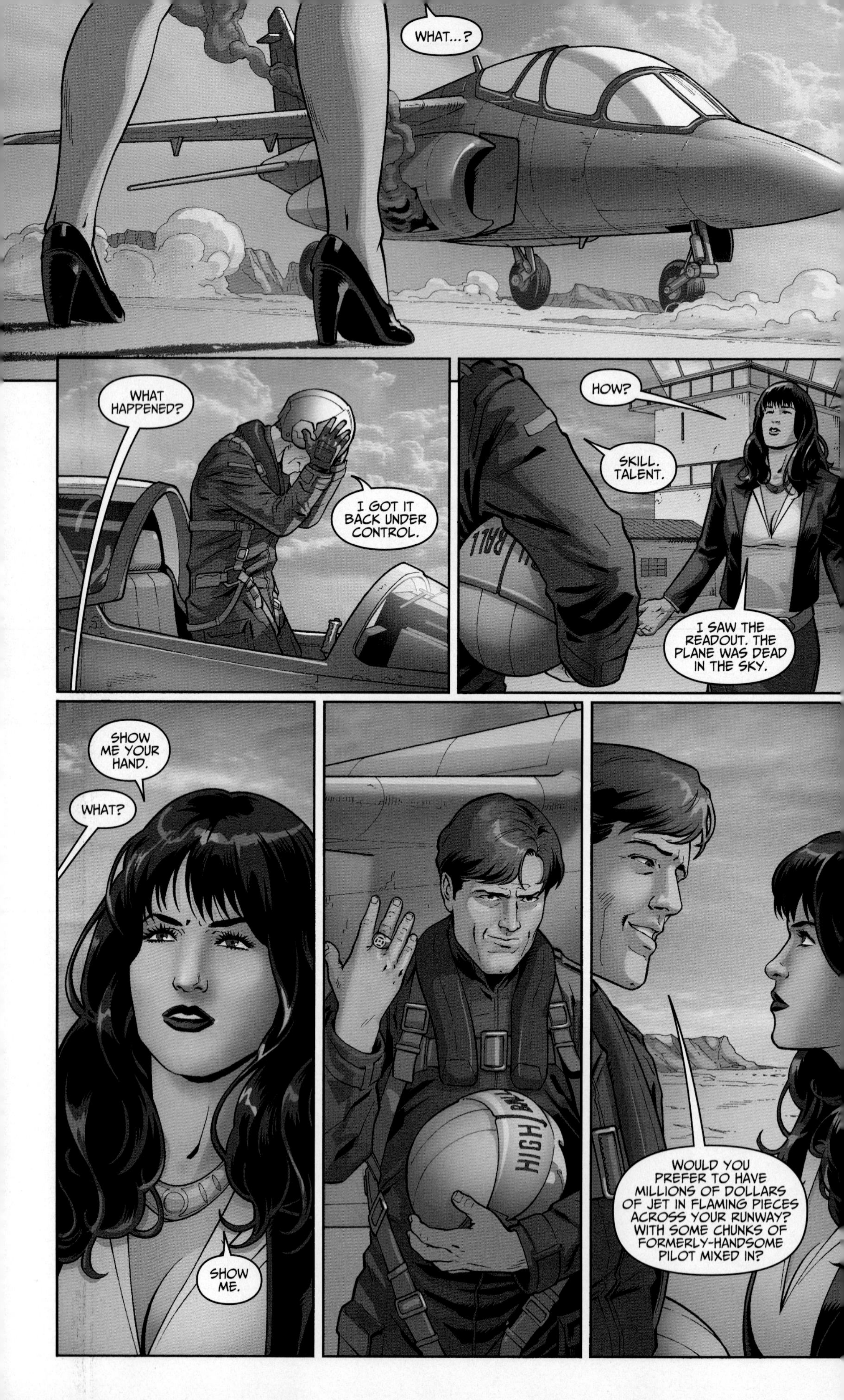

WHAT...?
WHAT HAPPENED?
I GOT IT BACK UNDER CONTROL.
HOW?
SKILL. TALENT.
I SAW THE READOUT. THE PLANE WAS DEAD IN THE SKY.
SHOW ME YOUR HAND.
WHAT?
SHOW ME.
HIGH BALL
WOULD YOU PREFER TO HAVE MILLIONS OF DOLLARS OF JET IN FLAMING PIECES ACROSS YOUR RUNWAY? WITH SOME CHUNKS OF FORMERLY-HANDSOME PILOT MIXED IN?

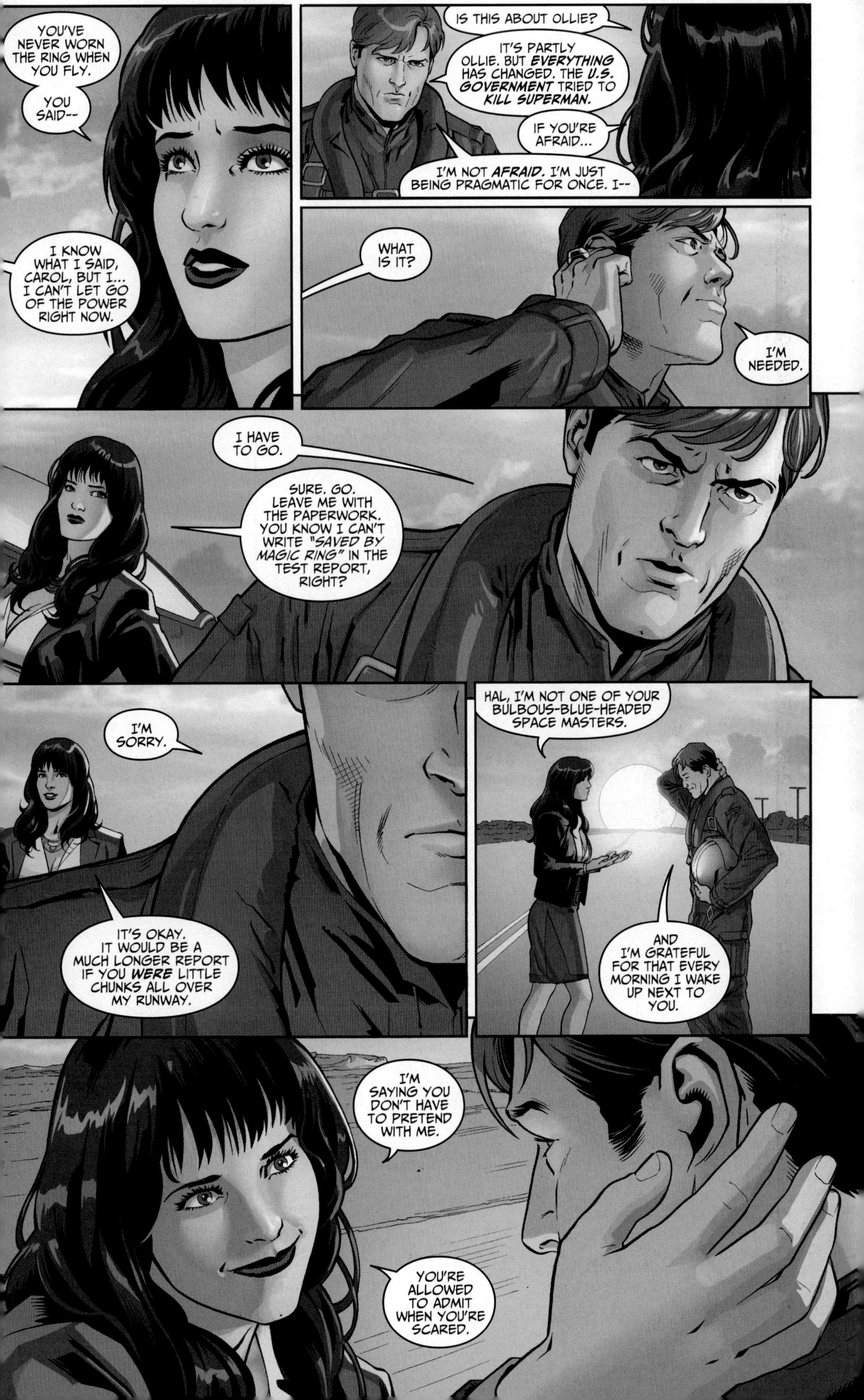

YOU'VE NEVER WORN THE RING WHEN YOU FLY.
YOU SAID--
IS THIS ABOUT OLLIE?
IT'S PARTLY OLLIE. BUT **EVERYTHING** HAS CHANGED. THE ***U.S. GOVERNMENT*** TRIED TO ***KILL SUPERMAN.***
IF YOU'RE AFRAID...
I'M NOT ***AFRAID.*** I'M JUST BEING PRAGMATIC FOR ONCE. I--
I KNOW WHAT I SAID, CAROL, BUT I... I CAN'T LET GO OF THE POWER RIGHT NOW.
WHAT IS IT?
I'M NEEDED.
I HAVE TO GO.
SURE. GO. LEAVE ME WITH THE PAPERWORK. YOU KNOW I CAN'T WRITE *"SAVED BY MAGIC RING"* IN THE TEST REPORT, RIGHT?
I'M SORRY.
IT'S OKAY. IT WOULD BE A MUCH LONGER REPORT IF YOU ***WERE*** LITTLE CHUNKS ALL OVER MY RUNWAY.
HAL, I'M NOT ONE OF YOUR BULBOUS-BLUE-HEADED SPACE MASTERS.
AND I'M GRATEFUL FOR THAT EVERY MORNING I WAKE UP NEXT TO YOU.
I'M SAYING YOU DON'T HAVE TO PRETEND WITH ME.
YOU'RE ALLOWED TO ADMIT WHEN YOU'RE SCARED.

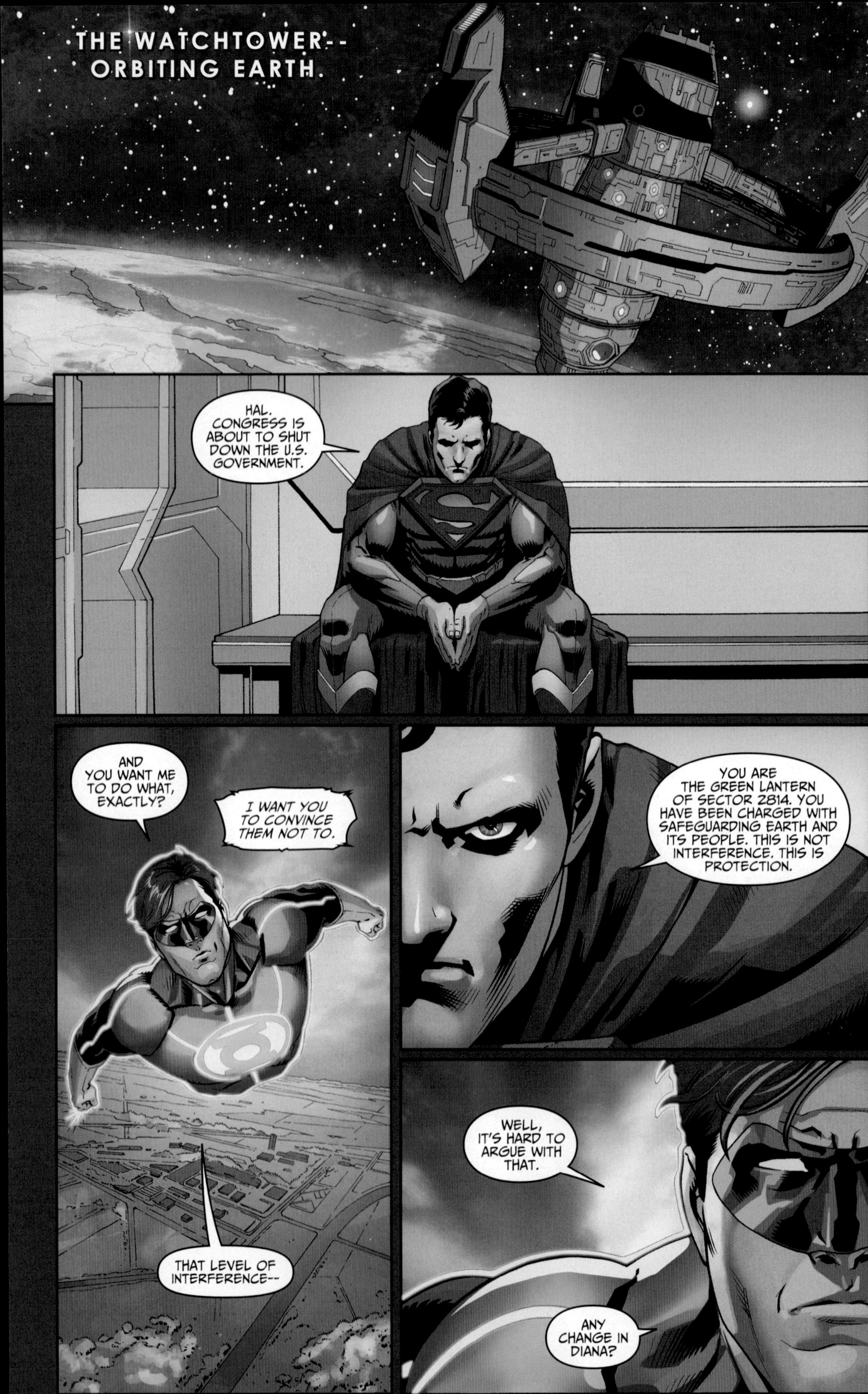
THE WATCHTOWER--
ORBITING EARTH.
HAL. CONGRESS IS ABOUT TO SHUT DOWN THE U.S. GOVERNMENT.
AND YOU WANT ME TO DO WHAT, EXACTLY?
I WANT YOU TO CONVINCE THEM NOT TO.
THAT LEVEL OF INTERFERENCE--
YOU ARE THE GREEN LANTERN OF SECTOR 2814. YOU HAVE BEEN CHARGED WITH SAFEGUARDING EARTH AND ITS PEOPLE. THIS IS NOT INTERFERENCE. THIS IS PROTECTION.
WELL, IT'S HARD TO ARGUE WITH THAT.
ANY CHANGE IN DIANA?

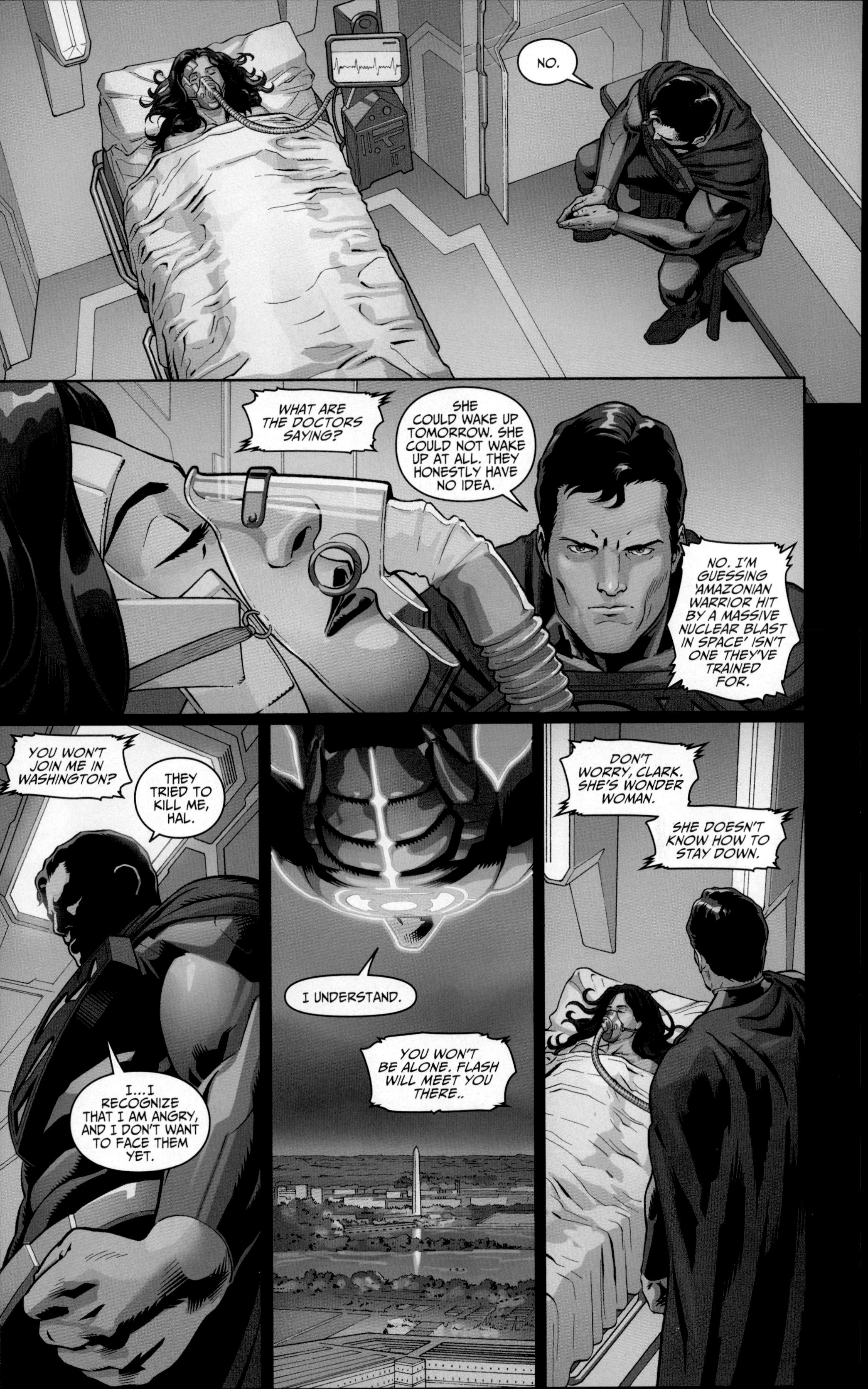
NO.
WHAT ARE THE DOCTORS SAYING?
SHE COULD WAKE UP TOMORROW. SHE COULD NOT WAKE UP AT ALL. THEY HONESTLY HAVE NO IDEA.
NO. I'M GUESSING 'AMAZONIAN WARRIOR HIT BY A MASSIVE NUCLEAR BLAST IN SPACE' ISN'T ONE THEY'VE TRAINED FOR.
YOU WON'T JOIN ME IN WASHINGTON?
THEY TRIED TO KILL ME, HAL.
I...I RECOGNIZE THAT I AM ANGRY, AND I DON'T WANT TO FACE THEM YET.
I UNDERSTAND.
YOU WON'T BE ALONE. FLASH WILL MEET YOU THERE..
DON'T WORRY, CLARK. SHE'S WONDER WOMAN.
SHE DOESN'T KNOW HOW TO STAY DOWN.

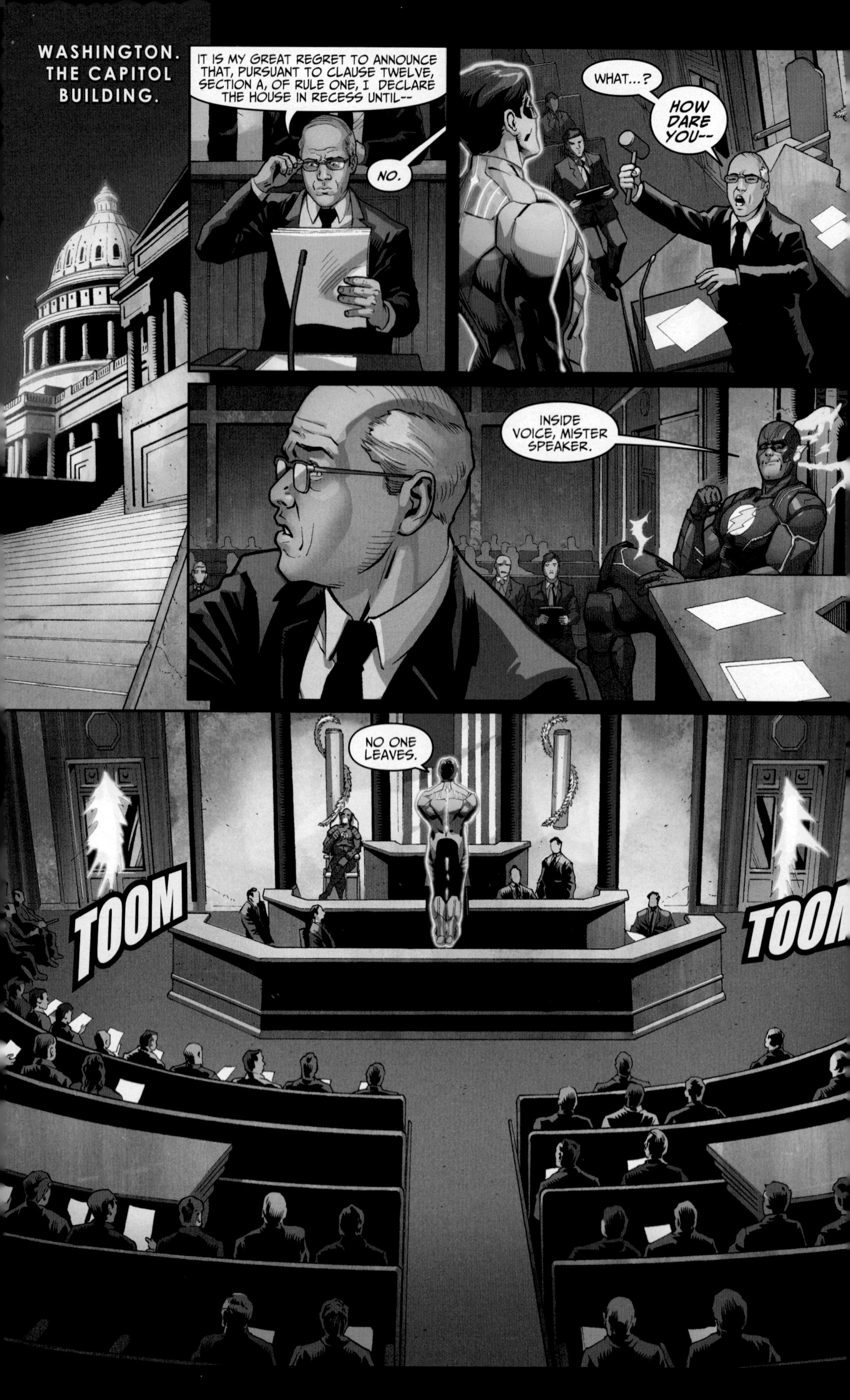
WASHINGTON. THE CAPITOL BUILDING.
IT IS MY GREAT REGRET TO ANNOUNCE THAT, PURSUANT TO CLAUSE TWELVE, SECTION A, OF RULE ONE, I DECLARE THE HOUSE IN RECESS UNTIL--
NO.
WHAT...?
HOW DARE YOU--
INSIDE VOICE, MISTER SPEAKER.
NO ONE LEAVES.
TOOM
TOOM

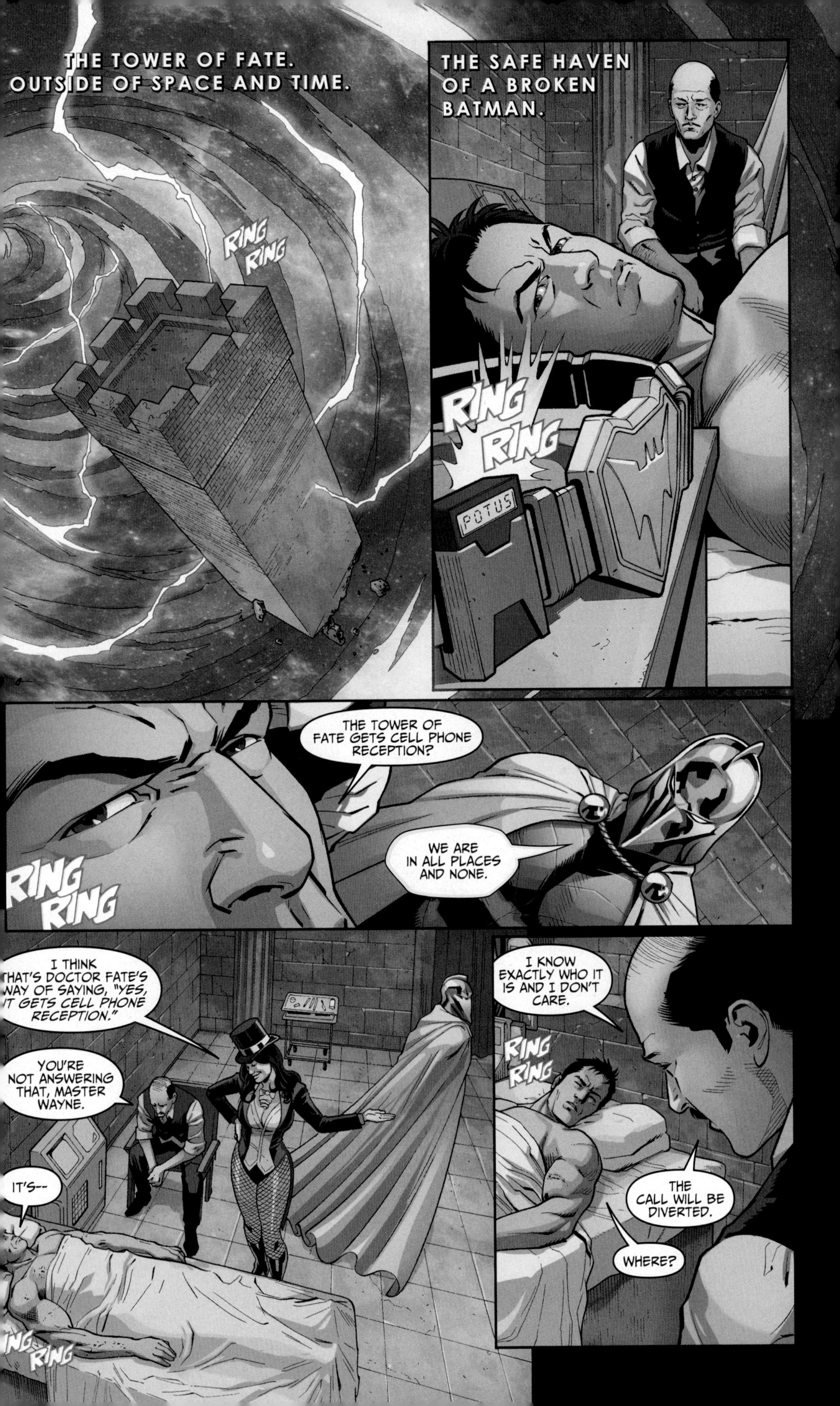
THE TOWER OF FATE. OUTSIDE OF SPACE AND TIME.
RING RING
THE SAFE HAVEN OF A BROKEN BATMAN.
RING RING
POTUS
THE TOWER OF FATE GETS CELL PHONE RECEPTION?
WE ARE IN ALL PLACES AND NONE.
RING RING
I THINK THAT'S DOCTOR FATE'S WAY OF SAYING, "YES, IT GETS CELL PHONE RECEPTION."
YOU'RE NOT ANSWERING THAT, MASTER WAYNE.
IT'S--
I KNOW EXACTLY WHO IT IS AND I DON'T CARE.
RING RING
THE CALL WILL BE DIVERTED.
WHERE?

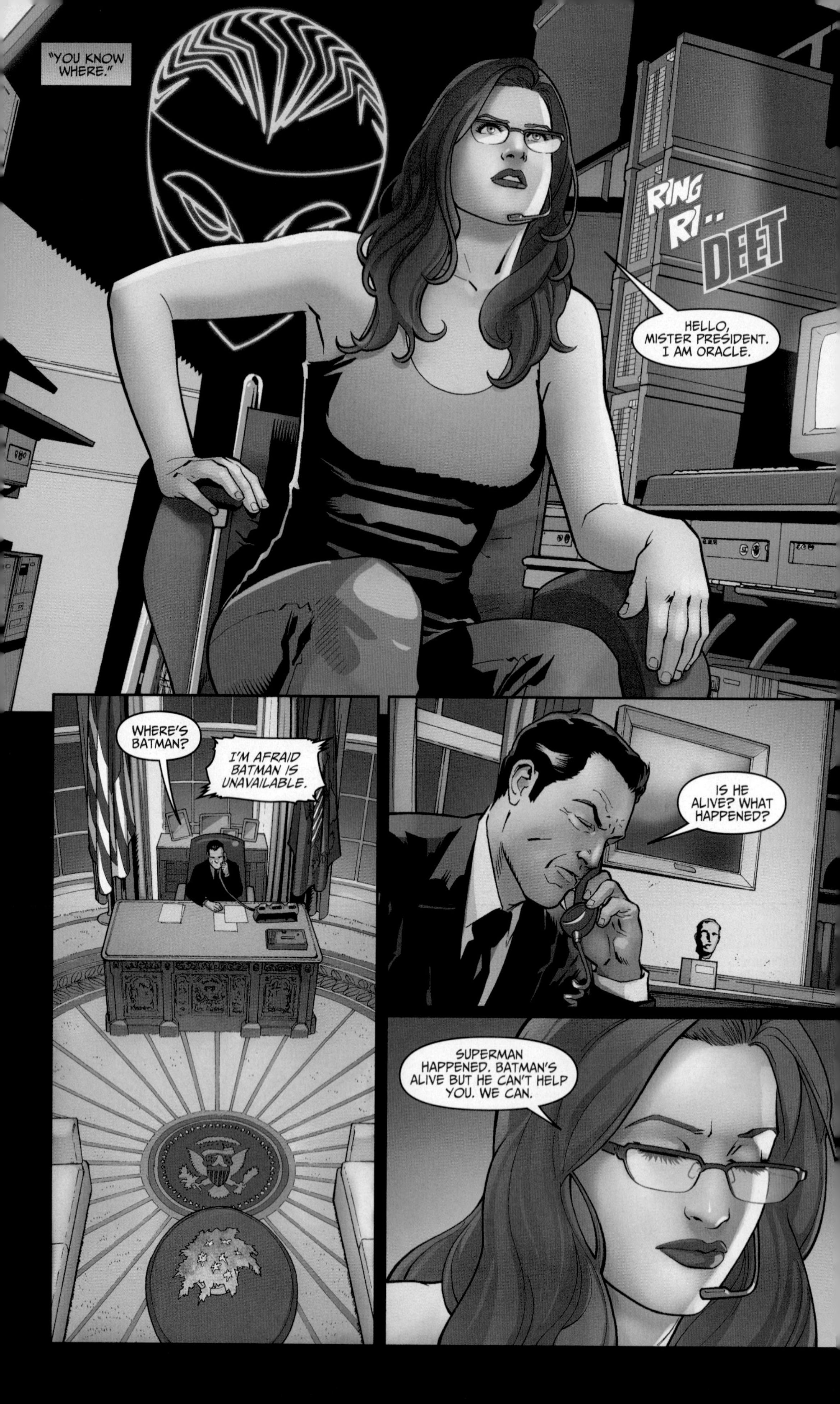
"YOU KNOW WHERE."
RING RI.. DEET
HELLO, MISTER PRESIDENT. I AM ORACLE.
WHERE'S BATMAN?
I'M AFRAID BATMAN IS UNAVAILABLE.
IS HE ALIVE? WHAT HAPPENED?
SUPERMAN HAPPENED. BATMAN'S ALIVE BUT HE CAN'T HELP YOU. WE CAN.

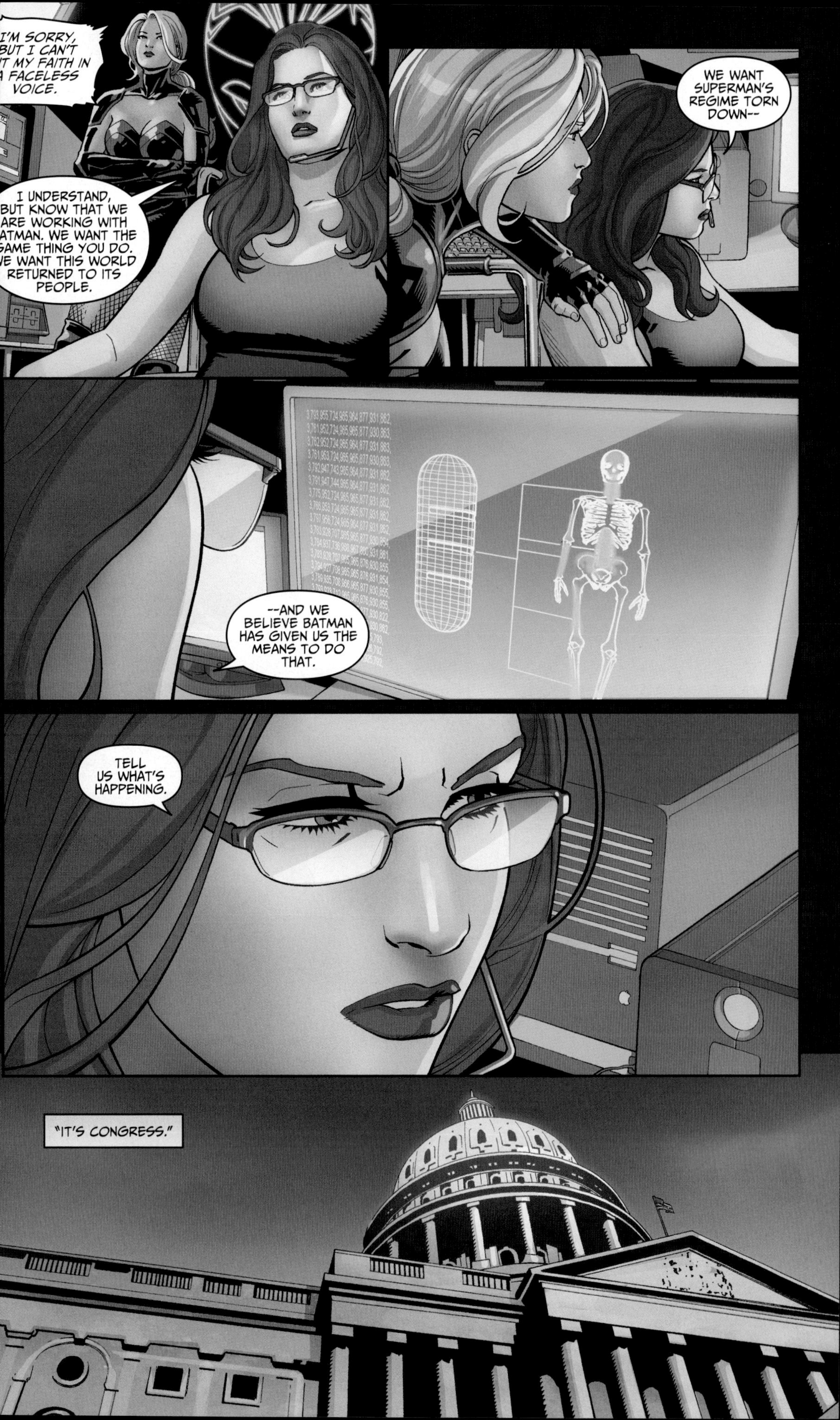
I'M SORRY, BUT I CAN'T T MY FAITH IN A FACELESS VOICE.
I UNDERSTAND, BUT KNOW THAT WE ARE WORKING WITH BATMAN. WE WANT THE SAME THING YOU DO. WE WANT THIS WORLD RETURNED TO ITS PEOPLE.
WE WANT SUPERMAN'S REGIME TORN DOWN--
--AND WE BELIEVE BATMAN HAS GIVEN US THE MEANS TO DO THAT.
TELL US WHAT'S HAPPENING.
"IT'S CONGRESS."

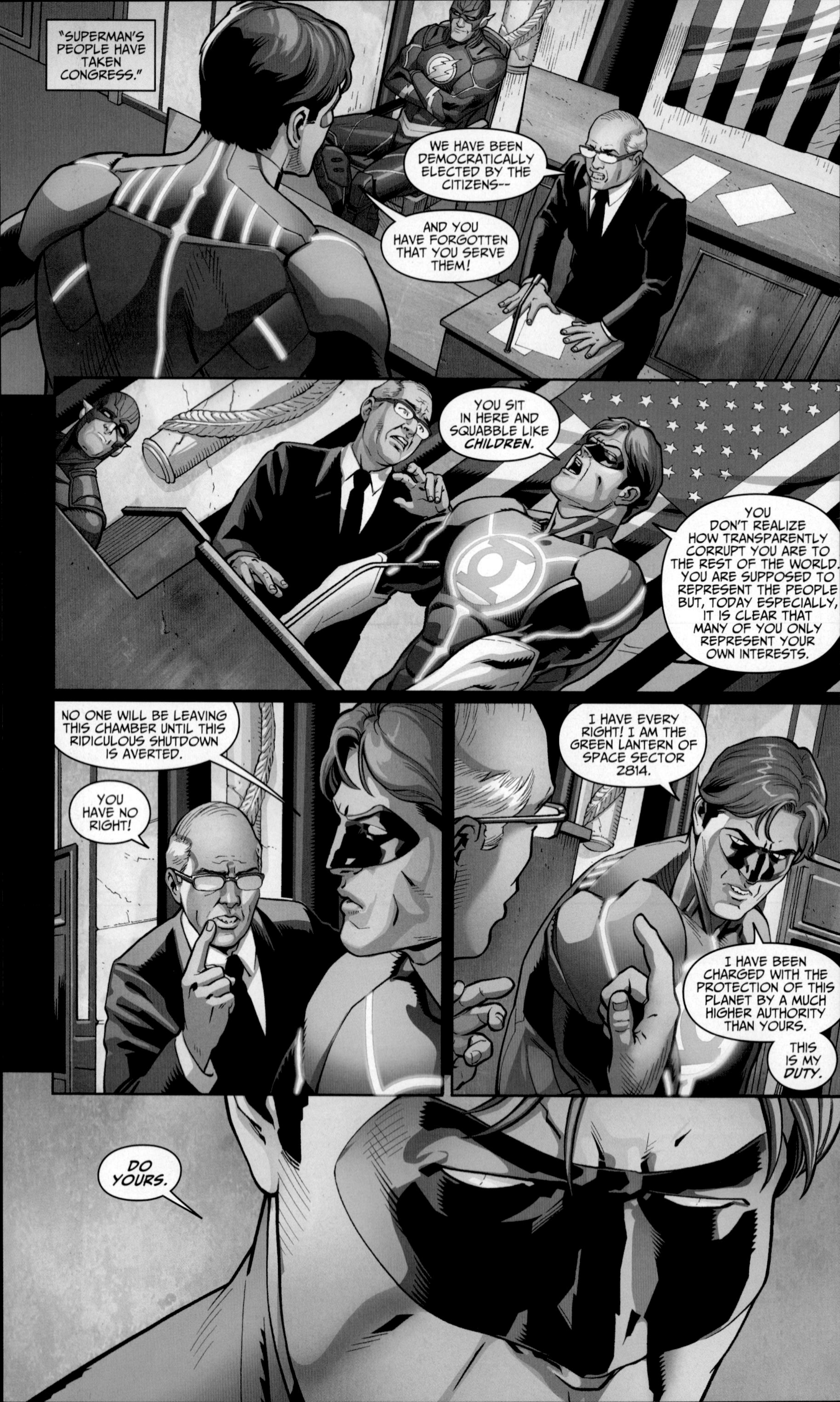
"SUPERMAN'S PEOPLE HAVE TAKEN CONGRESS."
WE HAVE BEEN DEMOCRATICALLY ELECTED BY THE CITIZENS--
AND YOU HAVE FORGOTTEN THAT YOU SERVE THEM!
YOU SIT IN HERE AND SQUABBLE LIKE CHILDREN.
YOU DON'T REALIZE HOW TRANSPARENTLY CORRUPT YOU ARE TO THE REST OF THE WORLD. YOU ARE SUPPOSED TO REPRESENT THE PEOPLE BUT, TODAY ESPECIALLY, IT IS CLEAR THAT MANY OF YOU ONLY REPRESENT YOUR OWN INTERESTS.
NO ONE WILL BE LEAVING THIS CHAMBER UNTIL THIS RIDICULOUS SHUTDOWN IS AVERTED.
YOU HAVE NO RIGHT!
I HAVE EVERY RIGHT! I AM THE GREEN LANTERN OF SPACE SECTOR 2814.
I HAVE BEEN CHARGED WITH THE PROTECTION OF THIS PLANET BY A MUCH HIGHER AUTHORITY THAN YOURS.
THIS IS MY DUTY.
DO YOURS.

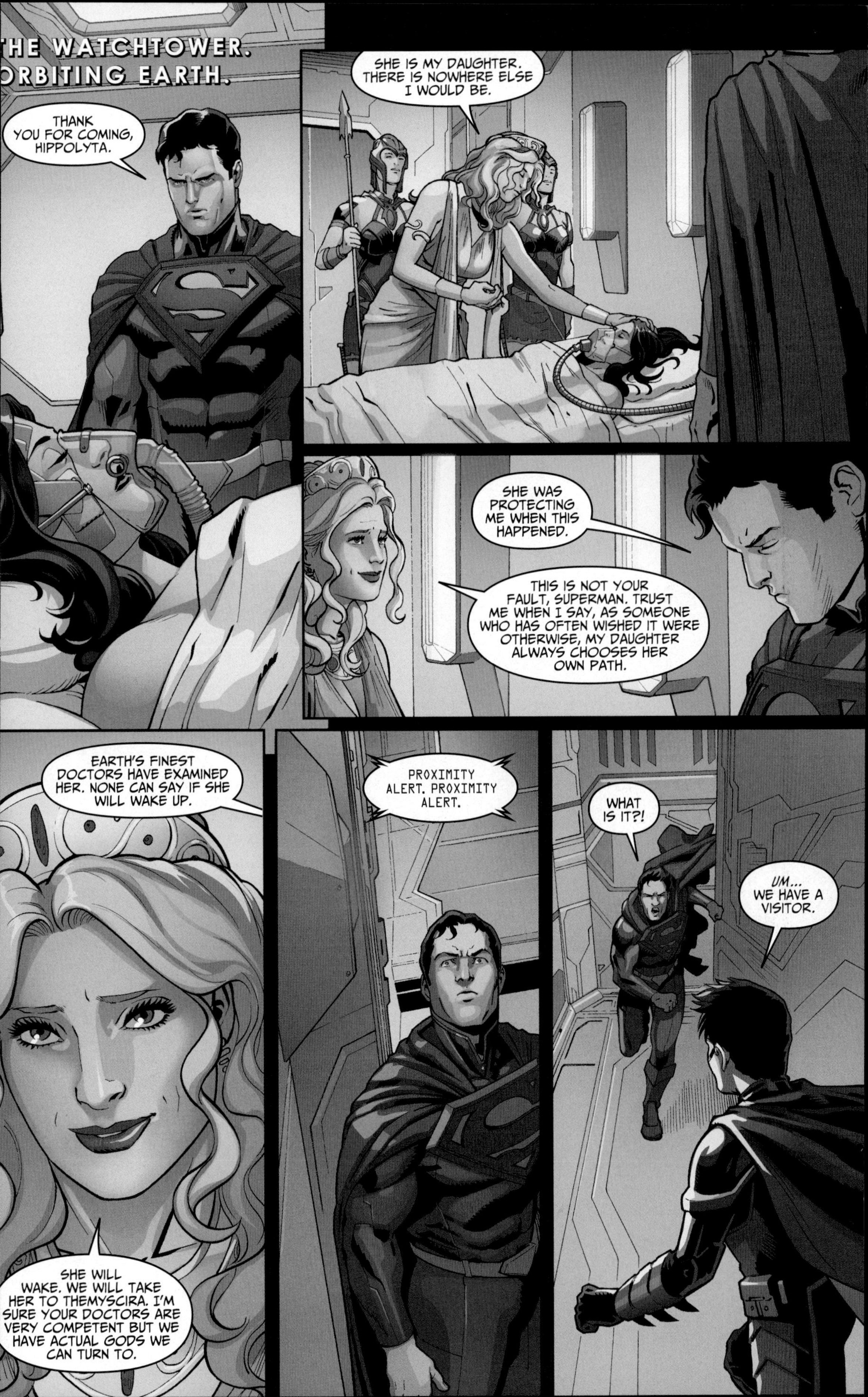
THE WATCHTOWER. ORBITING EARTH.
THANK YOU FOR COMING, HIPPOLYTA.
SHE IS MY DAUGHTER. THERE IS NOWHERE ELSE I WOULD BE.
SHE WAS PROTECTING ME WHEN THIS HAPPENED.
THIS IS NOT YOUR FAULT, SUPERMAN. TRUST ME WHEN I SAY, AS SOMEONE WHO HAS OFTEN WISHED IT WERE OTHERWISE, MY DAUGHTER ALWAYS CHOOSES HER OWN PATH.
EARTH'S FINEST DOCTORS HAVE EXAMINED HER. NONE CAN SAY IF SHE WILL WAKE UP.
SHE WILL WAKE. WE WILL TAKE HER TO THEMYSCIRA. I'M SURE YOUR DOCTORS ARE VERY COMPETENT BUT WE HAVE ACTUAL GODS WE CAN TURN TO.
PROXIMITY ALERT. PROXIMITY ALERT.
WHAT IS IT?!
UM... WE HAVE A VISITOR.

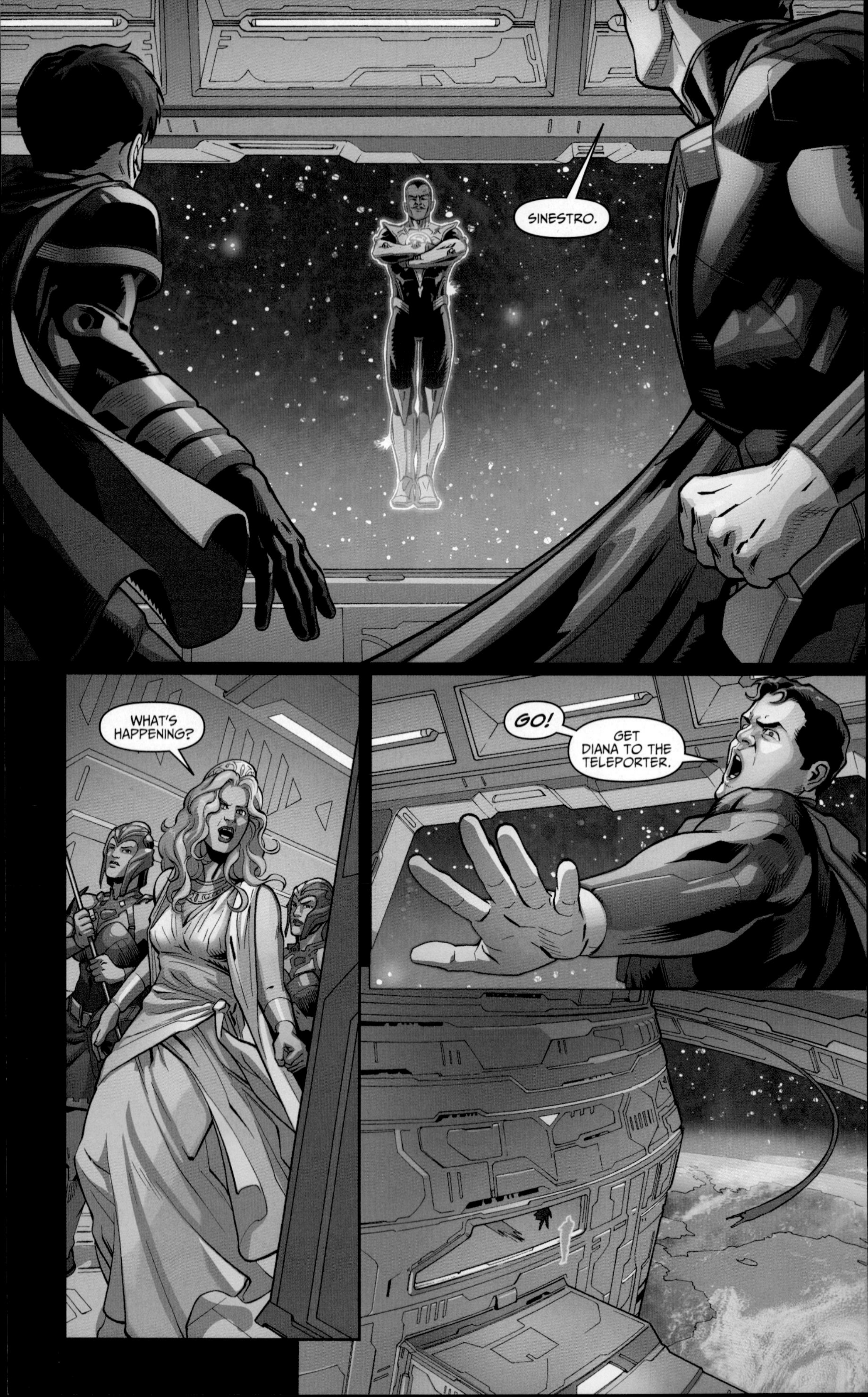
SINESTRO.
WHAT'S HAPPENING?
GO!
GET DIANA TO THE TELEPORTER.

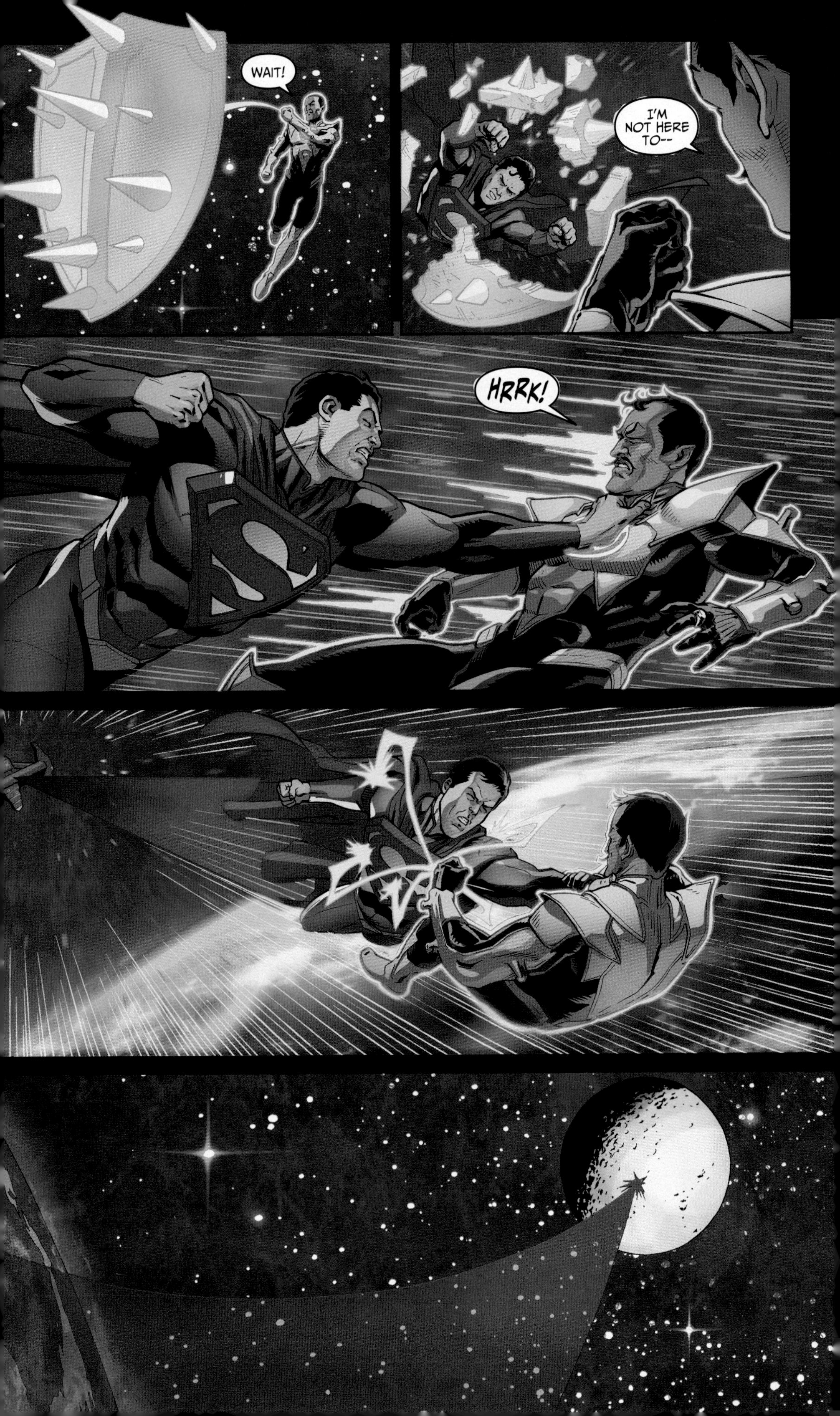
WAIT!
I'M NOT HERE TO--
HRRK!

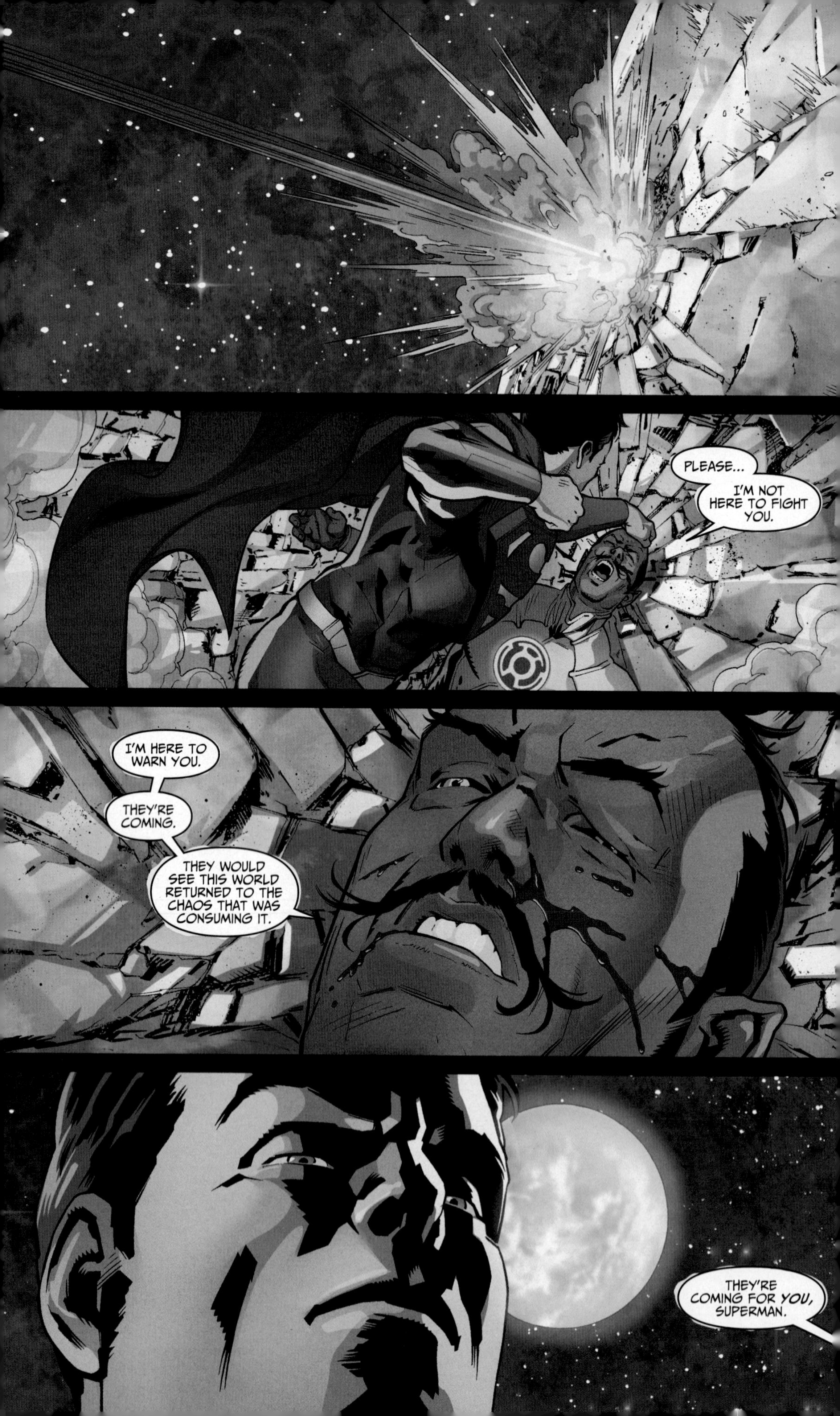
PLEASE...
I'M NOT HERE TO FIGHT YOU.
I'M HERE TO WARN YOU.
THEY'RE COMING.
THEY WOULD SEE THIS WORLD RETURNED TO THE CHAOS THAT WAS CONSUMING IT.
THEY'RE COMING FOR *YOU*, SUPERMAN.

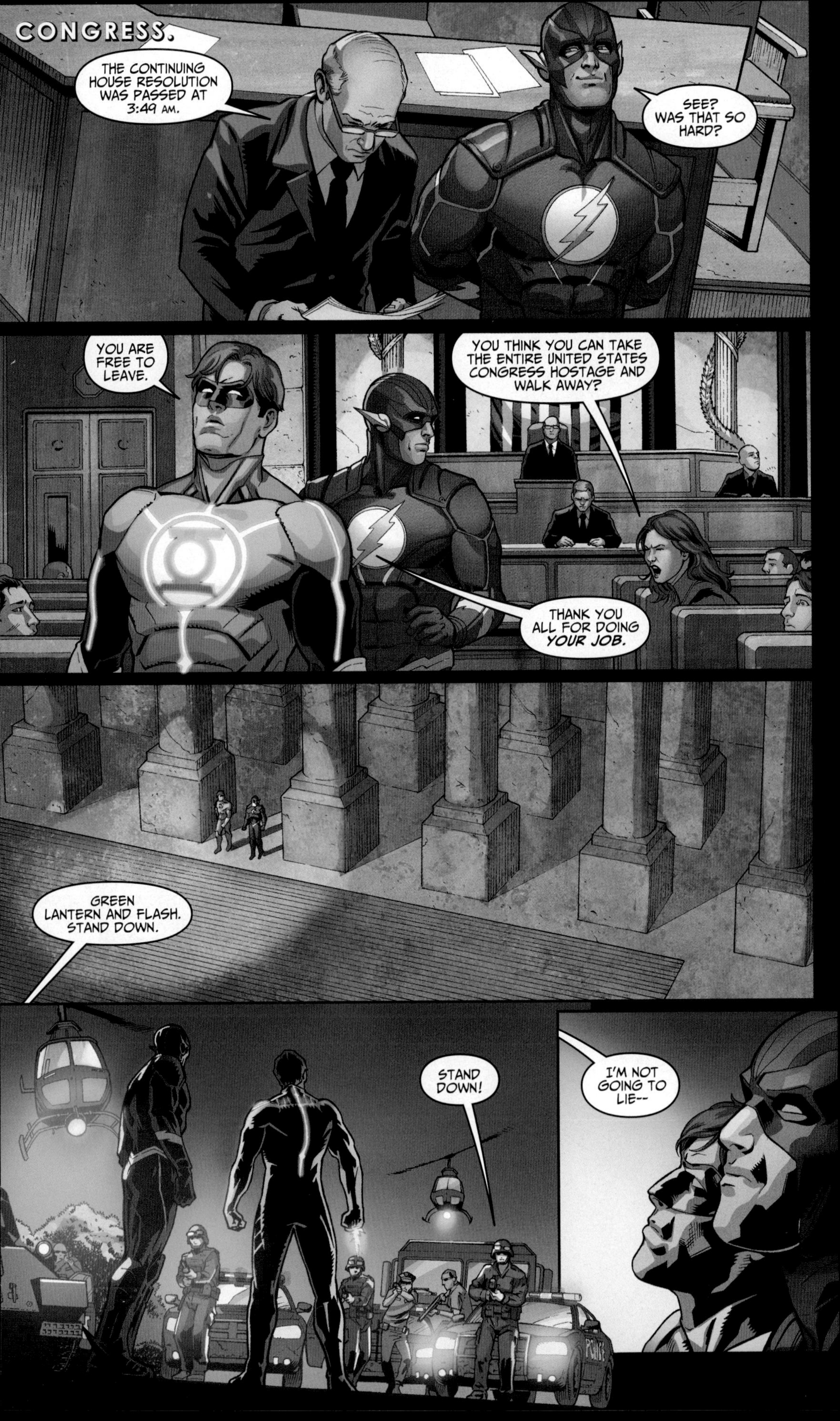
CONGRESS.
THE CONTINUING HOUSE RESOLUTION WAS PASSED AT 3:49 AM.
SEE? WAS THAT SO HARD?
YOU ARE FREE TO LEAVE.
YOU THINK YOU CAN TAKE THE ENTIRE UNITED STATES CONGRESS HOSTAGE AND WALK AWAY?
THANK YOU ALL FOR DOING *YOUR JOB.*
GREEN LANTERN AND FLASH. STAND DOWN.
STAND DOWN!
I'M NOT GOING TO LIE--

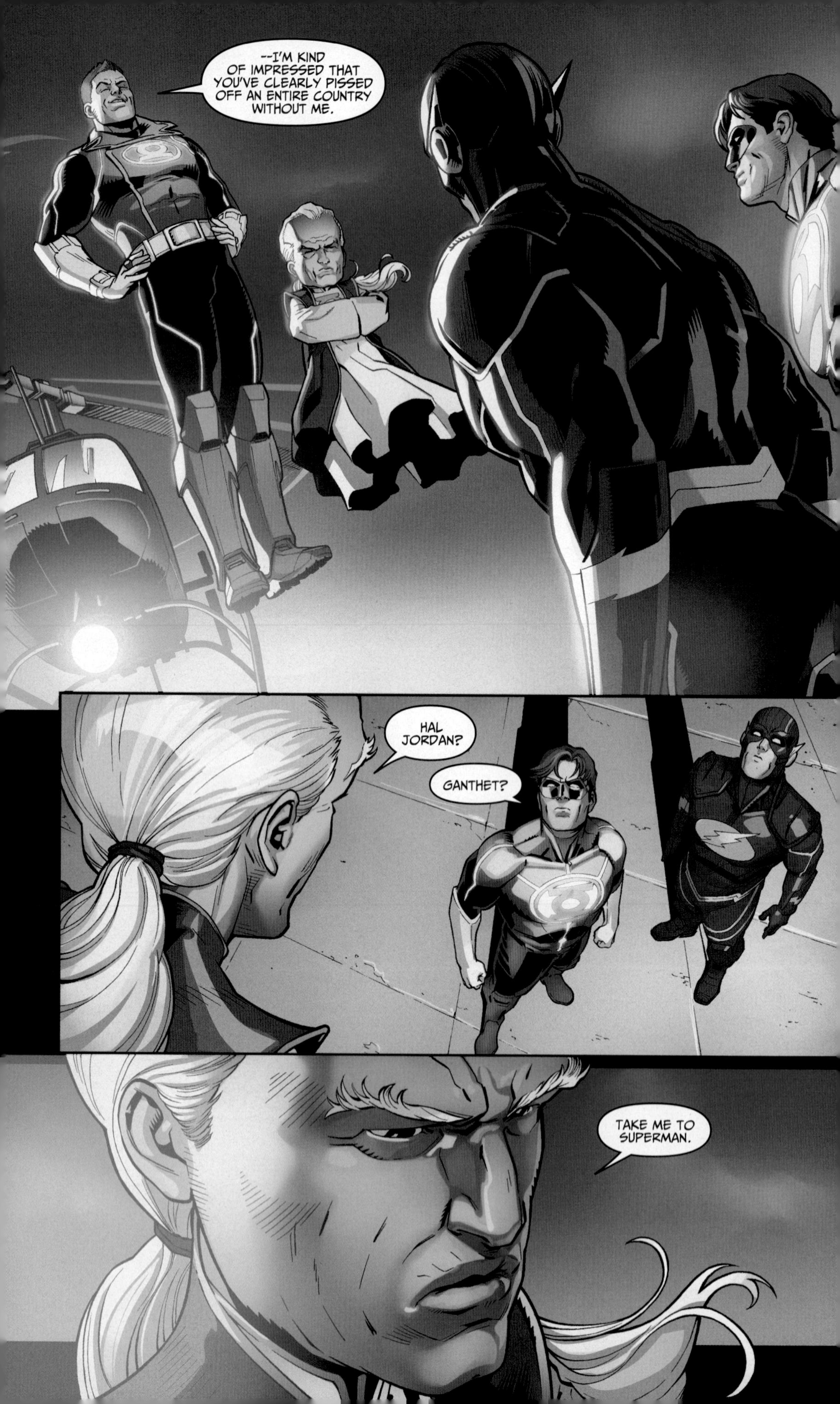
--I'M KIND OF IMPRESSED THAT YOU'VE CLEARLY PISSED OFF AN ENTIRE COUNTRY WITHOUT ME.
HAL JORDAN?
GANTHET?
TAKE ME TO SUPERMAN.

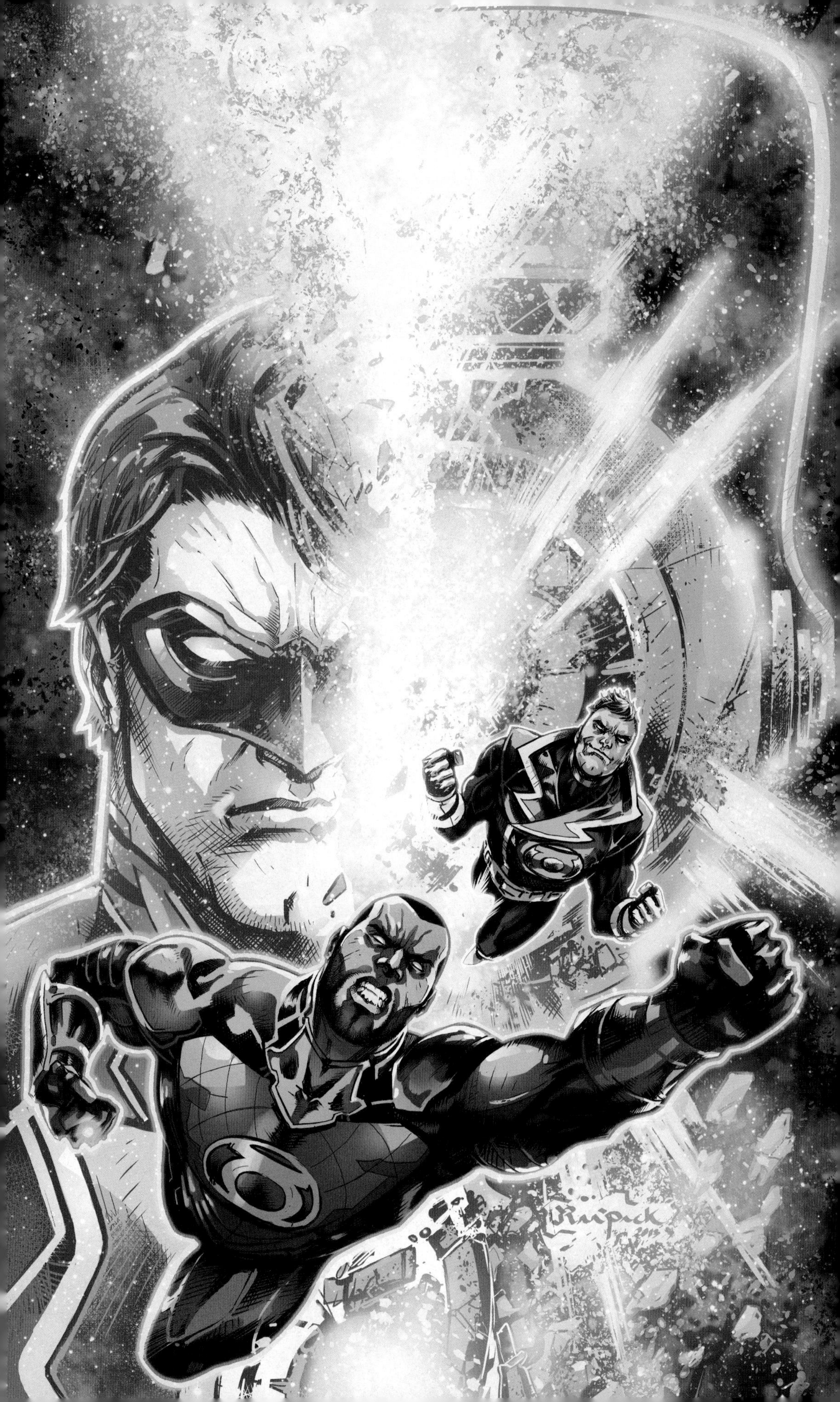

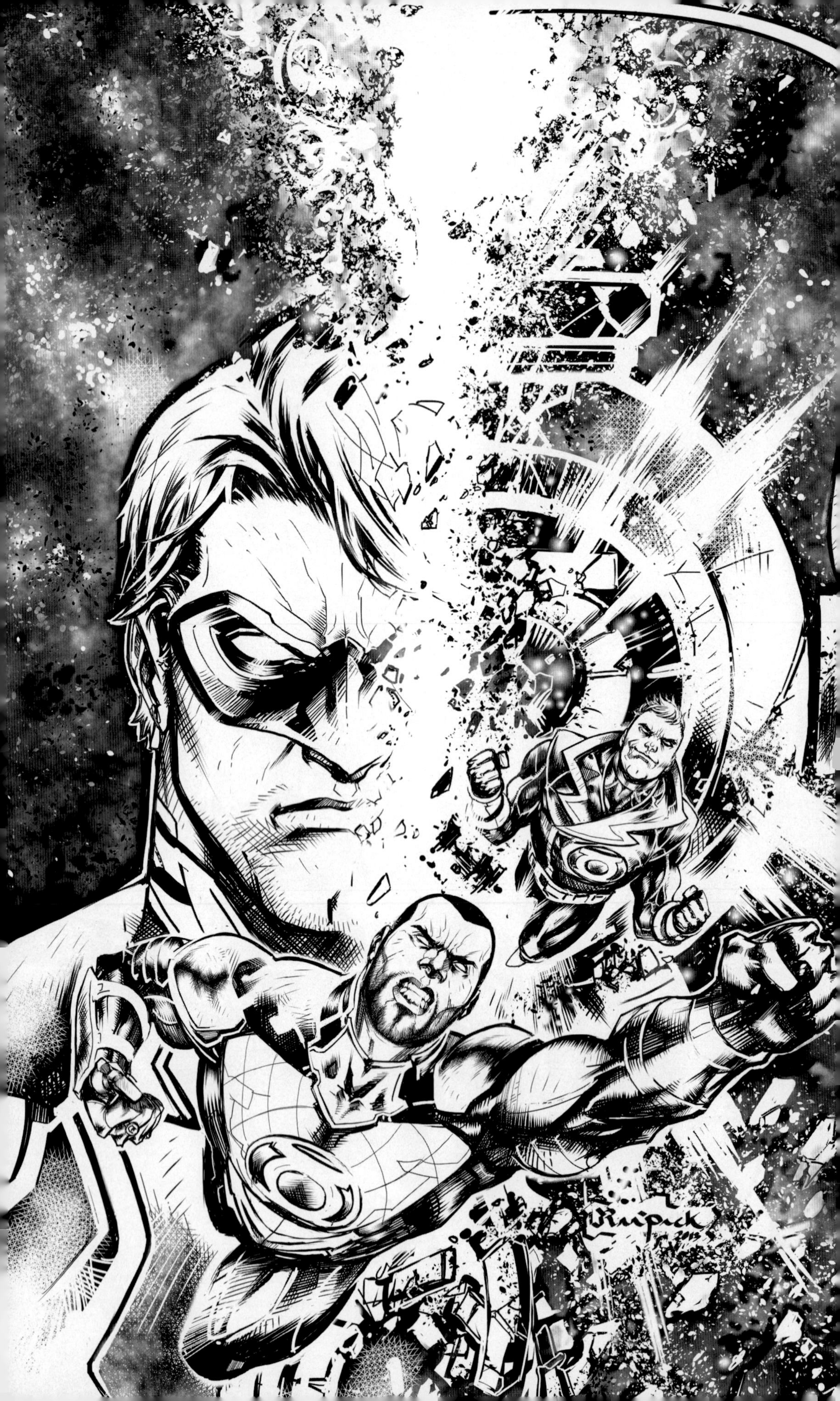

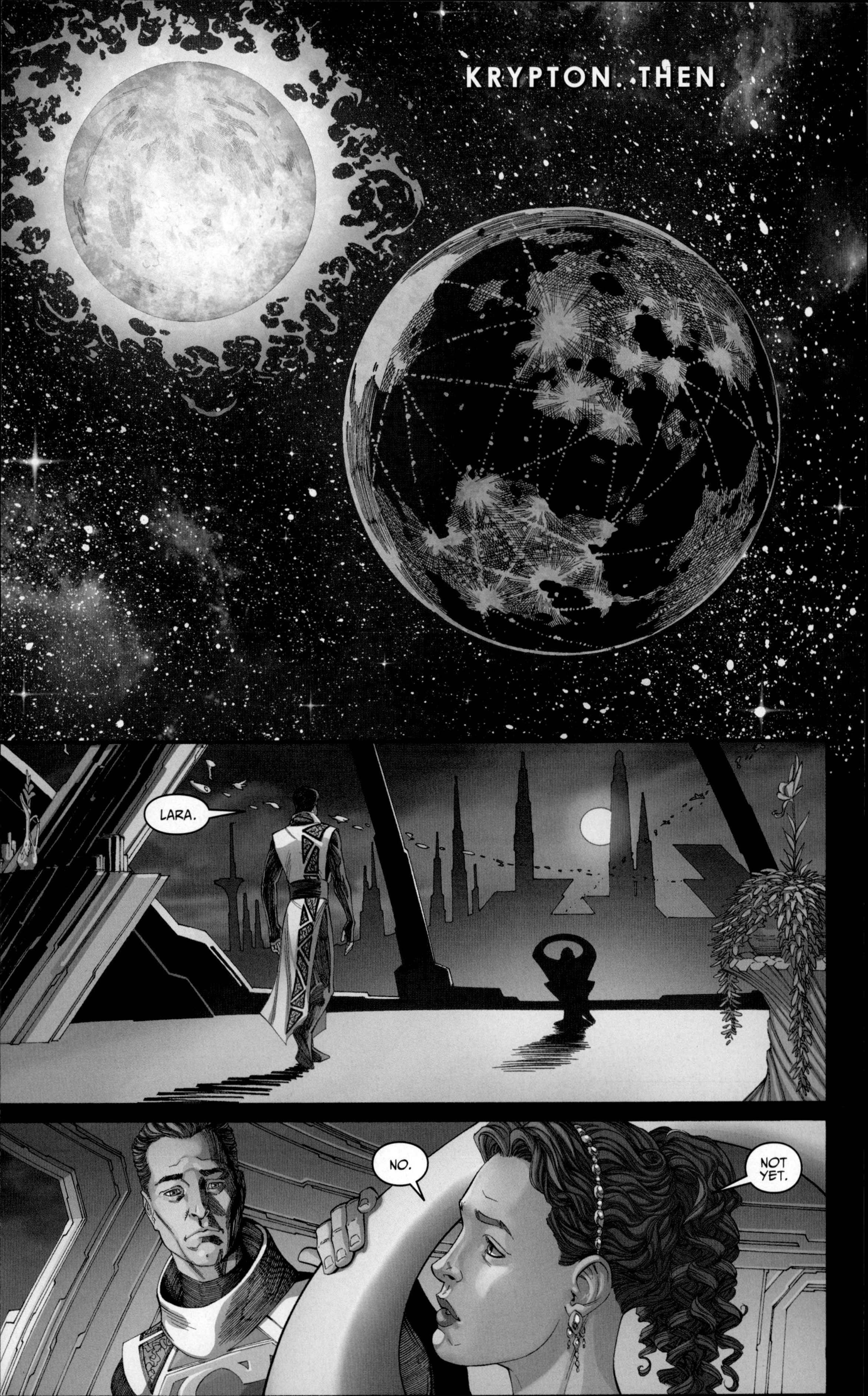
KRYPTON. THEN.
LARA.
NO.
NOT YET.

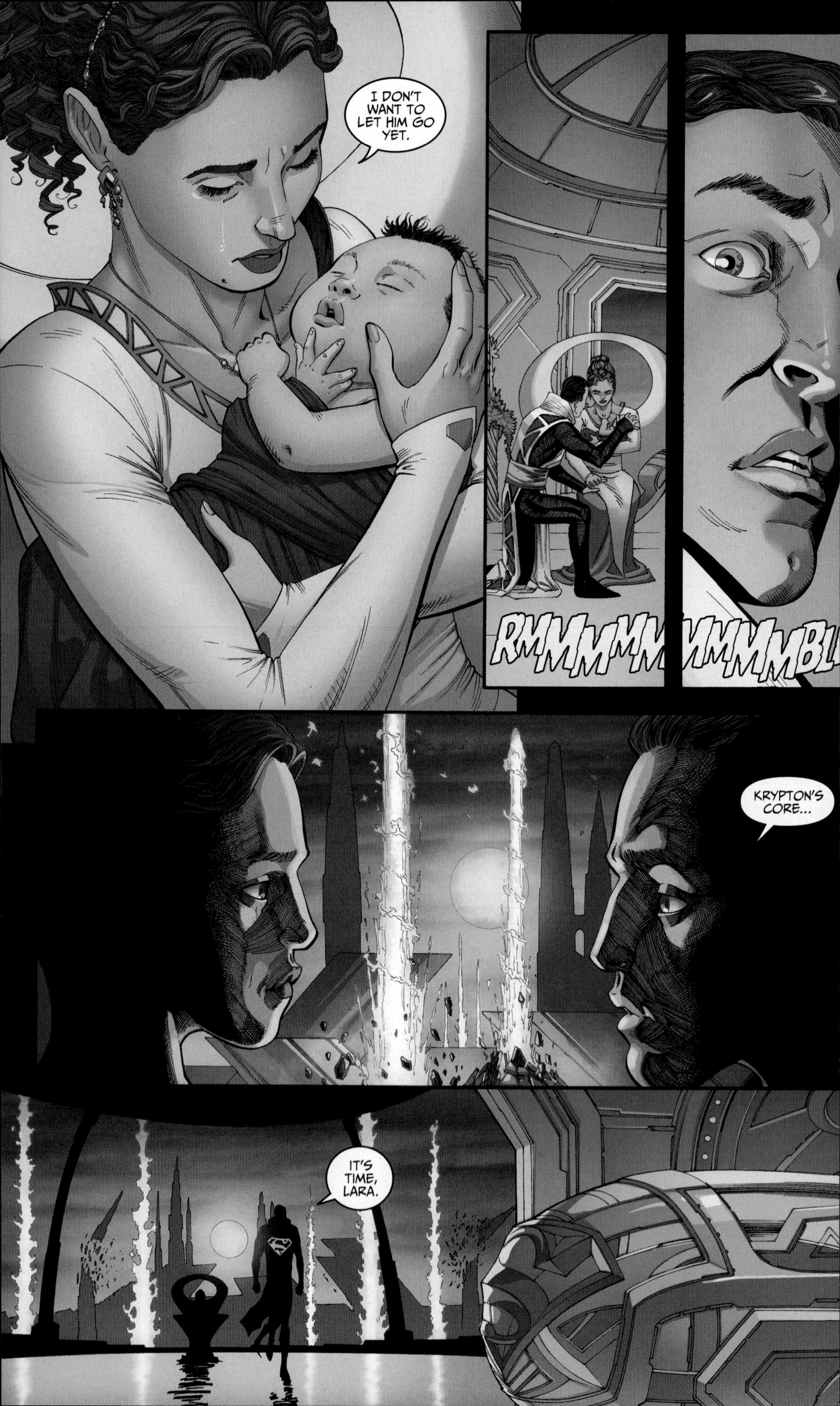
I DON'T WANT TO LET HIM GO YET.
RMMMMMMMMMMMBL
KRYPTON'S CORE...
IT'S TIME, LARA.

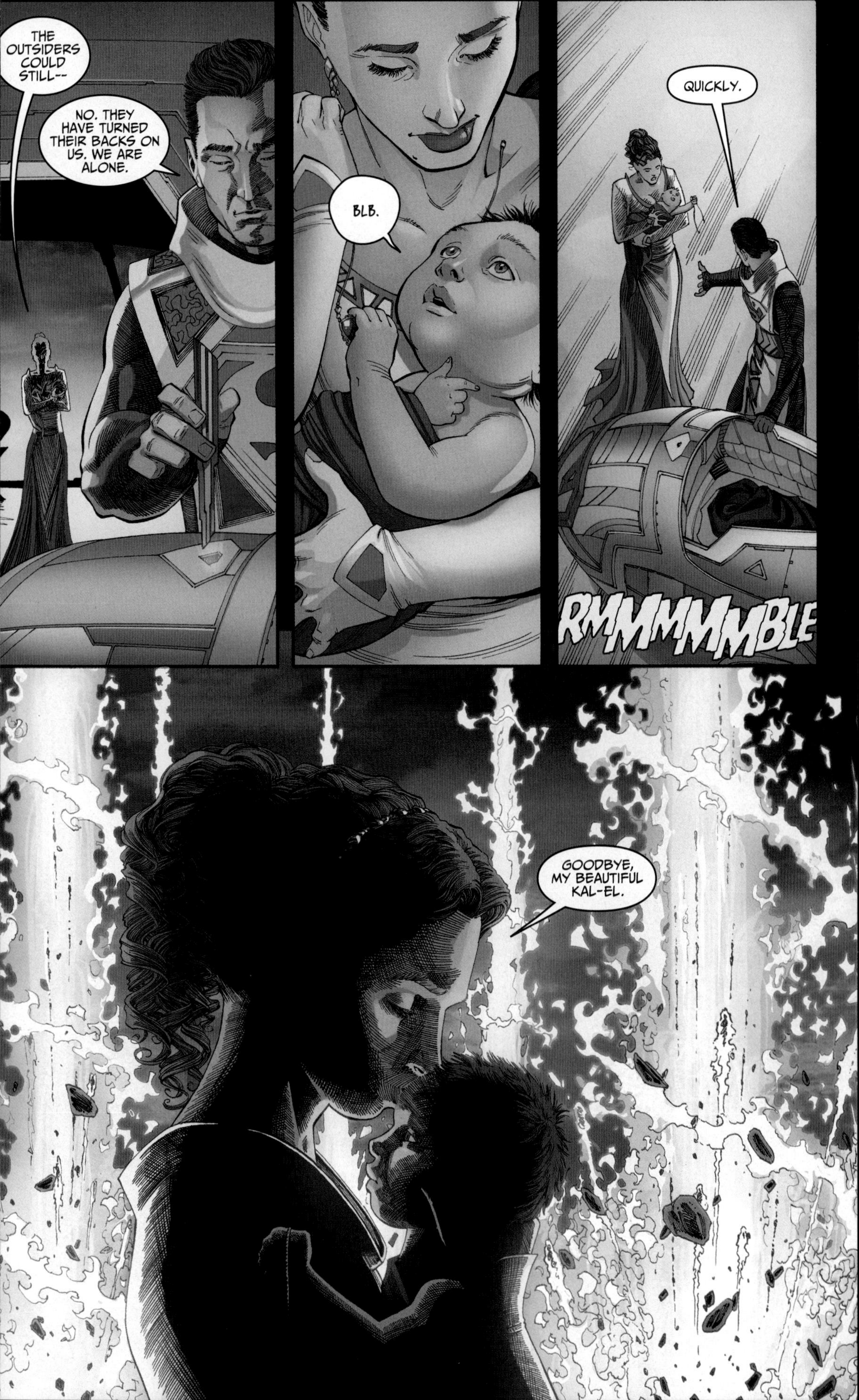

THE OUTSIDERS COULD STILL--
NO. THEY HAVE TURNED THEIR BACKS ON US. WE ARE ALONE.
BLB.
QUICKLY.
RMMMMMMBLE
GOODBYE, MY BEAUTIFUL KAL-EL.

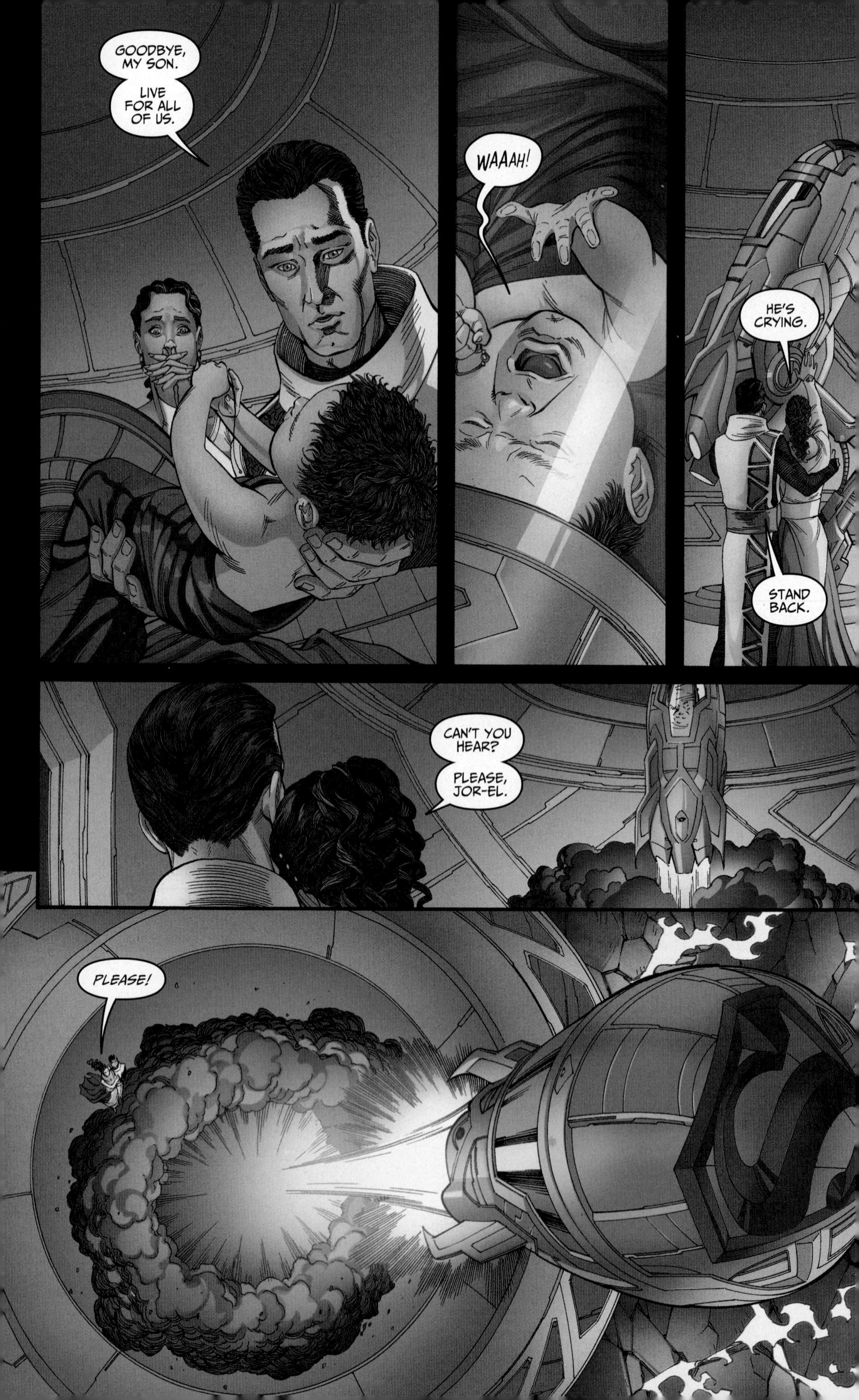
GOODBYE, MY SON.
LIVE FOR ALL OF US.
WAAAH!
HE'S CRYING.
STAND BACK.
CAN'T YOU HEAR?
PLEASE, JOR-EL.
PLEASE!

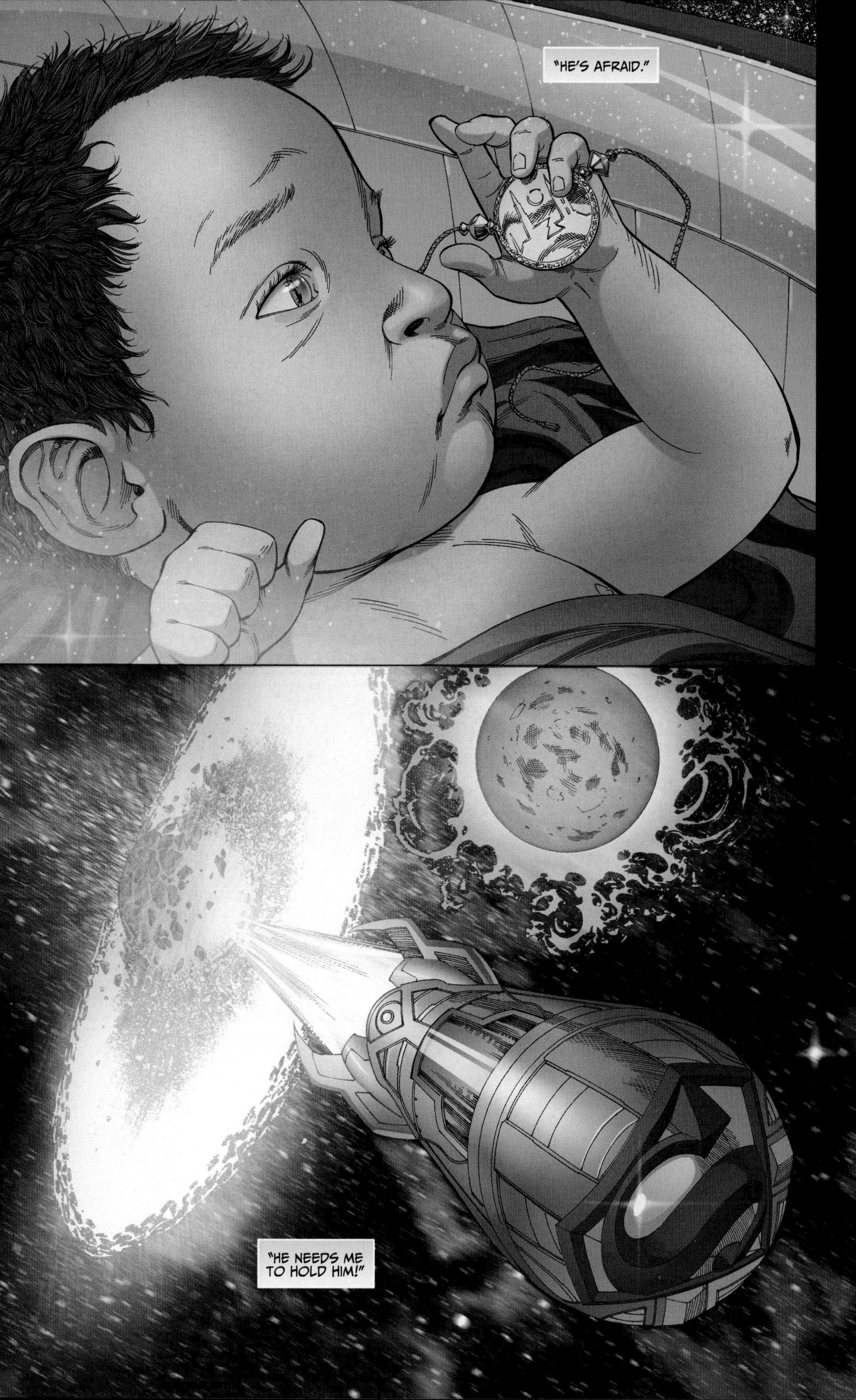
"HE'S AFRAID."
"HE NEEDS ME TO HOLD HIM!"

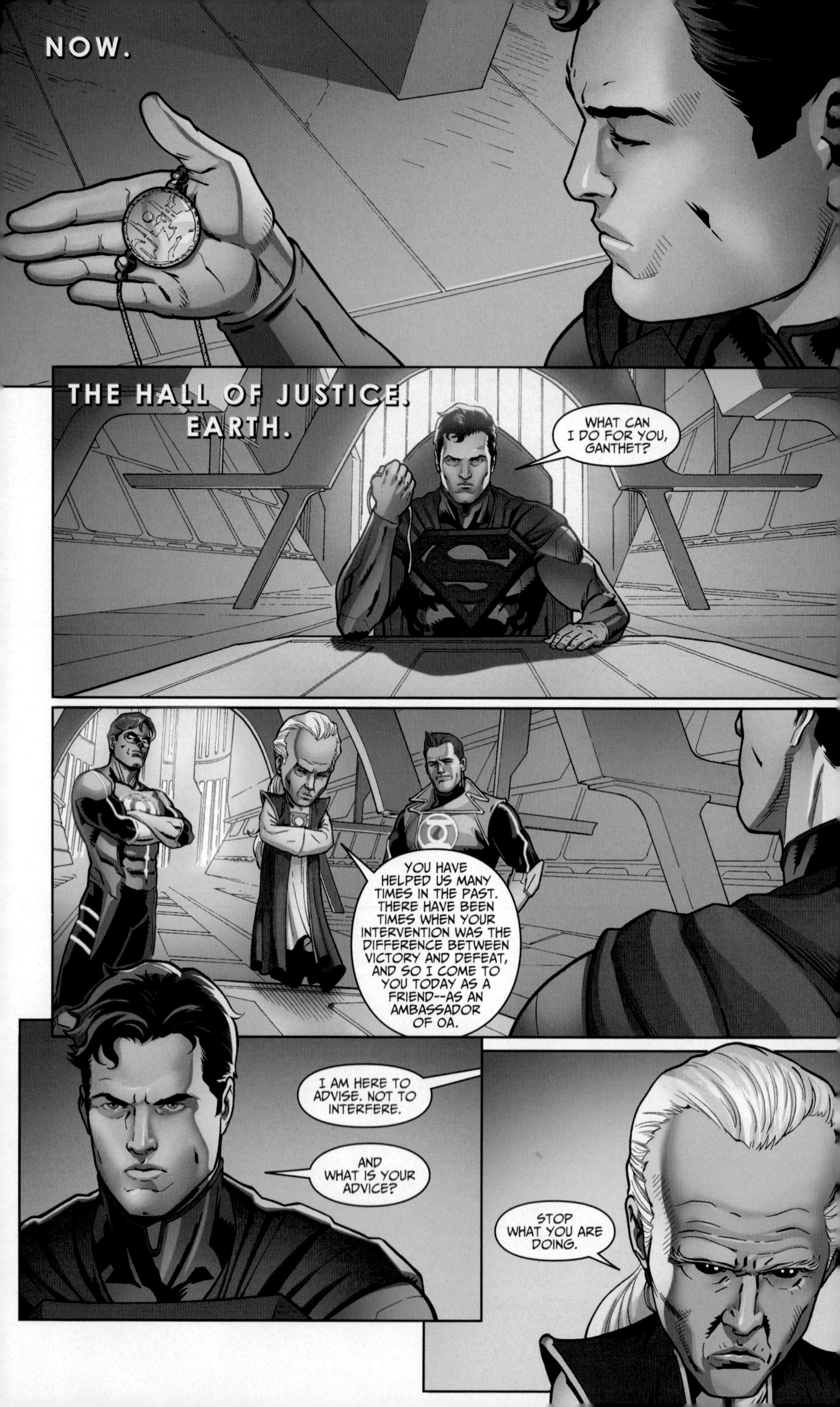
NOW.
THE HALL OF JUSTICE. EARTH.
WHAT CAN I DO FOR YOU, GANTHET?
YOU HAVE HELPED US MANY TIMES IN THE PAST. THERE HAVE BEEN TIMES WHEN YOUR INTERVENTION WAS THE DIFFERENCE BETWEEN VICTORY AND DEFEAT, AND SO I COME TO YOU TODAY AS A FRIEND--AS AN AMBASSADOR OF OA.
I AM HERE TO ADVISE. NOT TO INTERFERE.
AND WHAT IS YOUR ADVICE?
STOP WHAT YOU ARE DOING.

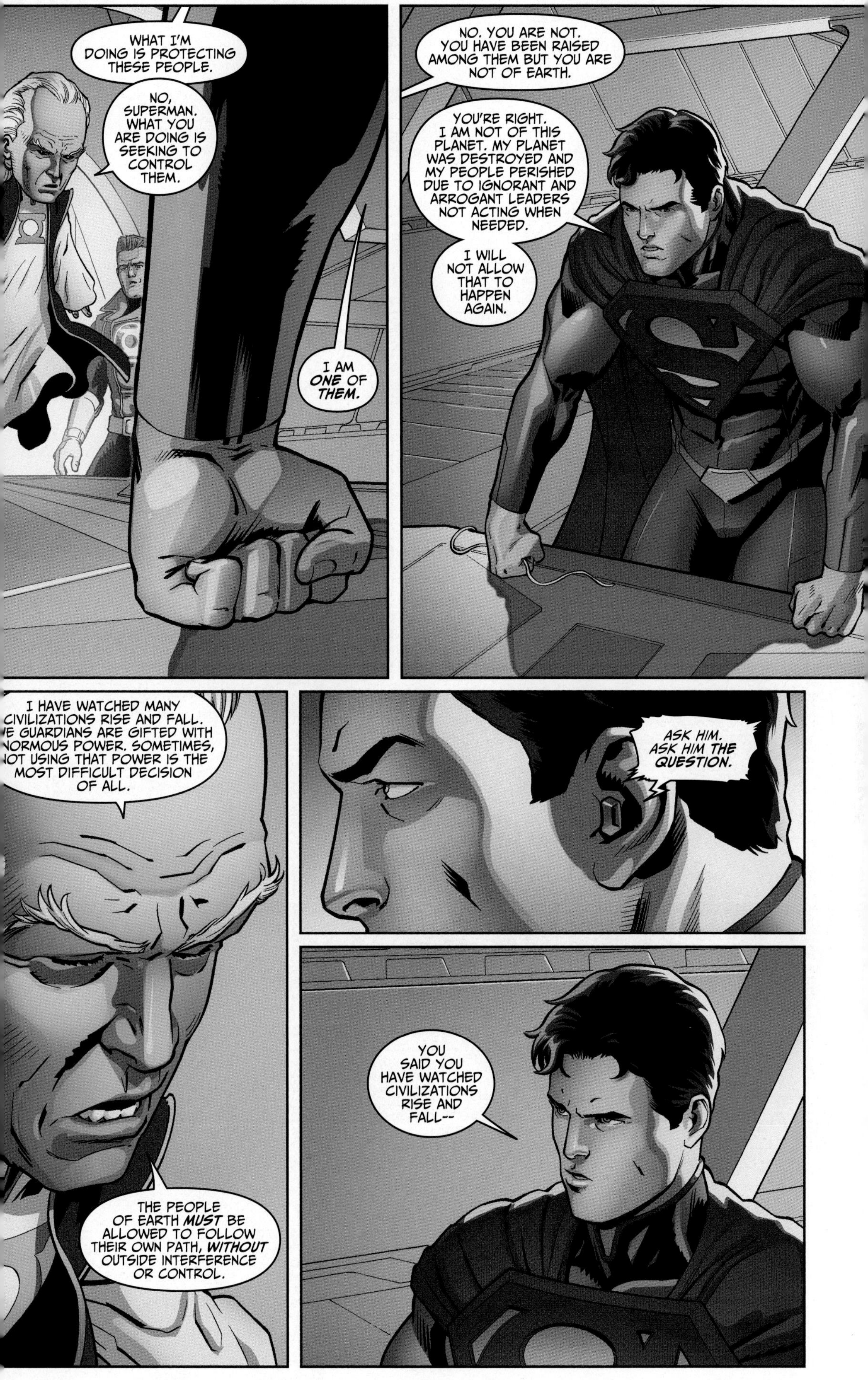
WHAT I'M DOING IS PROTECTING THESE PEOPLE.
NO, SUPERMAN. WHAT YOU ARE DOING IS SEEKING TO CONTROL THEM.
I AM *ONE* OF *THEM.*
NO. YOU ARE NOT. YOU HAVE BEEN RAISED AMONG THEM BUT YOU ARE NOT OF EARTH.
YOU'RE RIGHT. I AM NOT OF THIS PLANET. MY PLANET WAS DESTROYED AND MY PEOPLE PERISHED DUE TO IGNORANT AND ARROGANT LEADERS NOT ACTING WHEN NEEDED.
I WILL NOT ALLOW THAT TO HAPPEN AGAIN.
I HAVE WATCHED MANY CIVILIZATIONS RISE AND FALL. E GUARDIANS ARE GIFTED WITH NORMOUS POWER. SOMETIMES, NOT USING THAT POWER IS THE MOST DIFFICULT DECISION OF ALL.
THE PEOPLE OF EARTH *MUST* BE ALLOWED TO FOLLOW THEIR OWN PATH, *WITHOUT* OUTSIDE INTERFERENCE OR CONTROL.
ASK HIM. ASK HIM *THE QUESTION.*
YOU SAID YOU HAVE WATCHED CIVILIZATIONS RISE AND FALL--

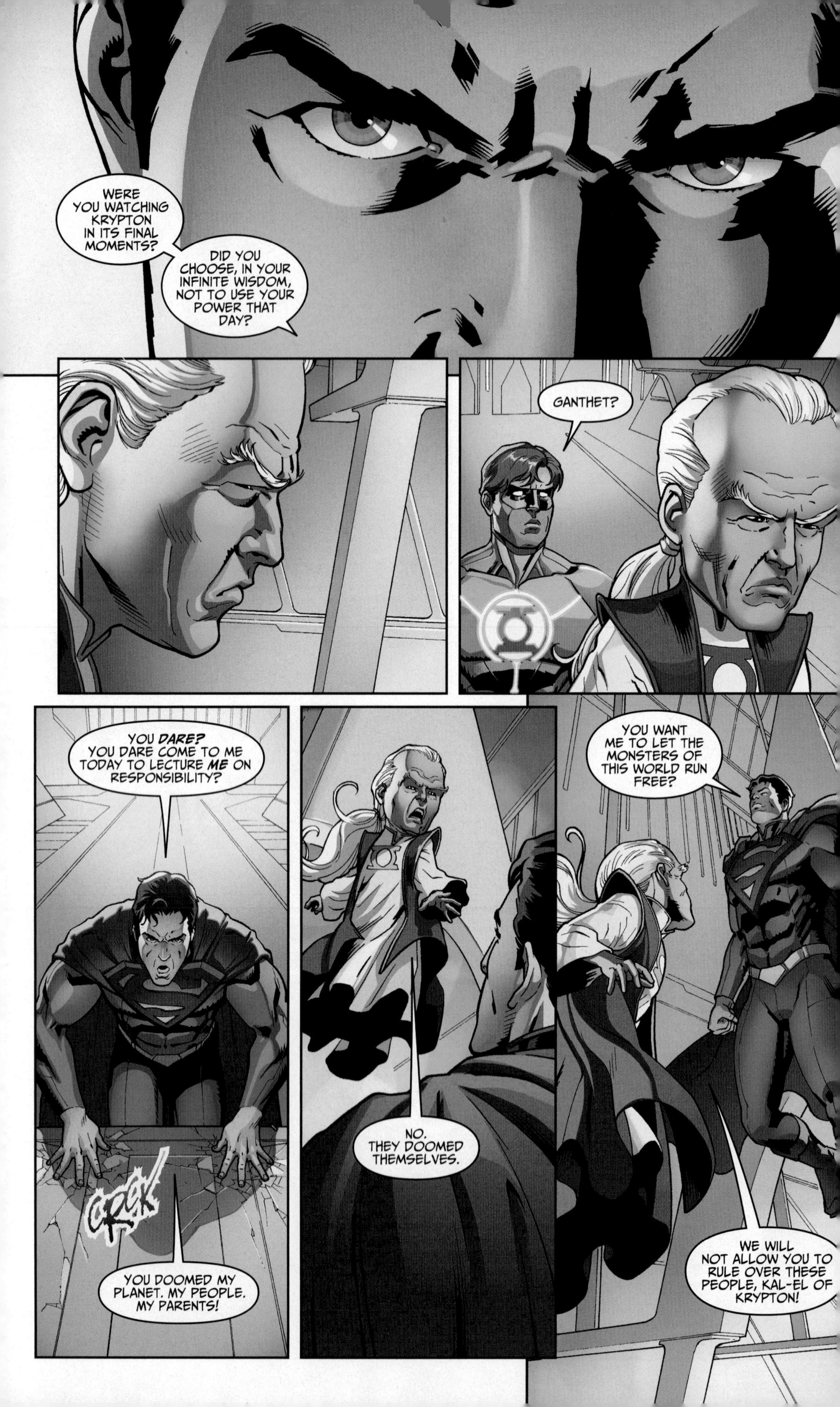
WERE YOU WATCHING KRYPTON IN ITS FINAL MOMENTS?
DID YOU CHOOSE, IN YOUR INFINITE WISDOM, NOT TO USE YOUR POWER THAT DAY?
GANTHET?
YOU DARE? YOU DARE COME TO ME TODAY TO LECTURE ME ON RESPONSIBILITY?
CRCK
YOU DOOMED MY PLANET. MY PEOPLE. MY PARENTS!
NO. THEY DOOMED THEMSELVES.
YOU WANT ME TO LET THE MONSTERS OF THIS WORLD RUN FREE?
WE WILL NOT ALLOW YOU TO RULE OVER THESE PEOPLE, KAL-EL OF KRYPTON!

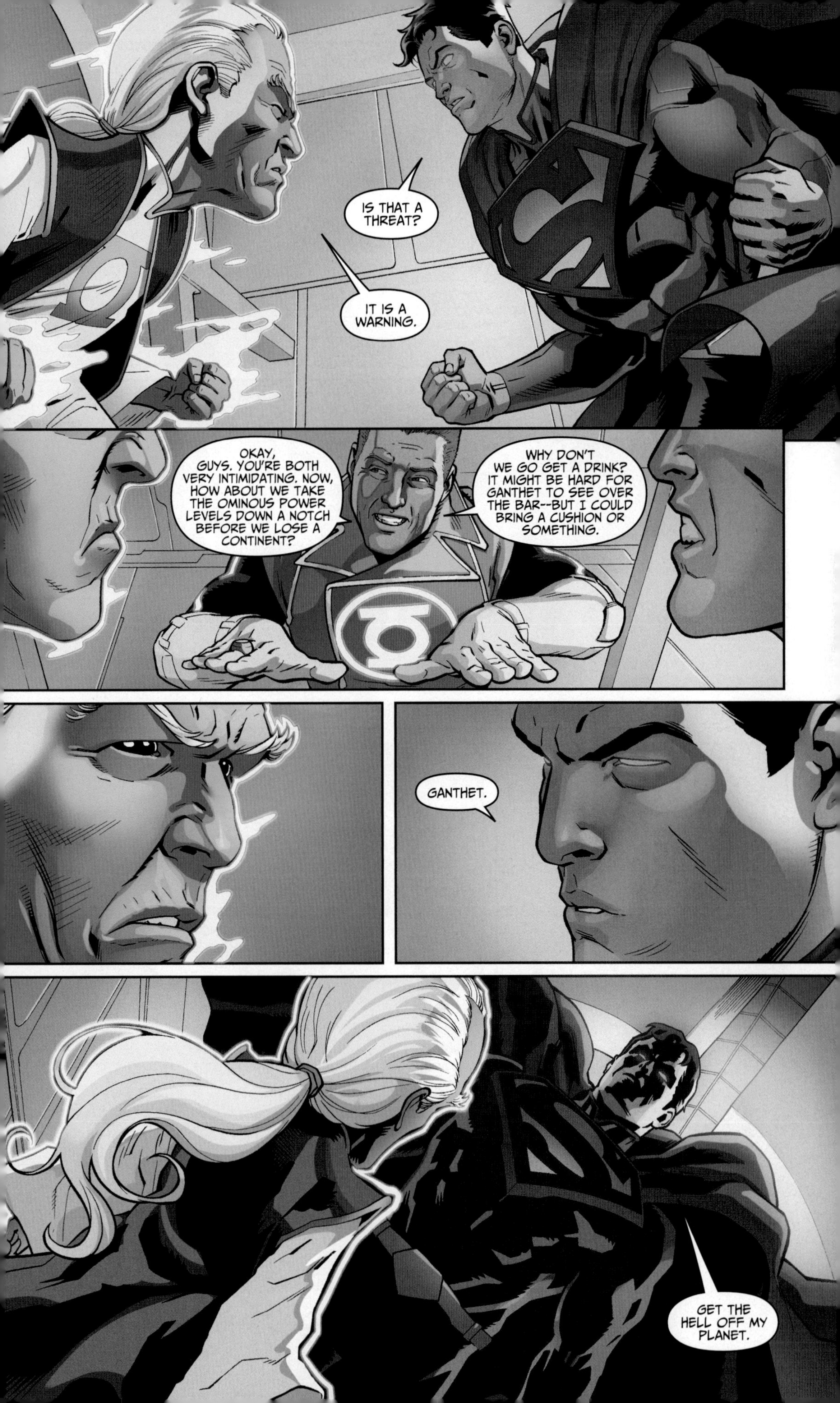
IS THAT A THREAT?
IT IS A WARNING.
OKAY, GUYS. YOU'RE BOTH VERY INTIMIDATING. NOW, HOW ABOUT WE TAKE THE OMINOUS POWER LEVELS DOWN A NOTCH BEFORE WE LOSE A CONTINENT?
WHY DON'T WE GO GET A DRINK? IT MIGHT BE HARD FOR GANTHET TO SEE OVER THE BAR--BUT I COULD BRING A CUSHION OR SOMETHING.
GANTHET.
GET THE HELL OFF MY PLANET.

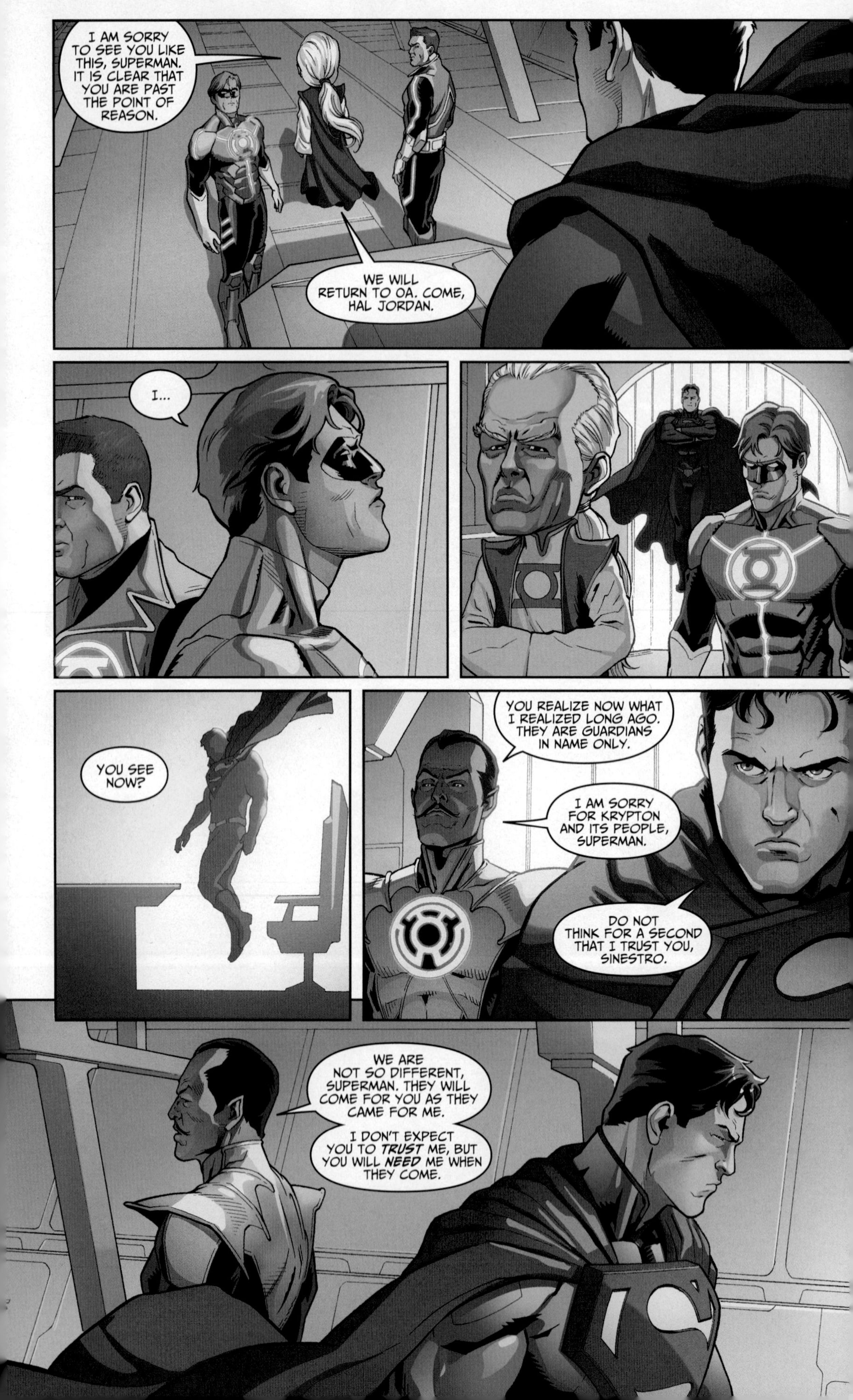
I AM SORRY TO SEE YOU LIKE THIS, SUPERMAN. IT IS CLEAR THAT YOU ARE PAST THE POINT OF REASON.
WE WILL RETURN TO OA. COME, HAL JORDAN.
I...
YOU SEE NOW?
YOU REALIZE NOW WHAT I REALIZED LONG AGO. THEY ARE GUARDIANS IN NAME ONLY.
I AM SORRY FOR KRYPTON AND ITS PEOPLE, SUPERMAN.
DO NOT THINK FOR A SECOND THAT I TRUST YOU, SINESTRO.
WE ARE NOT SO DIFFERENT, SUPERMAN. THEY WILL COME FOR YOU AS THEY CAME FOR ME.
I DON'T EXPECT YOU TO *TRUST* ME, BUT YOU WILL *NEED* ME WHEN THEY COME.

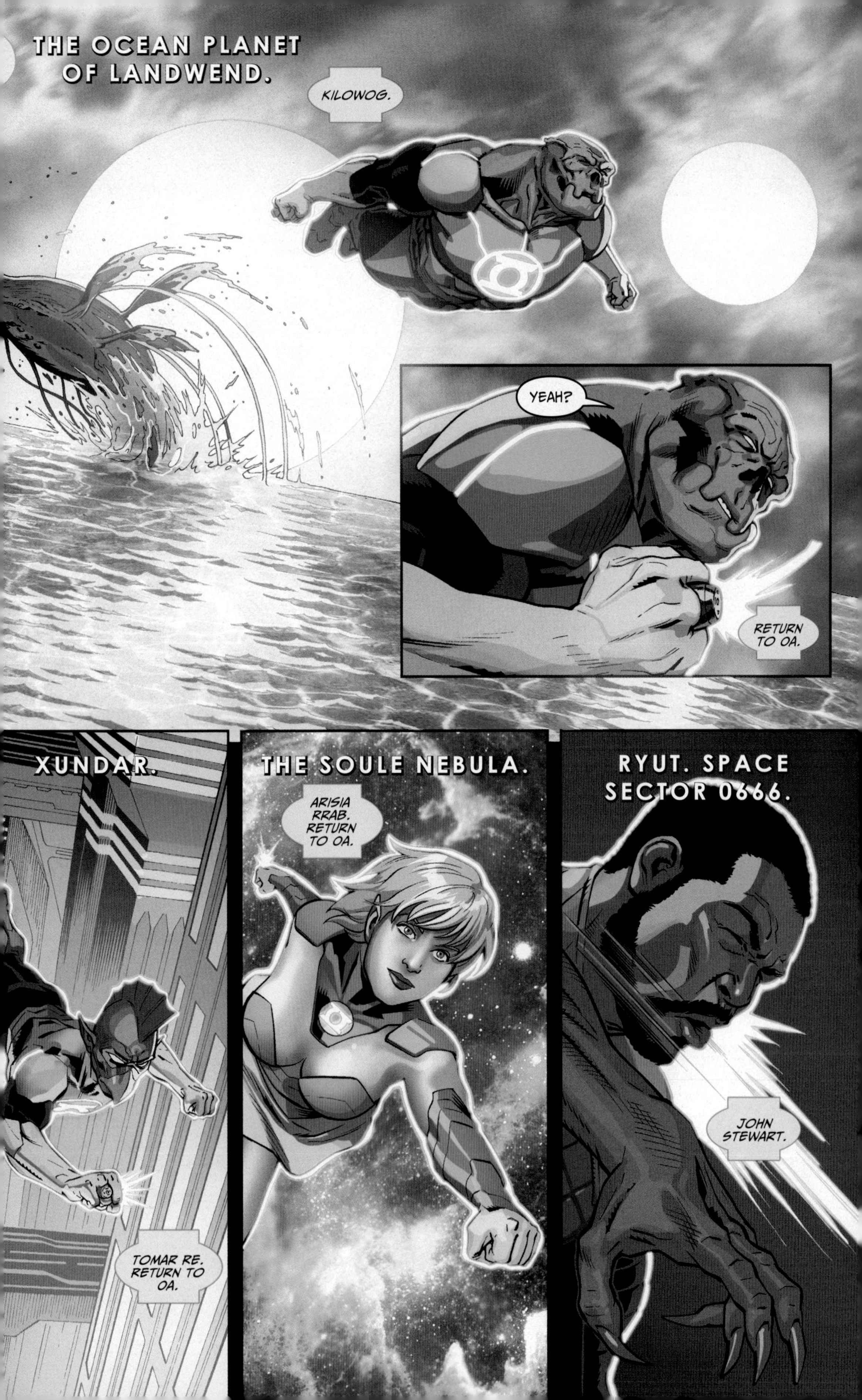
THE OCEAN PLANET OF LANDWEND.
KILOWOG.
YEAH?
RETURN TO OA.
XUNDAR.
TOMAR RE. RETURN TO OA.
THE SOULE NEBULA.
ARISIA RRAB. RETURN TO OA.
RYUT. SPACE SECTOR 0666.
JOHN STEWART.

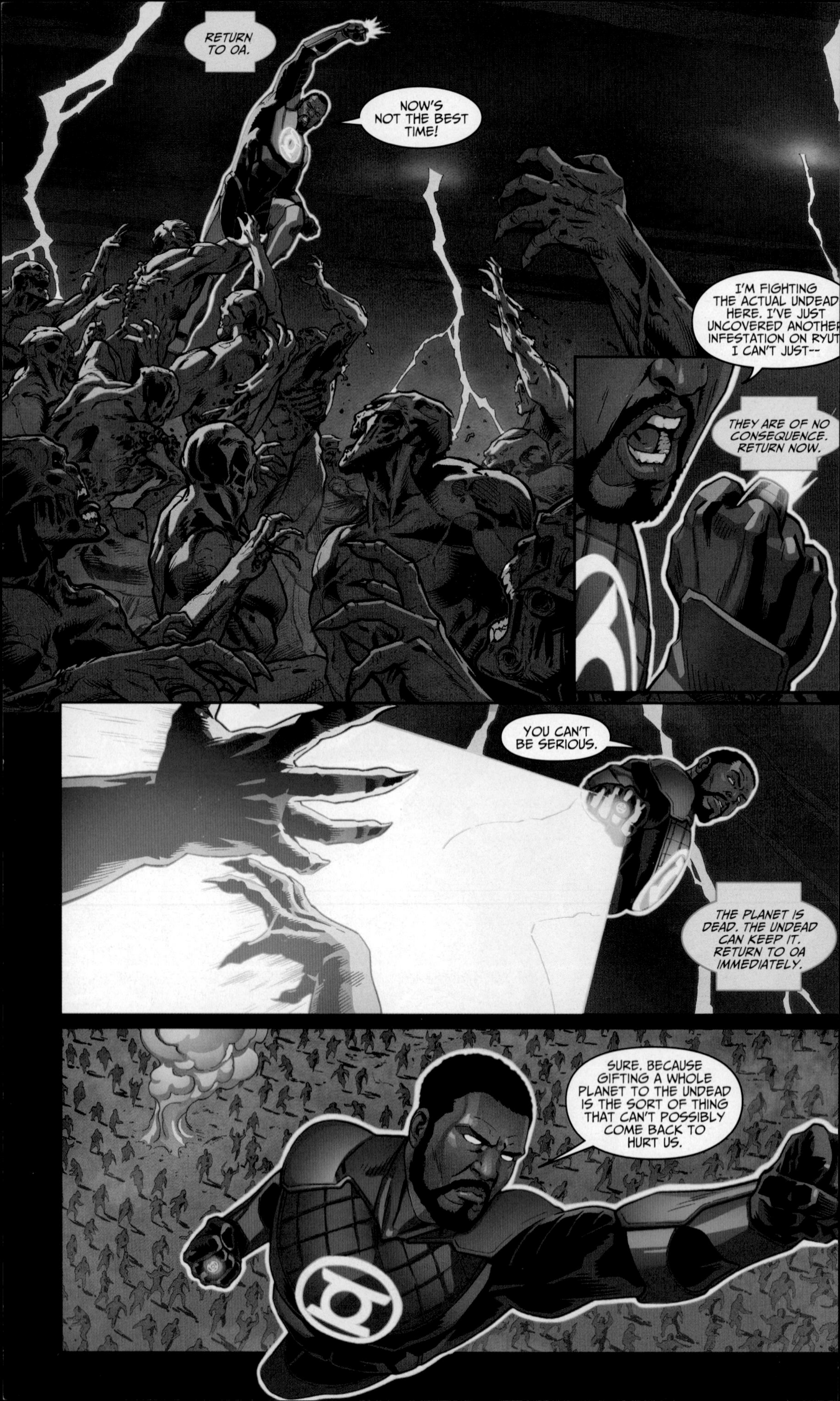
RETURN TO OA.
NOW'S NOT THE BEST TIME!
I'M FIGHTING THE ACTUAL UNDEAD HERE. I'VE JUST UNCOVERED ANOTHER INFESTATION ON RYUT. I CAN'T JUST--
THEY ARE OF NO CONSEQUENCE. RETURN NOW.
YOU CAN'T BE SERIOUS.
THE PLANET IS DEAD. THE UNDEAD CAN KEEP IT. RETURN TO OA IMMEDIATELY.
SURE. BECAUSE GIFTING A WHOLE PLANET TO THE UNDEAD IS THE SORT OF THING THAT CAN'T POSSIBLY COME BACK TO HURT US.

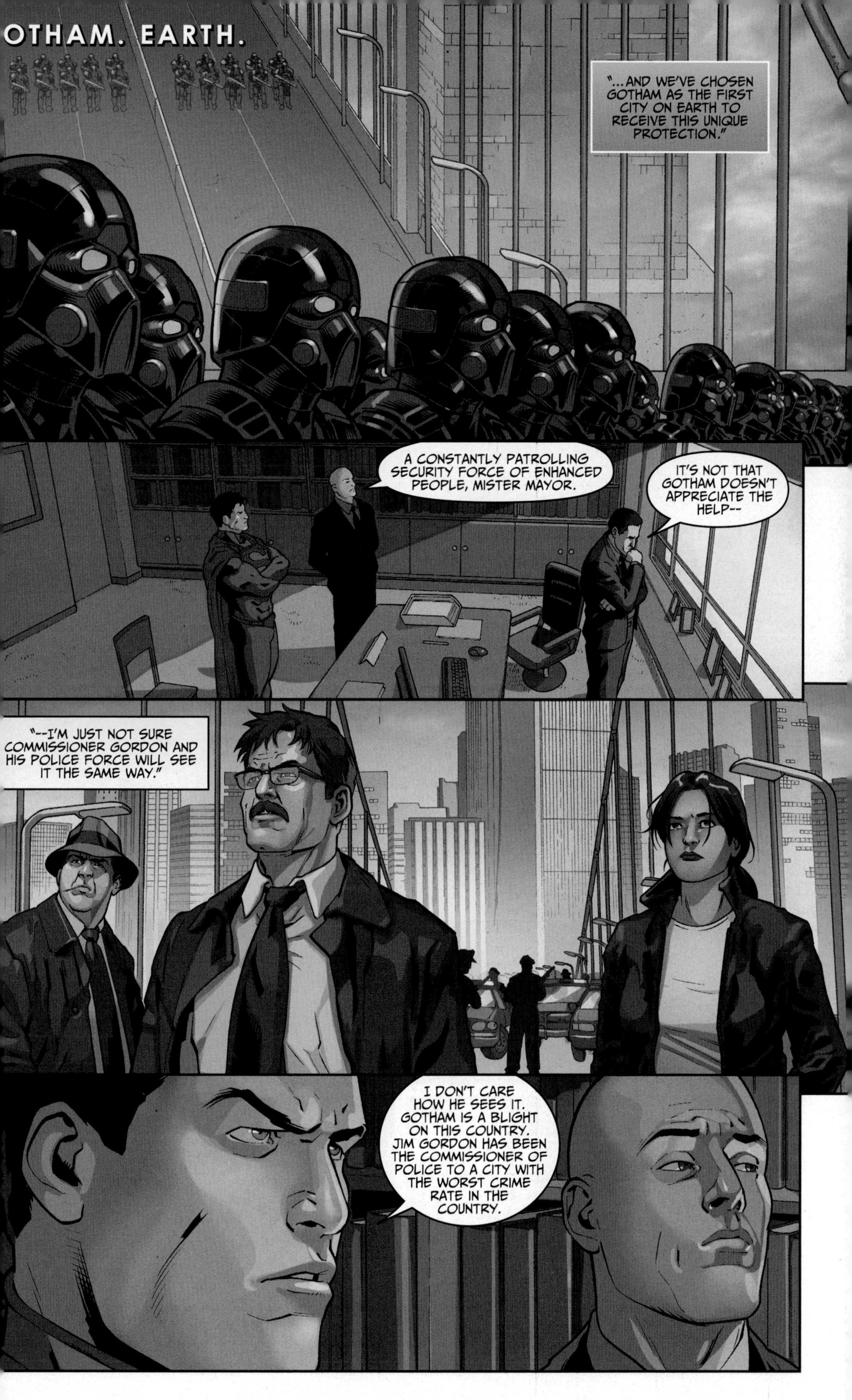
OTHAM. EARTH.
"...AND WE'VE CHOSEN GOTHAM AS THE FIRST CITY ON EARTH TO RECEIVE THIS UNIQUE PROTECTION."
A CONSTANTLY PATROLLING SECURITY FORCE OF ENHANCED PEOPLE, MISTER MAYOR.
IT'S NOT THAT GOTHAM DOESN'T APPRECIATE THE HELP--
"--I'M JUST NOT SURE COMMISSIONER GORDON AND HIS POLICE FORCE WILL SEE IT THE SAME WAY."
I DON'T CARE HOW HE SEES IT. GOTHAM IS A BLIGHT ON THIS COUNTRY. JIM GORDON HAS BEEN THE COMMISSIONER OF POLICE TO A CITY WITH THE WORST CRIME RATE IN THE COUNTRY.

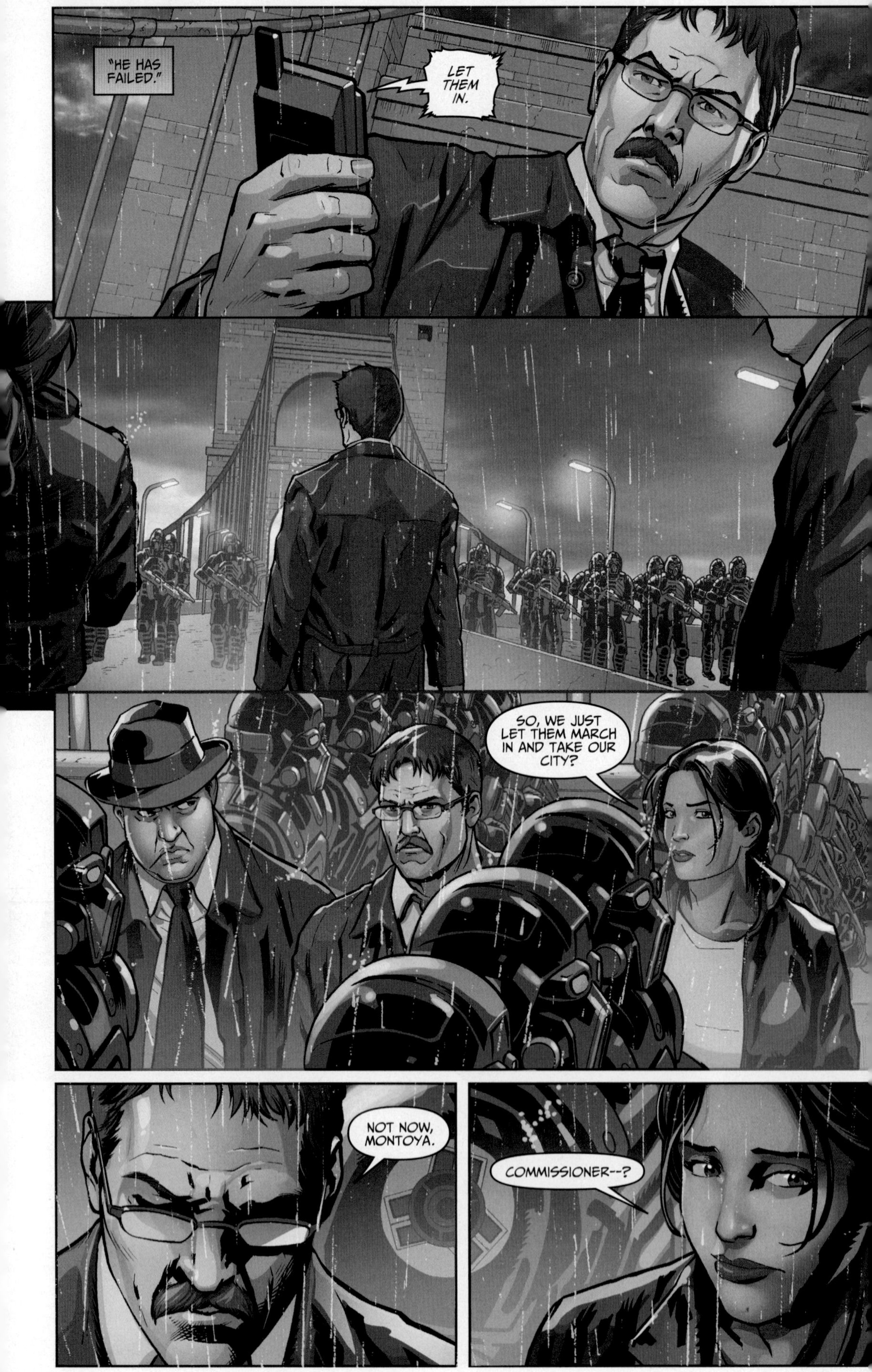

"HE HAS FAILED."
LET THEM IN.
SO, WE JUST LET THEM MARCH IN AND TAKE OUR CITY?
NOT NOW, MONTOYA.
COMMISSIONER--?

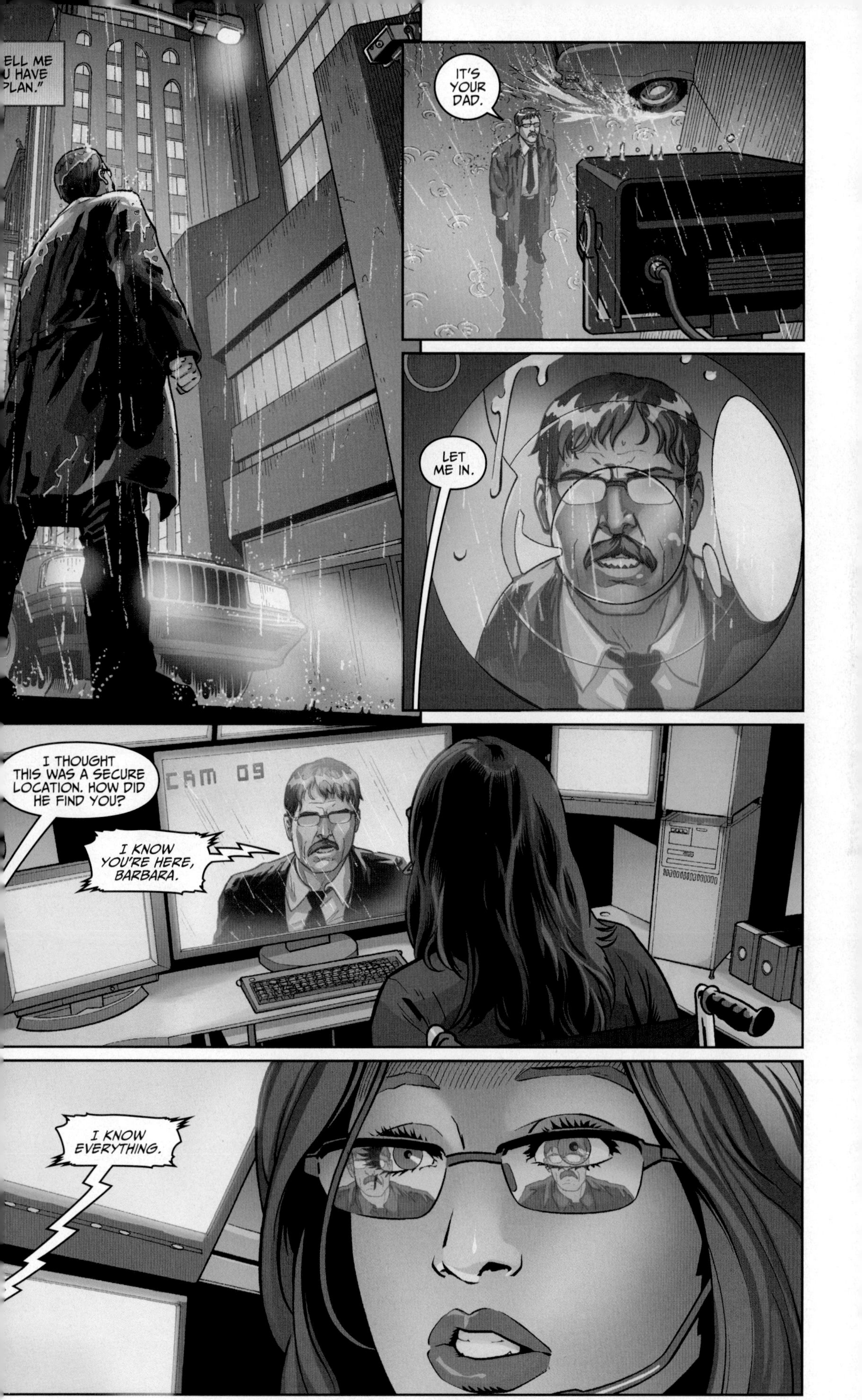
ELL ME
U HAVE
PLAN."
IT'S YOUR DAD.
LET ME IN.
I THOUGHT THIS WAS A SECURE LOCATION. HOW DID HE FIND YOU?
CAM 09
I KNOW YOU'RE HERE, BARBARA.
I KNOW EVERYTHING.

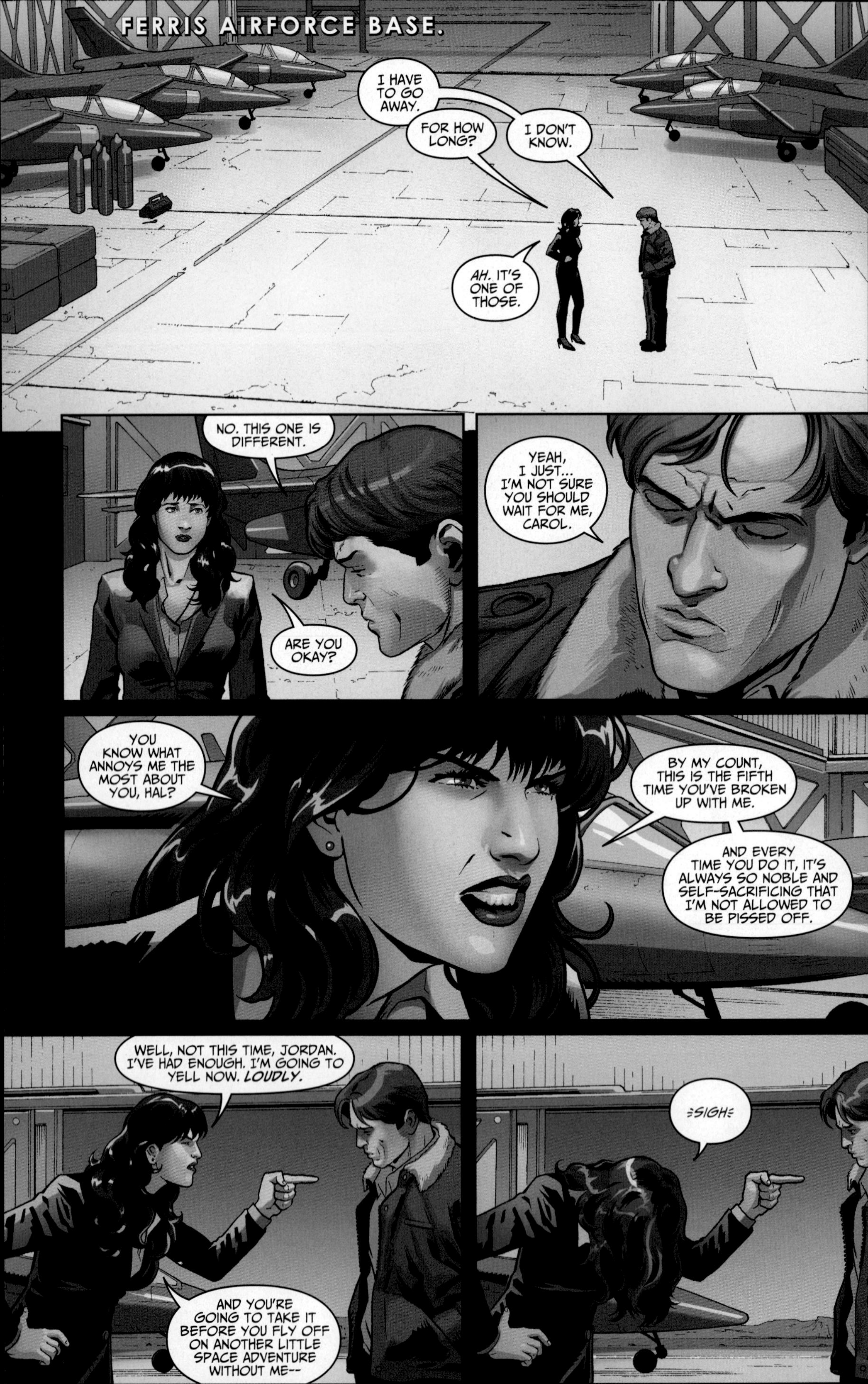
FERRIS AIRFORCE BASE.
I HAVE TO GO AWAY.
FOR HOW LONG?
I DON'T KNOW.
AH. IT'S ONE OF THOSE.
NO. THIS ONE IS DIFFERENT.
ARE YOU OKAY?
YEAH, I JUST... I'M NOT SURE YOU SHOULD WAIT FOR ME, CAROL.
YOU KNOW WHAT ANNOYS ME THE MOST ABOUT YOU, HAL?
BY MY COUNT, THIS IS THE FIFTH TIME YOU'VE BROKEN UP WITH ME.
AND EVERY TIME YOU DO IT, IT'S ALWAYS SO NOBLE AND SELF-SACRIFICING THAT I'M NOT ALLOWED TO BE PISSED OFF.
WELL, NOT THIS TIME, JORDAN. I'VE HAD ENOUGH. I'M GOING TO YELL NOW. LOUDLY.
AND YOU'RE GOING TO TAKE IT BEFORE YOU FLY OFF ON ANOTHER LITTLE SPACE ADVENTURE WITHOUT ME--
SIGH

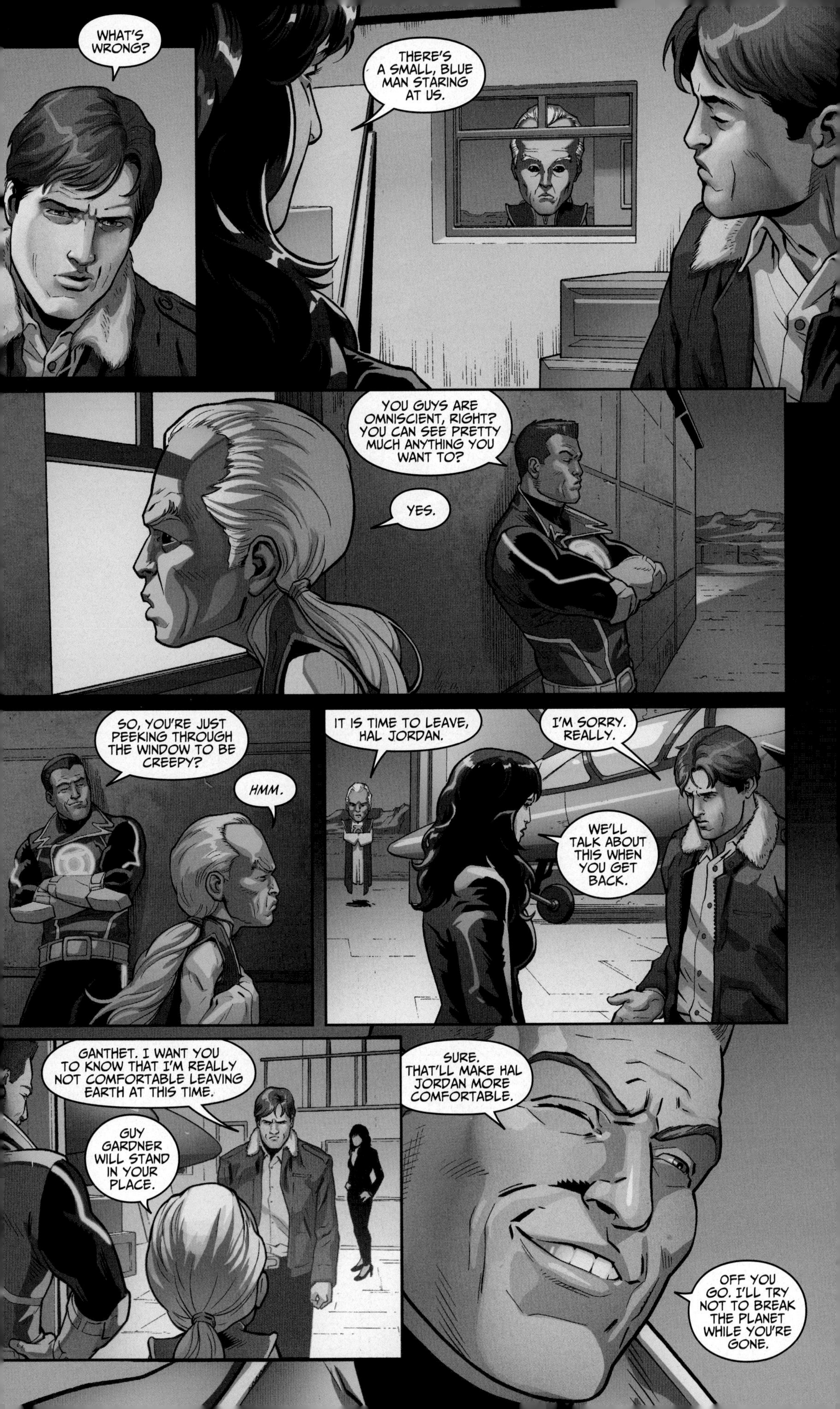
WHAT'S WRONG?
THERE'S A SMALL, BLUE MAN STARING AT US.
YOU GUYS ARE OMNISCIENT, RIGHT? YOU CAN SEE PRETTY MUCH ANYTHING YOU WANT TO?
YES.
SO, YOU'RE JUST PEEKING THROUGH THE WINDOW TO BE CREEPY?
HMM.
IT IS TIME TO LEAVE, HAL JORDAN.
I'M SORRY. REALLY.
WE'LL TALK ABOUT THIS WHEN YOU GET BACK.
GANTHET. I WANT YOU TO KNOW THAT I'M REALLY NOT COMFORTABLE LEAVING EARTH AT THIS TIME.
GUY GARDNER WILL STAND IN YOUR PLACE.
SURE. THAT'LL MAKE HAL JORDAN MORE COMFORTABLE.
OFF YOU GO. I'LL TRY NOT TO BREAK THE PLANET WHILE YOU'RE GONE.

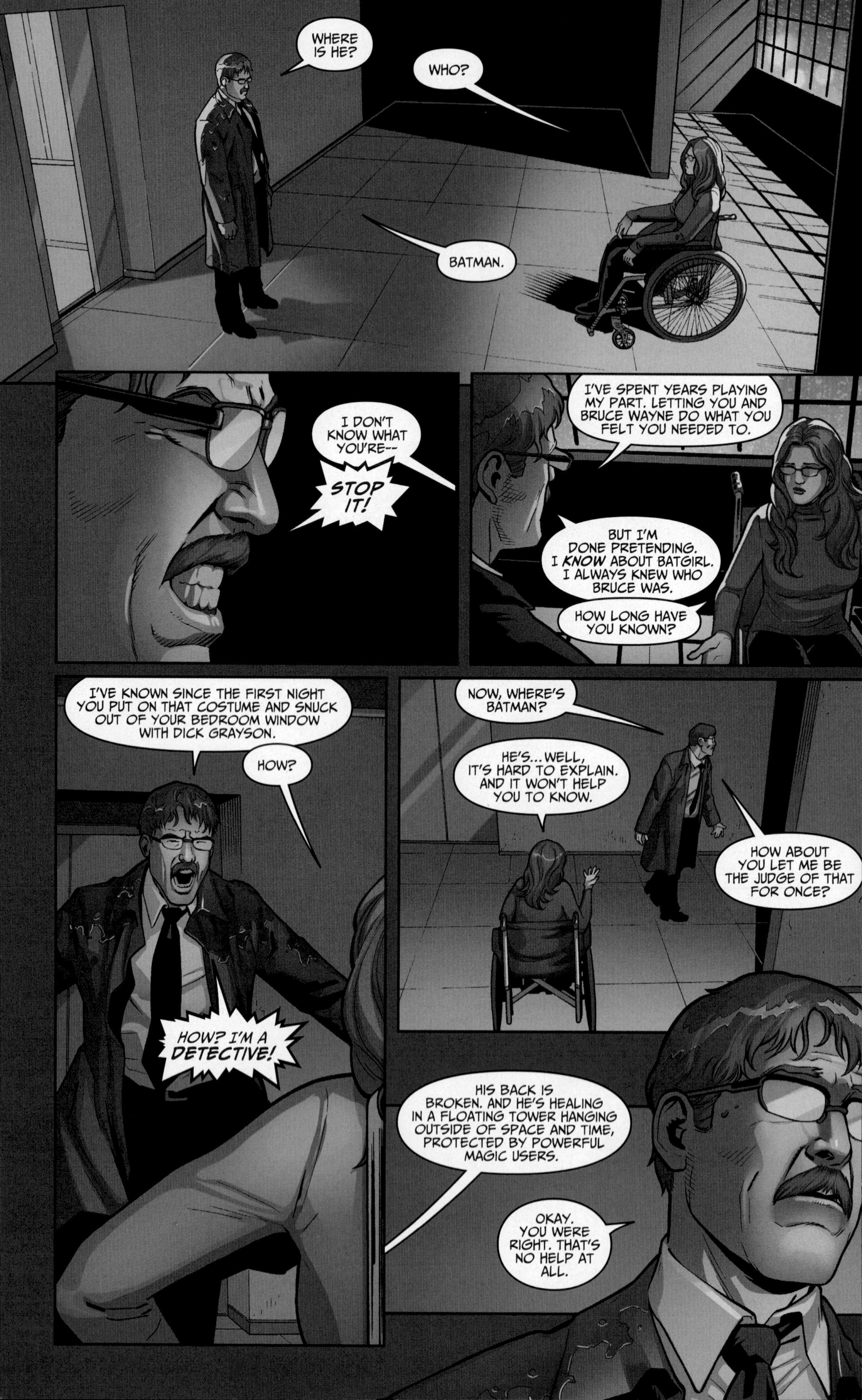
WHERE IS HE?
WHO?
BATMAN.
I DON'T KNOW WHAT YOU'RE--
STOP IT!
I'VE SPENT YEARS PLAYING MY PART. LETTING YOU AND BRUCE WAYNE DO WHAT YOU FELT YOU NEEDED TO.
BUT I'M DONE PRETENDING. I KNOW ABOUT BATGIRL. I ALWAYS KNEW WHO BRUCE WAS.
HOW LONG HAVE YOU KNOWN?
I'VE KNOWN SINCE THE FIRST NIGHT YOU PUT ON THAT COSTUME AND SNUCK OUT OF YOUR BEDROOM WINDOW WITH DICK GRAYSON.
HOW?
HOW? I'M A DETECTIVE!
NOW, WHERE'S BATMAN?
HE'S...WELL, IT'S HARD TO EXPLAIN. AND IT WON'T HELP YOU TO KNOW.
HOW ABOUT YOU LET ME BE THE JUDGE OF THAT FOR ONCE?
HIS BACK IS BROKEN. AND HE'S HEALING IN A FLOATING TOWER HANGING OUTSIDE OF SPACE AND TIME, PROTECTED BY POWERFUL MAGIC USERS.
OKAY. YOU WERE RIGHT. THAT'S NO HELP AT ALL.

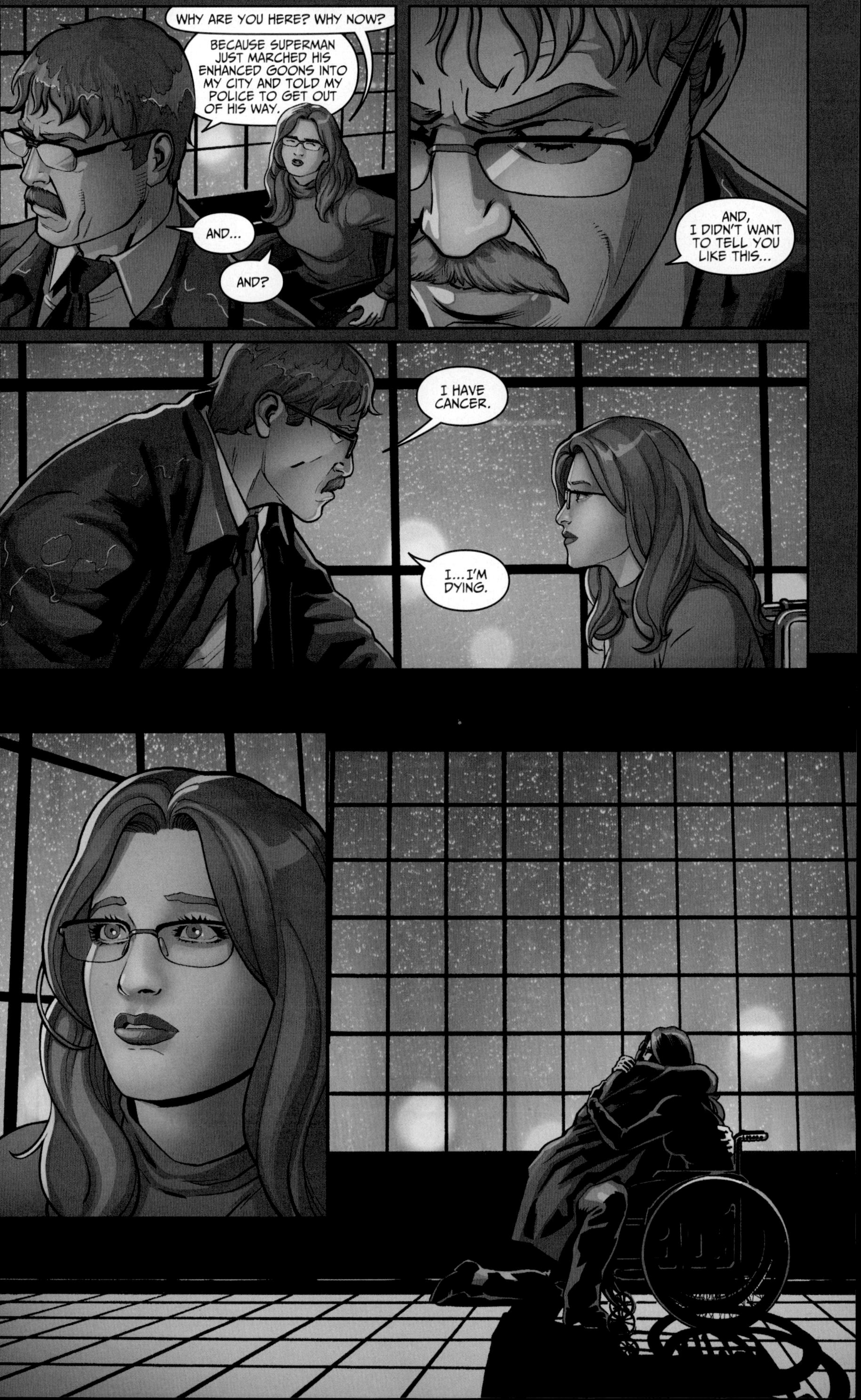
WHY ARE YOU HERE? WHY NOW?
BECAUSE SUPERMAN JUST MARCHED HIS ENHANCED GOONS INTO MY CITY AND TOLD MY POLICE TO GET OUT OF HIS WAY.
AND...
AND?
AND, I DIDN'T WANT TO TELL YOU LIKE THIS...
I HAVE CANCER.
I...I'M DYING.

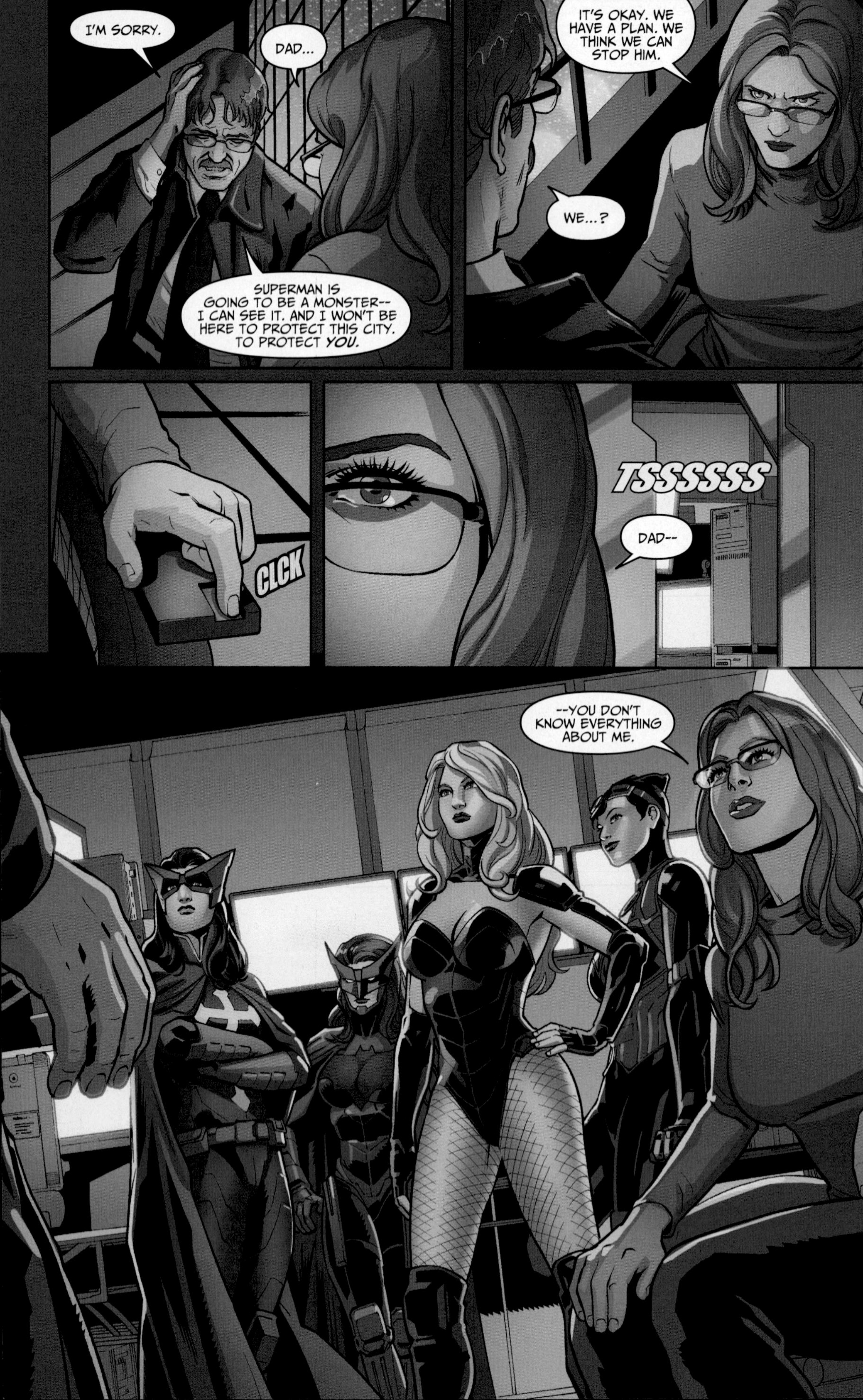
I'M SORRY.
DAD...
SUPERMAN IS GOING TO BE A MONSTER-- I CAN SEE IT. AND I WON'T BE HERE TO PROTECT THIS CITY. TO PROTECT *YOU.*
IT'S OKAY. WE HAVE A PLAN. WE THINK WE CAN STOP HIM.
WE...?
CLCK
TSSSSSS
DAD--
--YOU DON'T KNOW EVERYTHING ABOUT ME.

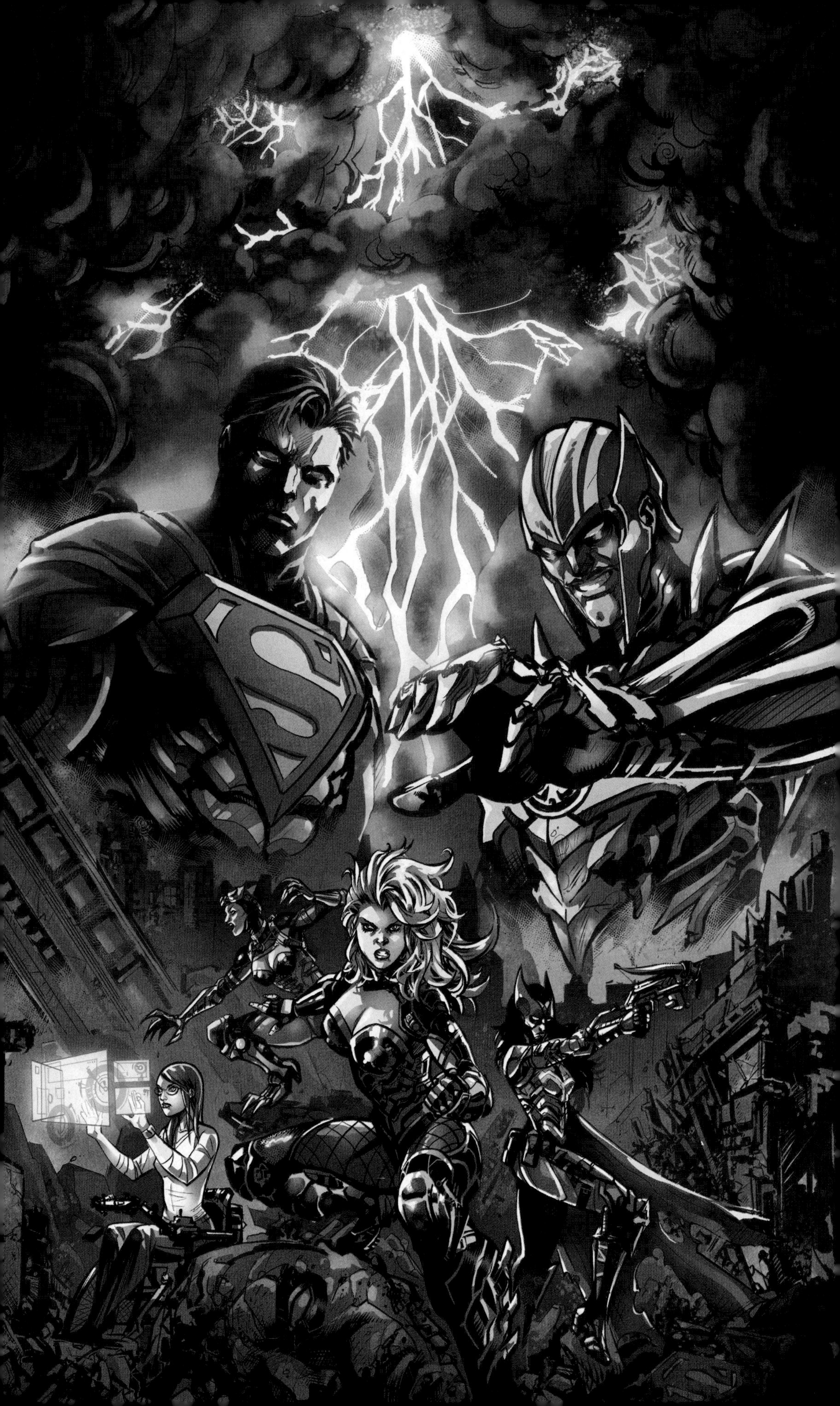

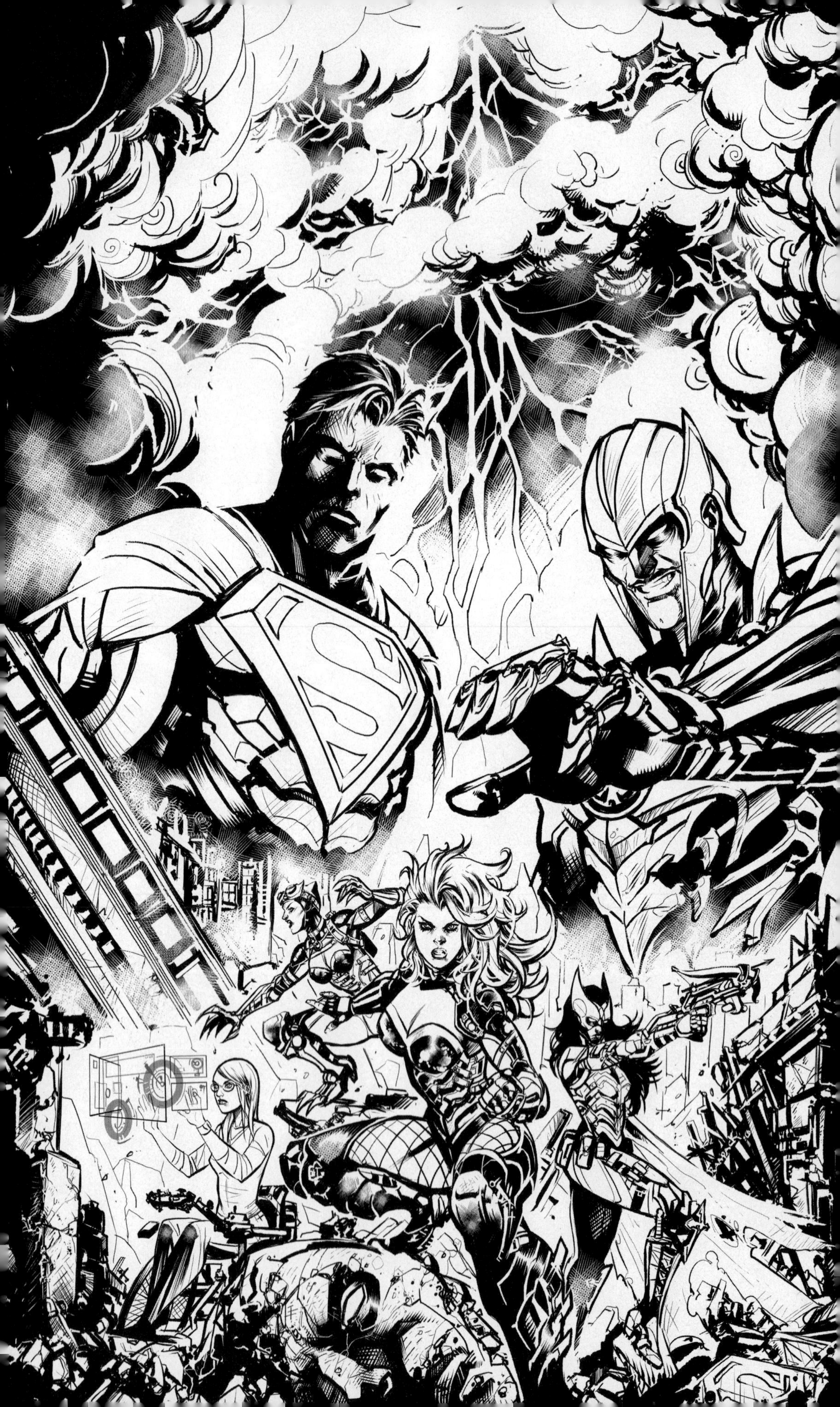

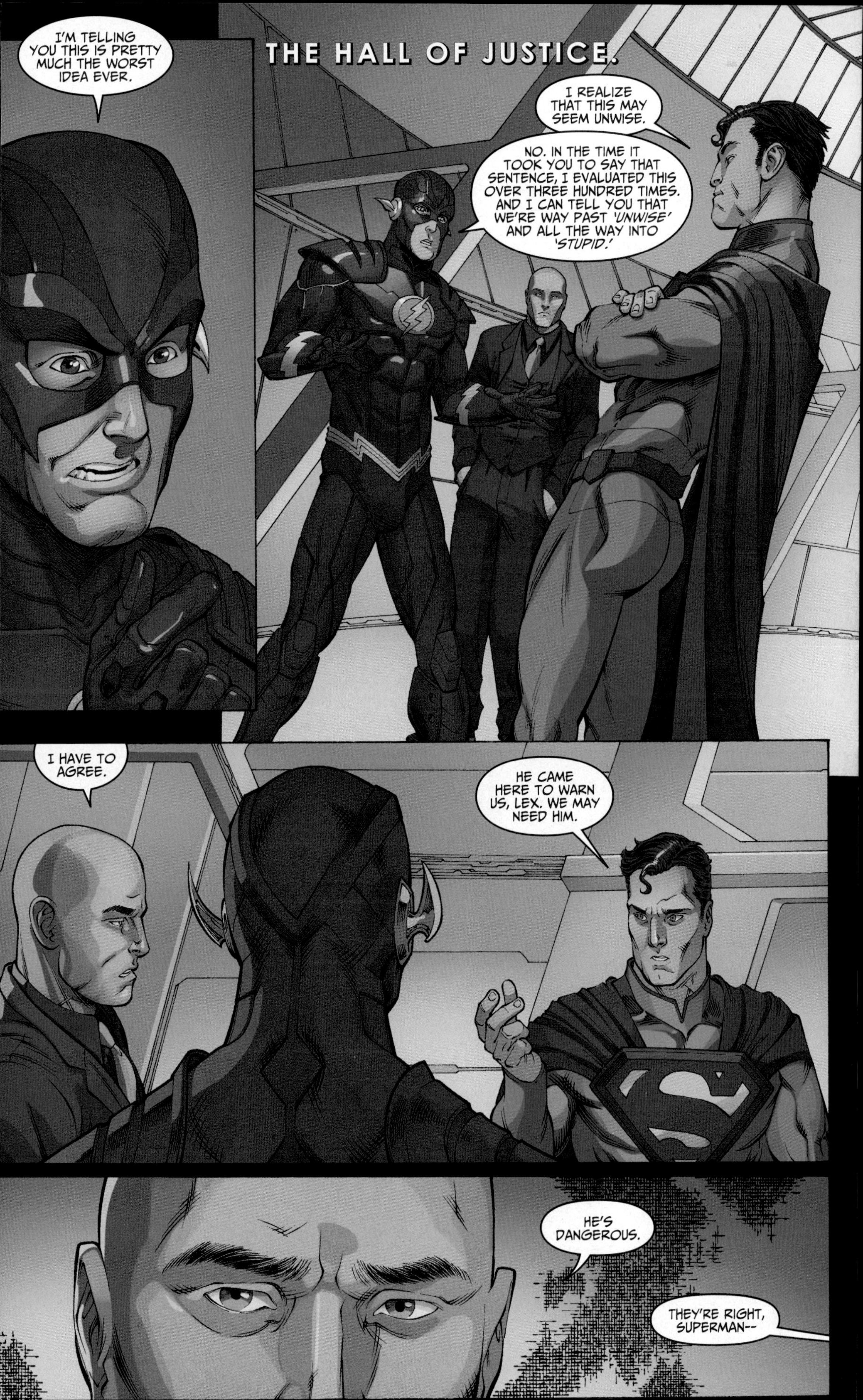
I'M TELLING YOU THIS IS PRETTY MUCH THE WORST IDEA EVER.
THE HALL OF JUSTICE.
I REALIZE THAT THIS MAY SEEM UNWISE.
NO. IN THE TIME IT TOOK YOU TO SAY THAT SENTENCE, I EVALUATED THIS OVER THREE HUNDRED TIMES. AND I CAN TELL YOU THAT WE'RE WAY PAST 'UNWISE' AND ALL THE WAY INTO 'STUPID.'
I HAVE TO AGREE.
HE CAME HERE TO WARN US, LEX. WE MAY NEED HIM.
HE'S DANGEROUS.
THEY'RE RIGHT, SUPERMAN--

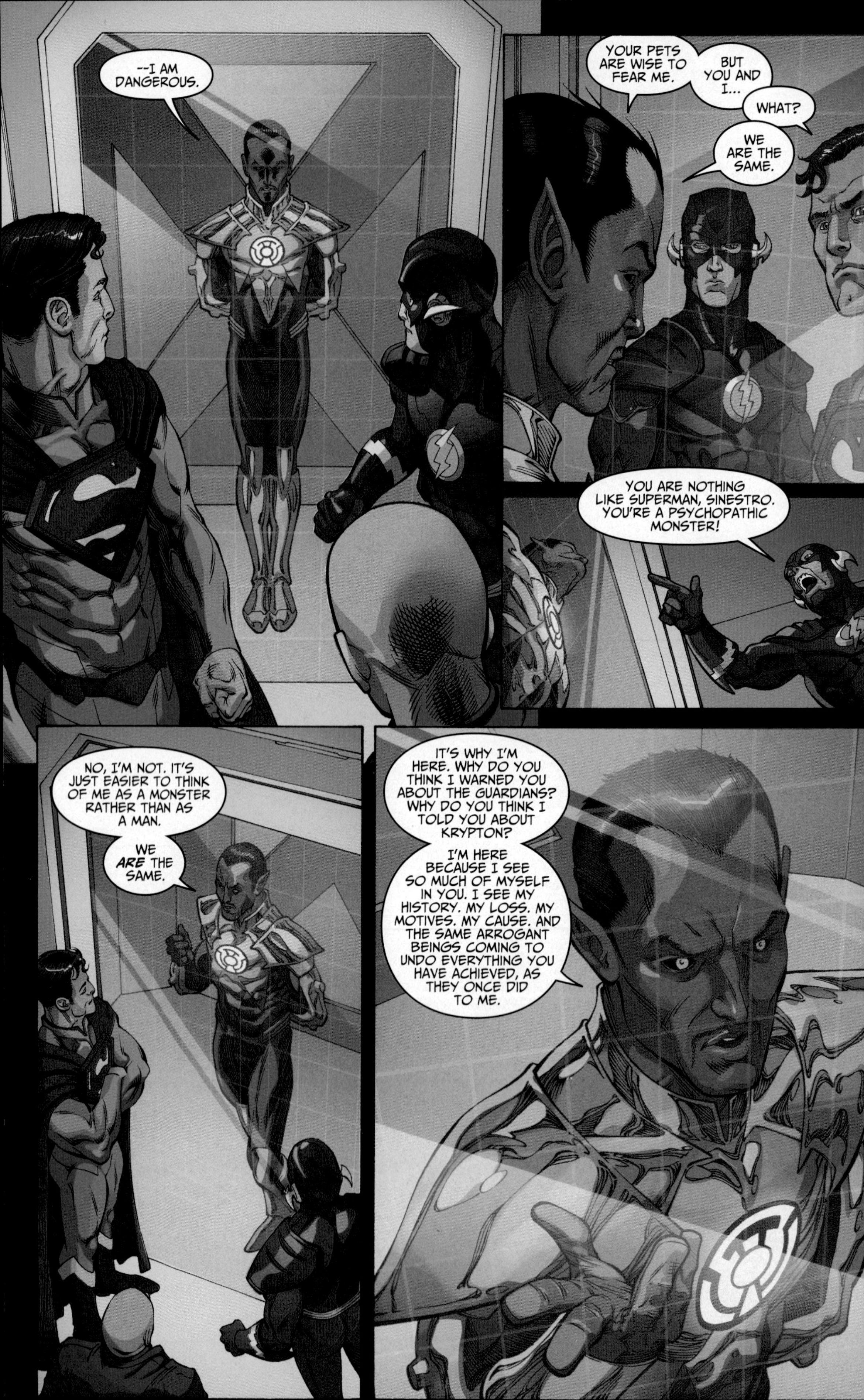
--I AM DANGEROUS.
YOUR PETS ARE WISE TO FEAR ME.
BUT YOU AND I...
WHAT?
WE ARE THE SAME.
YOU ARE NOTHING LIKE SUPERMAN, SINESTRO. YOU'RE A PSYCHOPATHIC MONSTER!
NO, I'M NOT. IT'S JUST EASIER TO THINK OF ME AS A MONSTER RATHER THAN AS A MAN.
WE ARE THE SAME.
IT'S WHY I'M HERE. WHY DO YOU THINK I WARNED YOU ABOUT THE GUARDIANS? WHY DO YOU THINK I TOLD YOU ABOUT KRYPTON?
I'M HERE BECAUSE I SEE SO MUCH OF MYSELF IN YOU. I SEE MY HISTORY. MY LOSS. MY MOTIVES. MY CAUSE. AND THE SAME ARROGANT BEINGS COMING TO UNDO EVERYTHING YOU HAVE ACHIEVED, AS THEY ONCE DID TO ME.

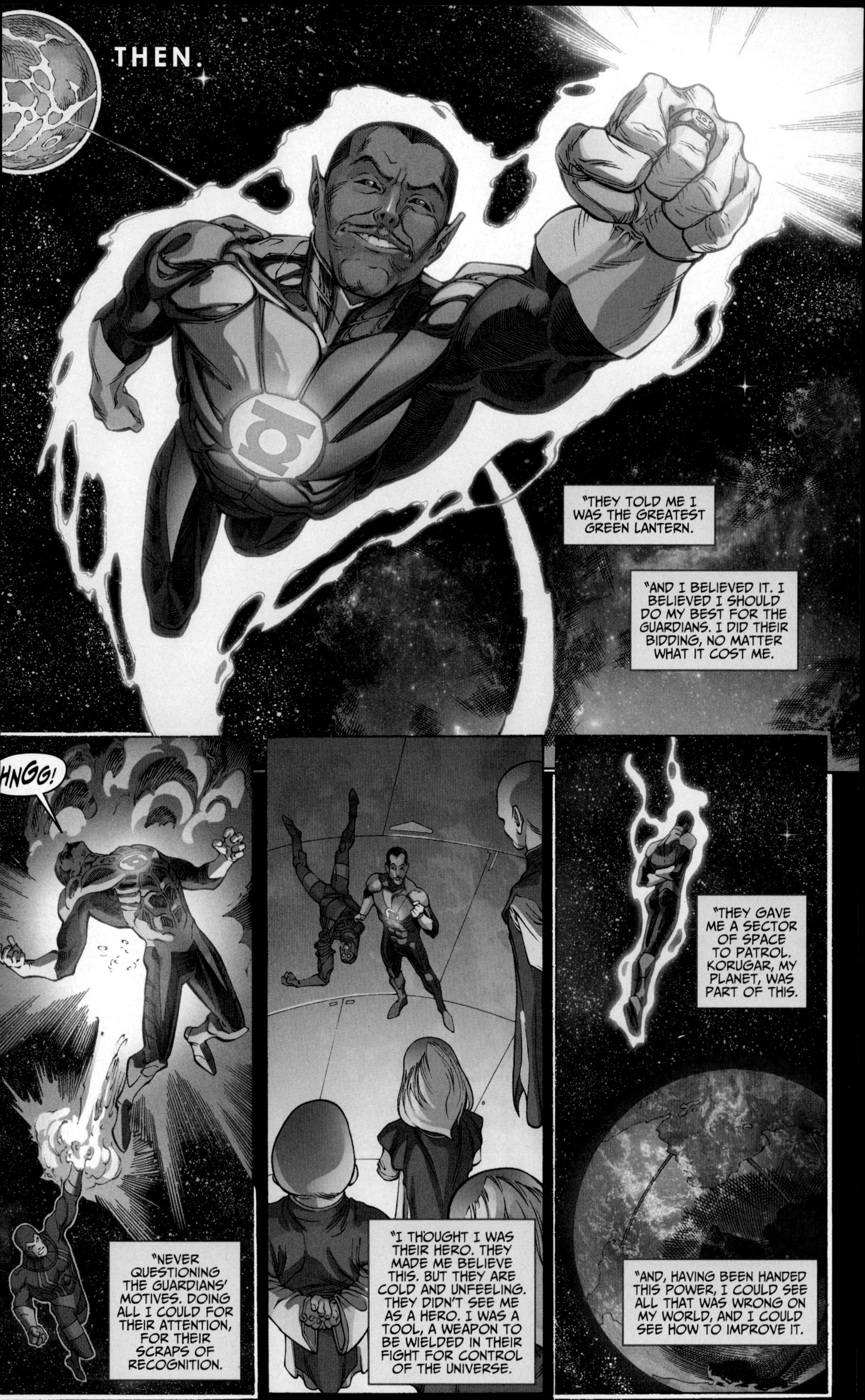
THEN.
"THEY TOLD ME I WAS THE GREATEST GREEN LANTERN.
"AND I BELIEVED IT. I BELIEVED I SHOULD DO MY BEST FOR THE GUARDIANS. I DID THEIR BIDDING, NO MATTER WHAT IT COST ME.
HNGG!
"NEVER QUESTIONING THE GUARDIANS' MOTIVES. DOING ALL I COULD FOR THEIR ATTENTION, FOR THEIR SCRAPS OF RECOGNITION.
"I THOUGHT I WAS THEIR HERO. THEY MADE ME BELIEVE THIS. BUT THEY ARE COLD AND UNFEELING. THEY DIDN'T SEE ME AS A HERO. I WAS A TOOL, A WEAPON TO BE WIELDED IN THEIR FIGHT FOR CONTROL OF THE UNIVERSE.
"THEY GAVE ME A SECTOR OF SPACE TO PATROL. KORUGAR, MY PLANET, WAS PART OF THIS.
"AND, HAVING BEEN HANDED THIS POWER, I COULD SEE ALL THAT WAS WRONG ON MY WORLD, AND I COULD SEE HOW TO IMPROVE IT.

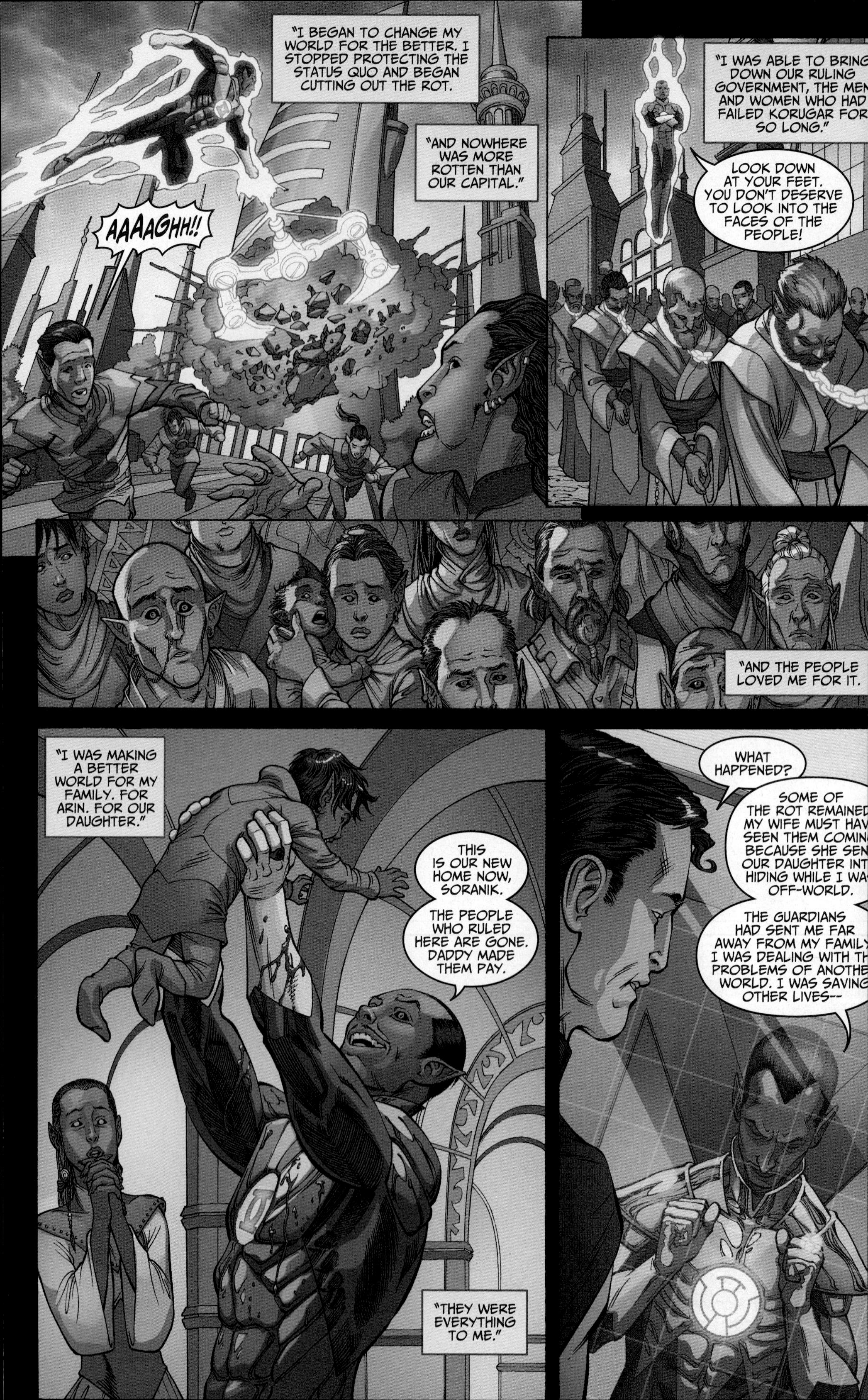
"I BEGAN TO CHANGE MY WORLD FOR THE BETTER. I STOPPED PROTECTING THE STATUS QUO AND BEGAN CUTTING OUT THE ROT.
"AND NOWHERE WAS MORE ROTTEN THAN OUR CAPITAL."
AAAAGHH!!
"I WAS ABLE TO BRING DOWN OUR RULING GOVERNMENT, THE MEN AND WOMEN WHO HAD FAILED KORUGAR FOR SO LONG."
LOOK DOWN AT YOUR FEET. YOU DON'T DESERVE TO LOOK INTO THE FACES OF THE PEOPLE!
"AND THE PEOPLE LOVED ME FOR IT.
"I WAS MAKING A BETTER WORLD FOR MY FAMILY. FOR ARIN. FOR OUR DAUGHTER."
THIS IS OUR NEW HOME NOW, SORANIK.
THE PEOPLE WHO RULED HERE ARE GONE. DADDY MADE THEM PAY.
"THEY WERE EVERYTHING TO ME."
WHAT HAPPENED?
SOME OF THE ROT REMAINED. MY WIFE MUST HAV SEEN THEM COMIN BECAUSE SHE SEN OUR DAUGHTER INT HIDING WHILE I WA OFF-WORLD.
THE GUARDIANS HAD SENT ME FAR AWAY FROM MY FAMILY I WAS DEALING WITH TH PROBLEMS OF ANOTHE WORLD. I WAS SAVING OTHER LIVES--

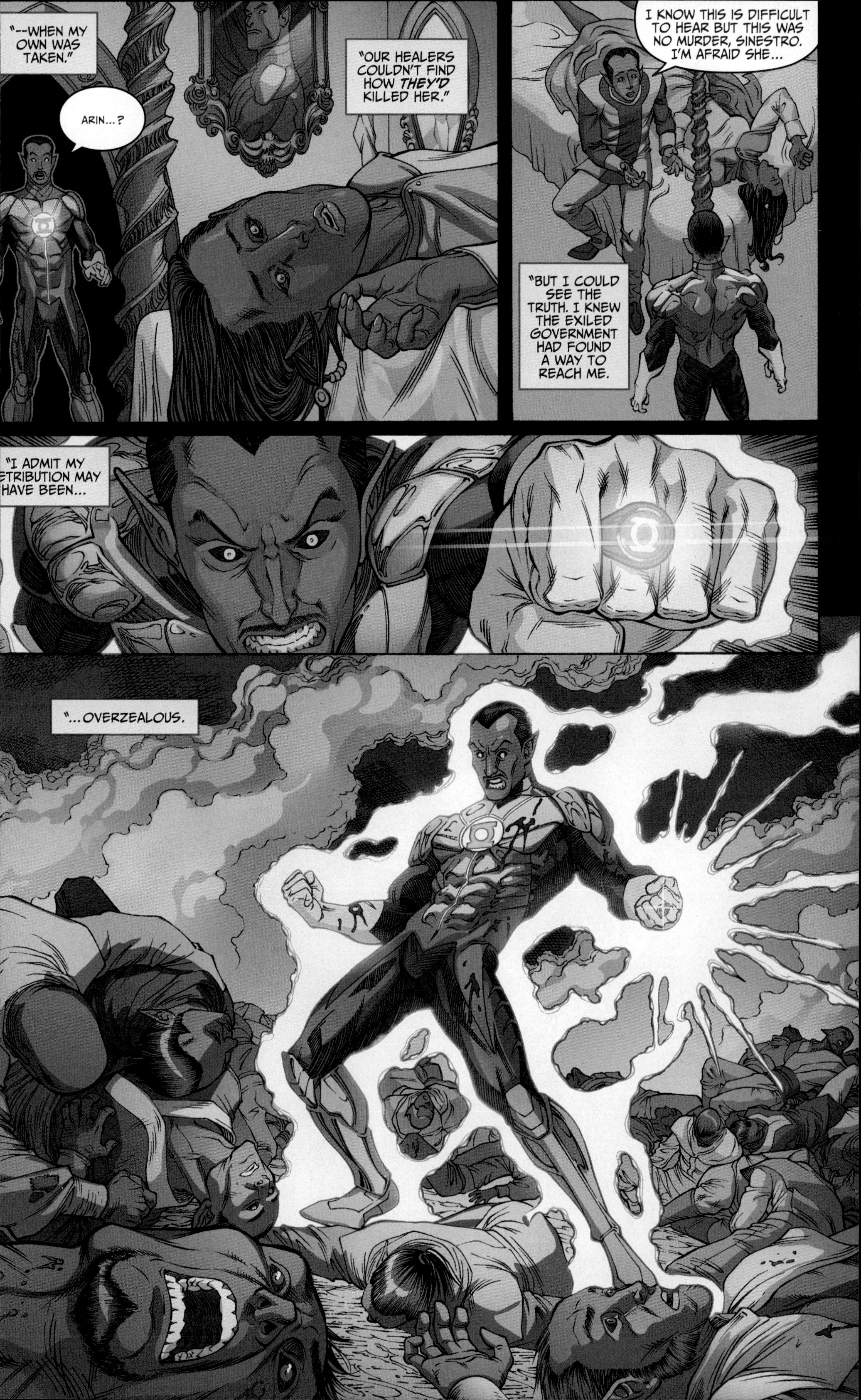
"--WHEN MY OWN WAS TAKEN."
ARIN...?
"OUR HEALERS COULDN'T FIND HOW *THEY'D* KILLED HER."
I KNOW THIS IS DIFFICULT TO HEAR BUT THIS WAS NO MURDER, SINESTRO. I'M AFRAID SHE...
"BUT I COULD SEE THE TRUTH. I KNEW THE EXILED GOVERNMENT HAD FOUND A WAY TO REACH ME.
"I ADMIT MY RETRIBUTION MAY HAVE BEEN...
"...OVERZEALOUS.

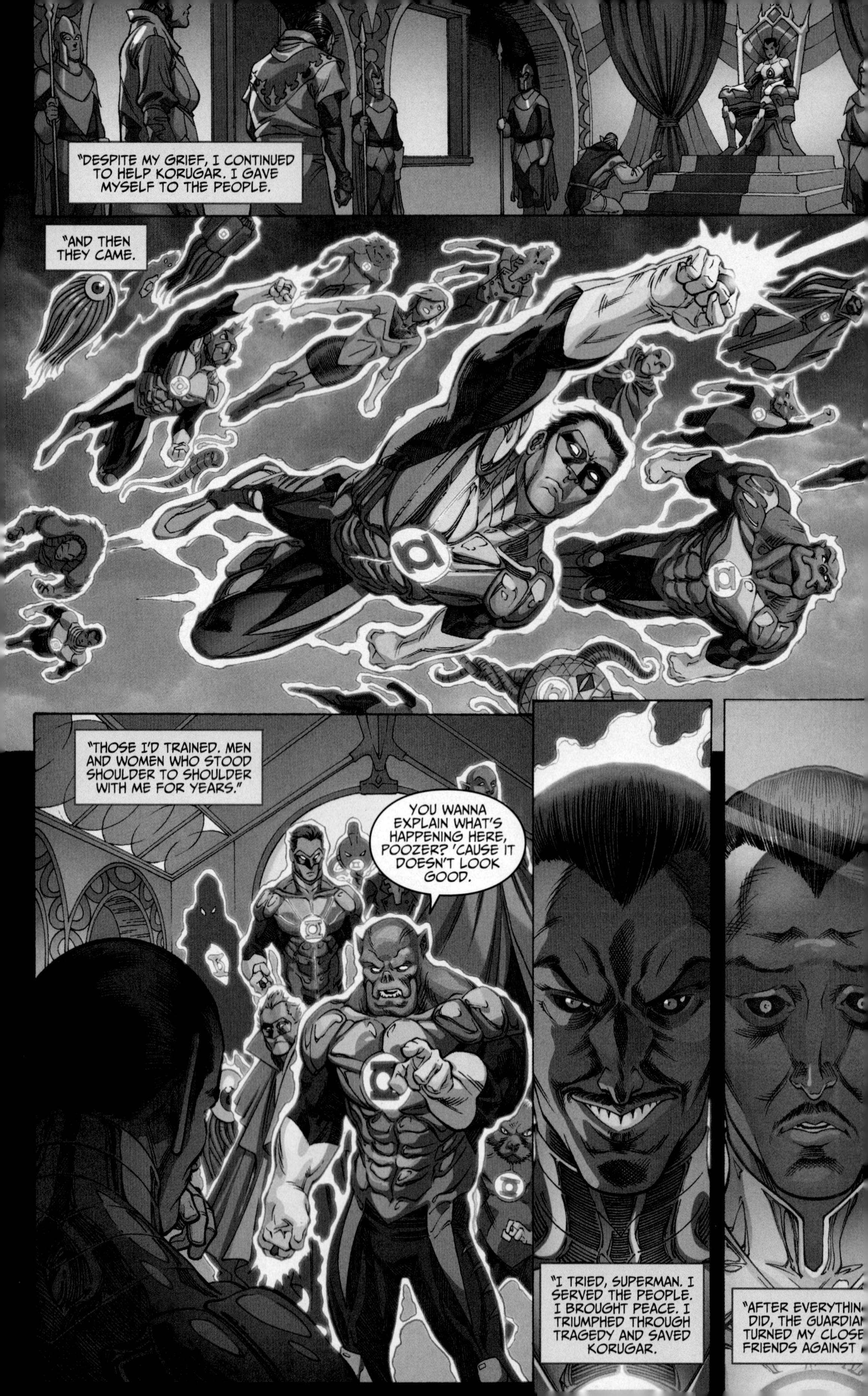

"DESPITE MY GRIEF, I CONTINUED TO HELP KORUGAR. I GAVE MYSELF TO THE PEOPLE.
"AND THEN THEY CAME.
"THOSE I'D TRAINED. MEN AND WOMEN WHO STOOD SHOULDER TO SHOULDER WITH ME FOR YEARS."
YOU WANNA EXPLAIN WHAT'S HAPPENING HERE, POOZER? 'CAUSE IT DOESN'T LOOK GOOD.
"I TRIED, SUPERMAN. I SERVED THE PEOPLE. I BROUGHT PEACE. I TRIUMPHED THROUGH TRAGEDY AND SAVED KORUGAR.
"AFTER EVERYTHIN DID, THE GUARDIA TURNED MY CLOSE FRIENDS AGAINST

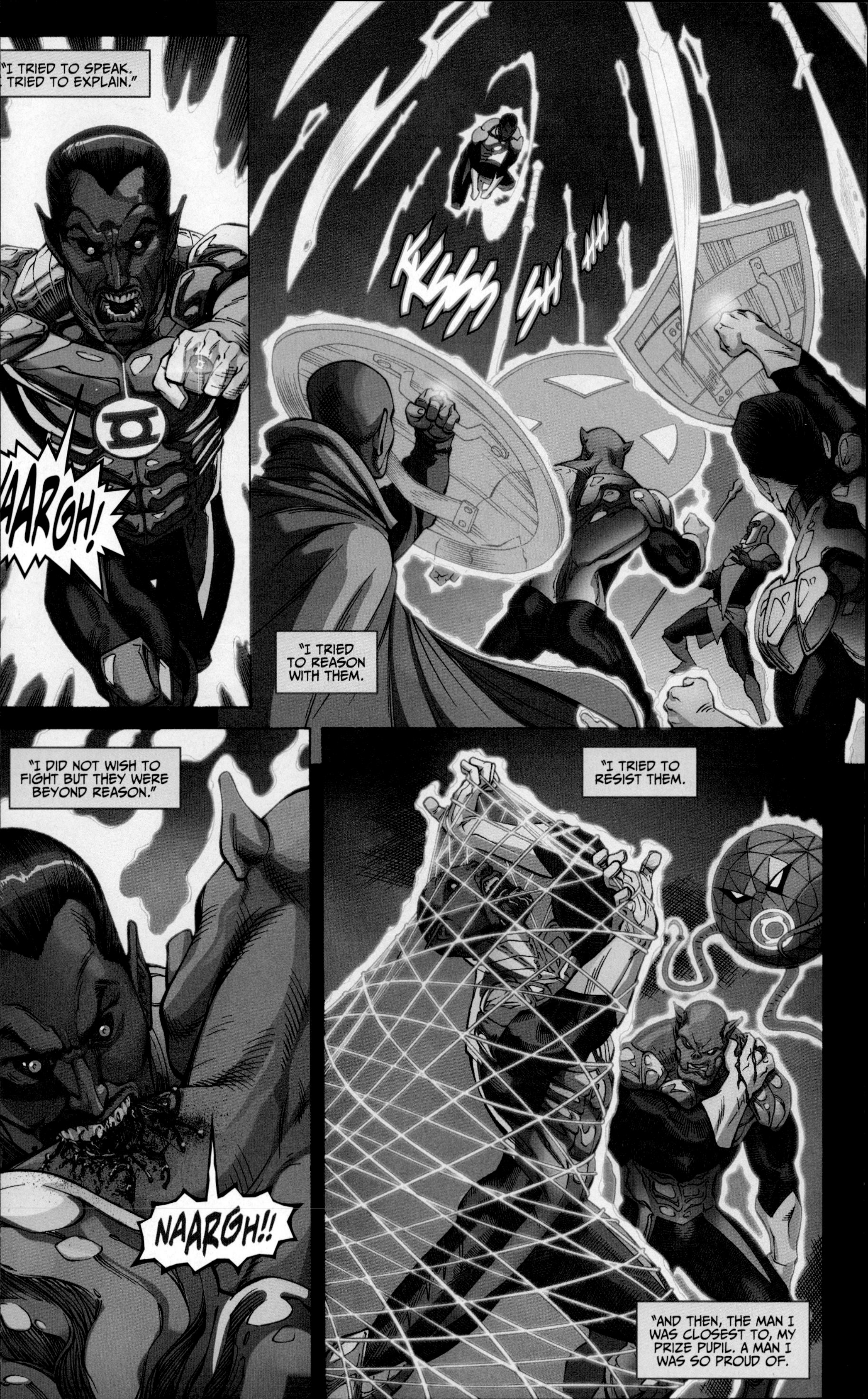
"I TRIED TO SPEAK.
TRIED TO EXPLAIN."
AARGH!
KSSSSSHHHH
"I TRIED
TO REASON
WITH THEM.
"I DID NOT WISH TO
FIGHT BUT THEY WERE
BEYOND REASON."
NAARGH!!
"I TRIED TO
RESIST THEM.
"AND THEN, THE MAN I
WAS CLOSEST TO, MY
PRIZE PUPIL. A MAN I
WAS SO PROUD OF.

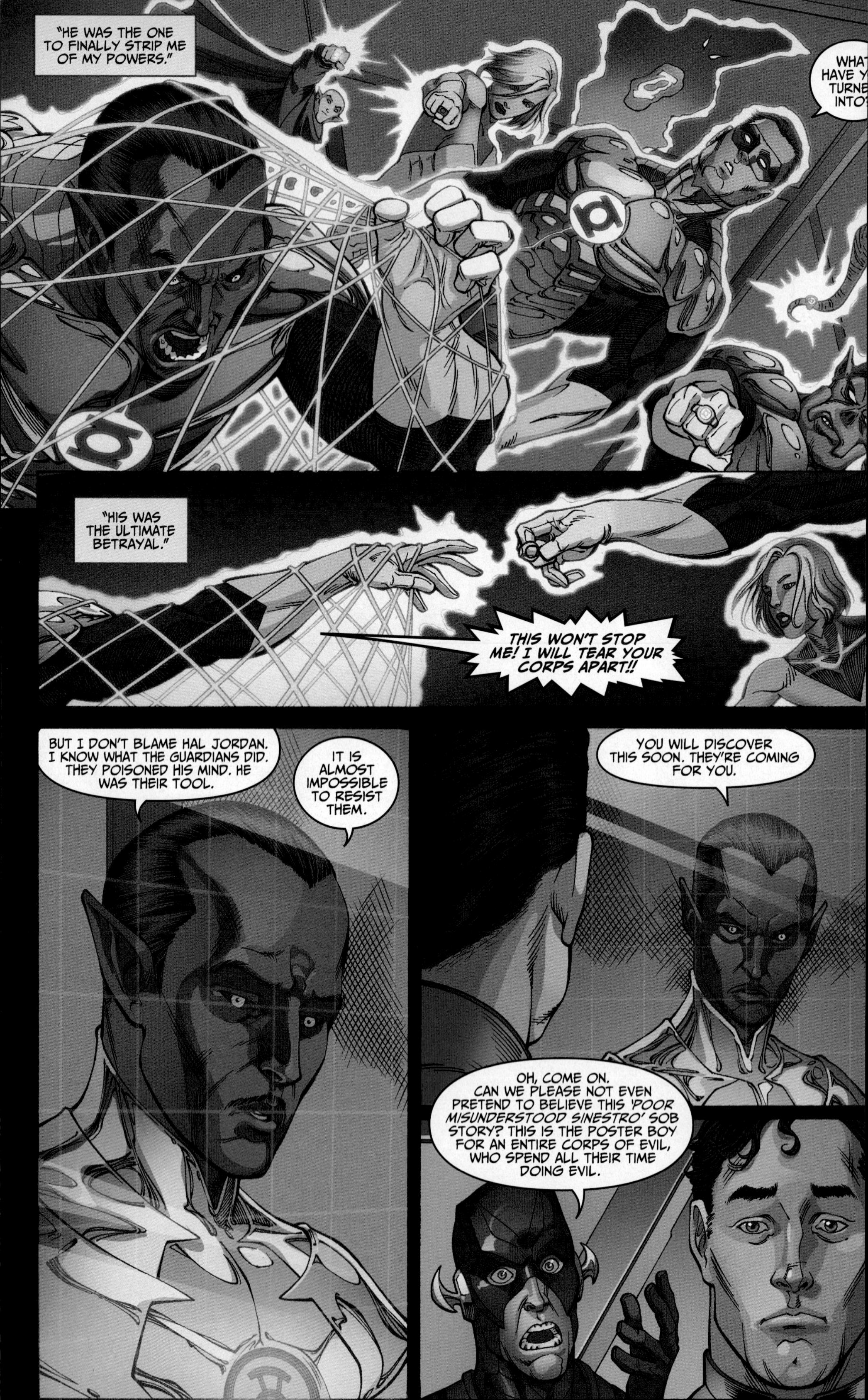
"HE WAS THE ONE TO FINALLY STRIP ME OF MY POWERS."
WHAT HAVE Y TURNE INTO?
"HIS WAS THE ULTIMATE BETRAYAL."
THIS WON'T STOP ME! I WILL TEAR YOUR CORPS APART!!
BUT I DON'T BLAME HAL JORDAN. I KNOW WHAT THE GUARDIANS DID. THEY POISONED HIS MIND. HE WAS THEIR TOOL.
IT IS ALMOST IMPOSSIBLE TO RESIST THEM.
YOU WILL DISCOVER THIS SOON. THEY'RE COMING FOR YOU.
OH, COME ON. CAN WE PLEASE NOT EVEN PRETEND TO BELIEVE THIS *'POOR MISUNDERSTOOD SINESTRO'* SOB STORY? THIS IS THE POSTER BOY FOR AN ENTIRE CORPS OF EVIL, WHO SPEND ALL THEIR TIME DOING EVIL.

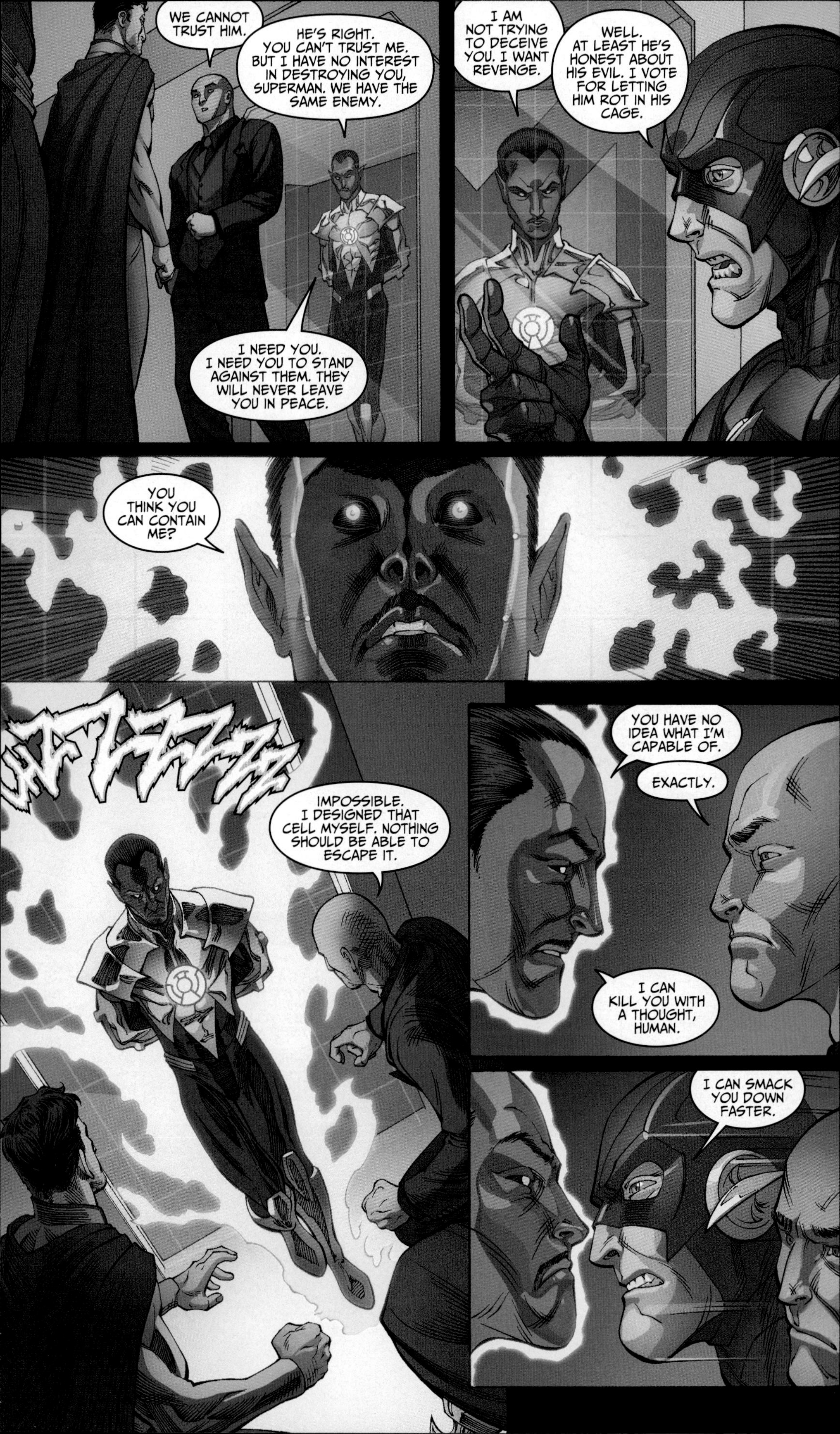
WE CANNOT TRUST HIM.
HE'S RIGHT. YOU CAN'T TRUST ME. BUT I HAVE NO INTEREST IN DESTROYING YOU, SUPERMAN. WE HAVE THE SAME ENEMY.
I NEED YOU. I NEED YOU TO STAND AGAINST THEM. THEY WILL NEVER LEAVE YOU IN PEACE.
I AM NOT TRYING TO DECEIVE YOU. I WANT REVENGE.
WELL. AT LEAST HE'S HONEST ABOUT HIS EVIL. I VOTE FOR LETTING HIM ROT IN HIS CAGE.
YOU THINK YOU CAN CONTAIN ME?
IMPOSSIBLE. I DESIGNED THAT CELL MYSELF. NOTHING SHOULD BE ABLE TO ESCAPE IT.
YOU HAVE NO IDEA WHAT I'M CAPABLE OF.
EXACTLY.
I CAN KILL YOU WITH A THOUGHT, HUMAN.
I CAN SMACK YOU DOWN FASTER.

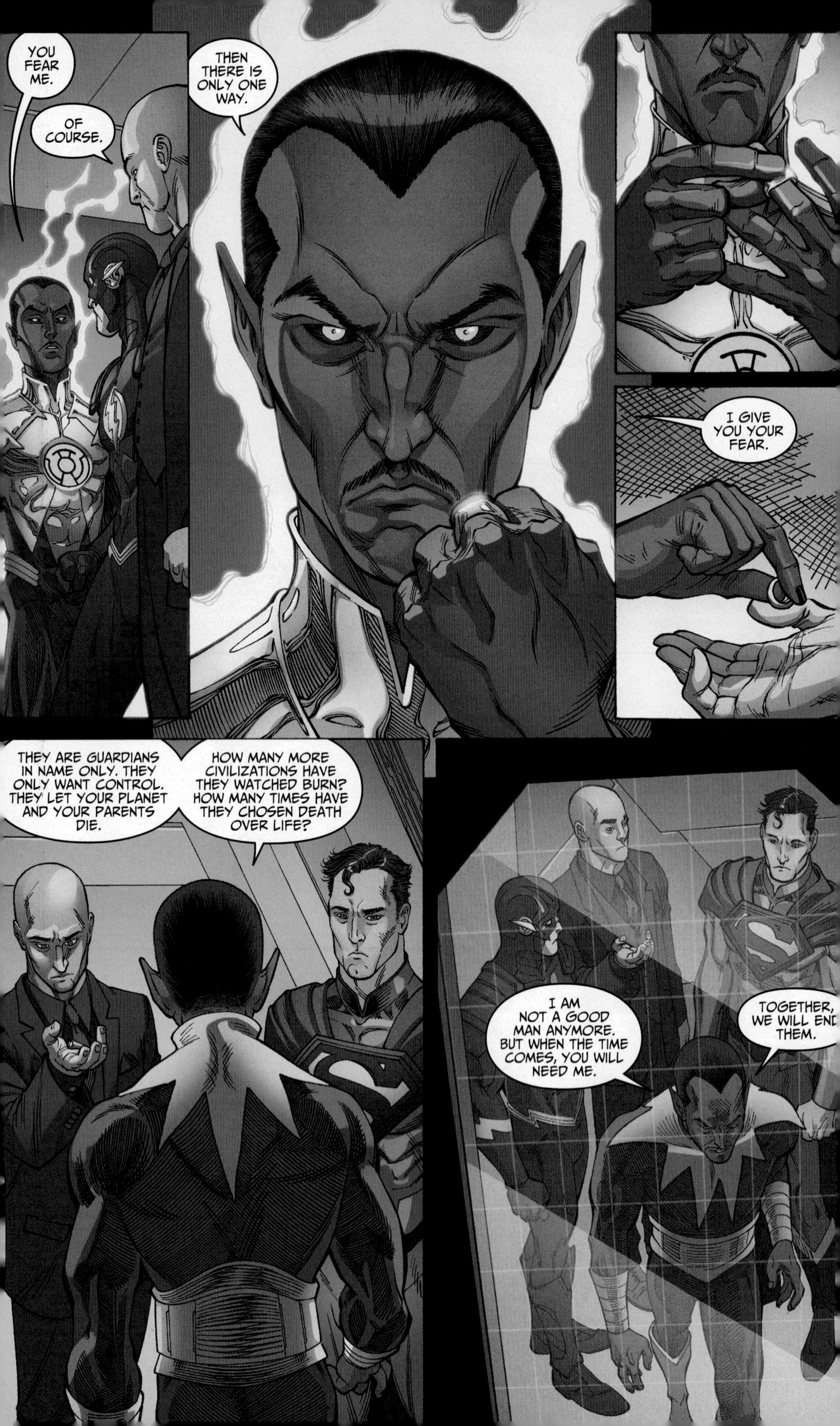
YOU FEAR ME.
OF COURSE.
THEN THERE IS ONLY ONE WAY.
I GIVE YOU YOUR FEAR.
THEY ARE GUARDIANS IN NAME ONLY. THEY ONLY WANT CONTROL. THEY LET YOUR PLANET AND YOUR PARENTS DIE.
HOW MANY MORE CIVILIZATIONS HAVE THEY WATCHED BURN? HOW MANY TIMES HAVE THEY CHOSEN DEATH OVER LIFE?
I AM NOT A GOOD MAN ANYMORE. BUT WHEN THE TIME COMES, YOU WILL NEED ME.
TOGETHER, WE WILL END THEM.

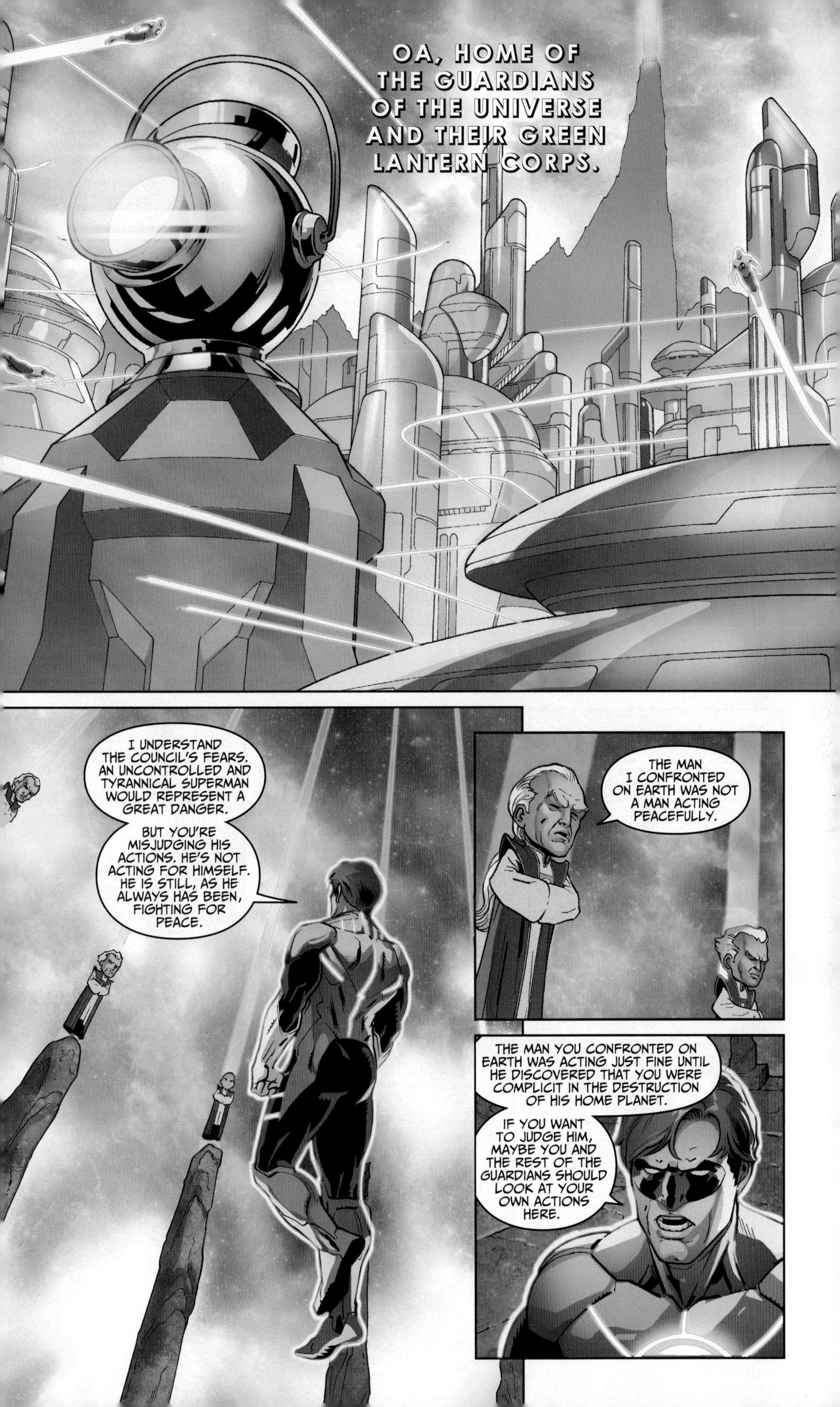

OA, HOME OF THE GUARDIANS OF THE UNIVERSE AND THEIR GREEN LANTERN CORPS.
I UNDERSTAND THE COUNCIL'S FEARS. AN UNCONTROLLED AND TYRANNICAL SUPERMAN WOULD REPRESENT A GREAT DANGER.
BUT YOU'RE MISJUDGING HIS ACTIONS. HE'S NOT ACTING FOR HIMSELF. HE IS STILL, AS HE ALWAYS HAS BEEN, FIGHTING FOR PEACE.
THE MAN I CONFRONTED ON EARTH WAS NOT A MAN ACTING PEACEFULLY.
THE MAN YOU CONFRONTED ON EARTH WAS ACTING JUST FINE UNTIL HE DISCOVERED THAT YOU WERE COMPLICIT IN THE DESTRUCTION OF HIS HOME PLANET.
IF YOU WANT TO JUDGE HIM, MAYBE YOU AND THE REST OF THE GUARDIANS SHOULD LOOK AT YOUR OWN ACTIONS HERE.

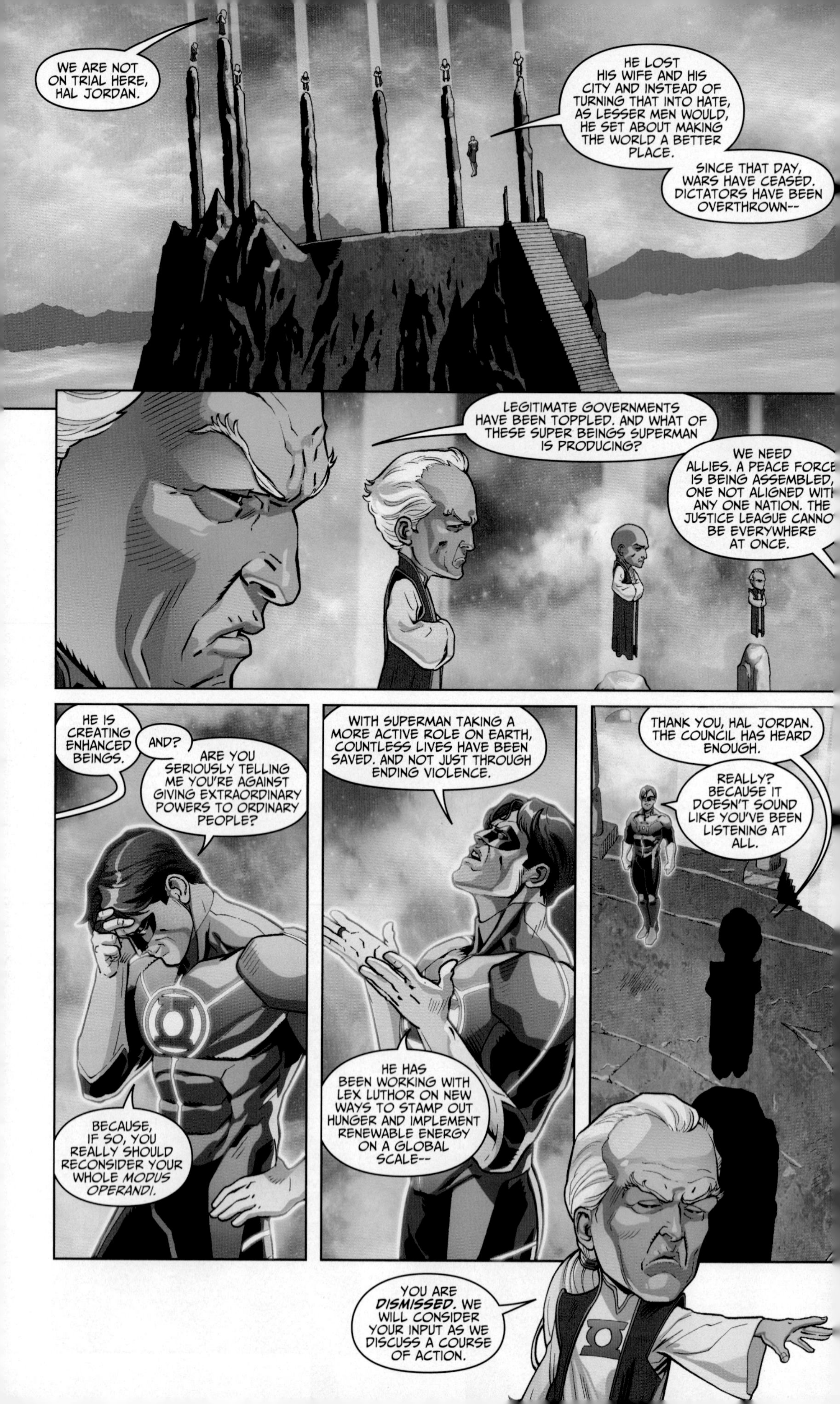

WE ARE NOT ON TRIAL HERE, HAL JORDAN.
HE LOST HIS WIFE AND HIS CITY AND INSTEAD OF TURNING THAT INTO HATE, AS LESSER MEN WOULD, HE SET ABOUT MAKING THE WORLD A BETTER PLACE.
SINCE THAT DAY, WARS HAVE CEASED. DICTATORS HAVE BEEN OVERTHROWN--
LEGITIMATE GOVERNMENTS HAVE BEEN TOPPLED. AND WHAT OF THESE SUPER BEINGS SUPERMAN IS PRODUCING?
WE NEED ALLIES. A PEACE FORCE IS BEING ASSEMBLED, ONE NOT ALIGNED WITH ANY ONE NATION. THE JUSTICE LEAGUE CANNOT BE EVERYWHERE AT ONCE.
HE IS CREATING ENHANCED BEINGS.
AND?
ARE YOU SERIOUSLY TELLING ME YOU'RE AGAINST GIVING EXTRAORDINARY POWERS TO ORDINARY PEOPLE?
BECAUSE, IF SO, YOU REALLY SHOULD RECONSIDER YOUR WHOLE *MODUS OPERANDI.*
WITH SUPERMAN TAKING A MORE ACTIVE ROLE ON EARTH, COUNTLESS LIVES HAVE BEEN SAVED. AND NOT JUST THROUGH ENDING VIOLENCE.
HE HAS BEEN WORKING WITH LEX LUTHOR ON NEW WAYS TO STAMP OUT HUNGER AND IMPLEMENT RENEWABLE ENERGY ON A GLOBAL SCALE--
THANK YOU, HAL JORDAN. THE COUNCIL HAS HEARD ENOUGH.
REALLY? BECAUSE IT DOESN'T SOUND LIKE YOU'VE BEEN LISTENING AT ALL.
YOU ARE ***DISMISSED.*** WE WILL CONSIDER YOUR INPUT AS WE DISCUSS A COURSE OF ACTION.

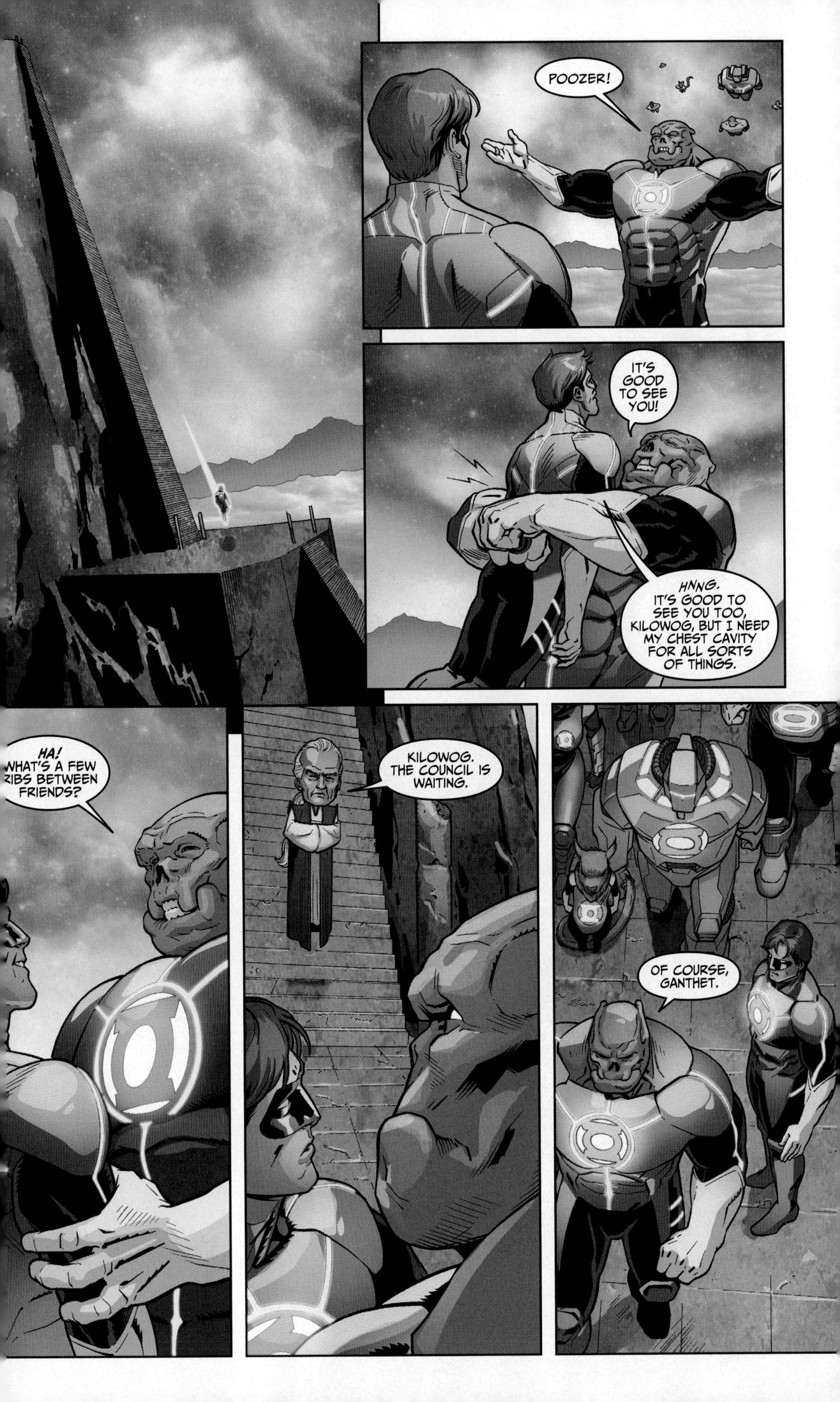
POOZER!
IT'S GOOD TO SEE YOU!
HNNG. IT'S GOOD TO SEE YOU TOO, KILOWOG, BUT I NEED MY CHEST CAVITY FOR ALL SORTS OF THINGS.
HA! WHAT'S A FEW RIBS BETWEEN FRIENDS?
KILOWOG. THE COUNCIL IS WAITING.
OF COURSE, GANTHET.

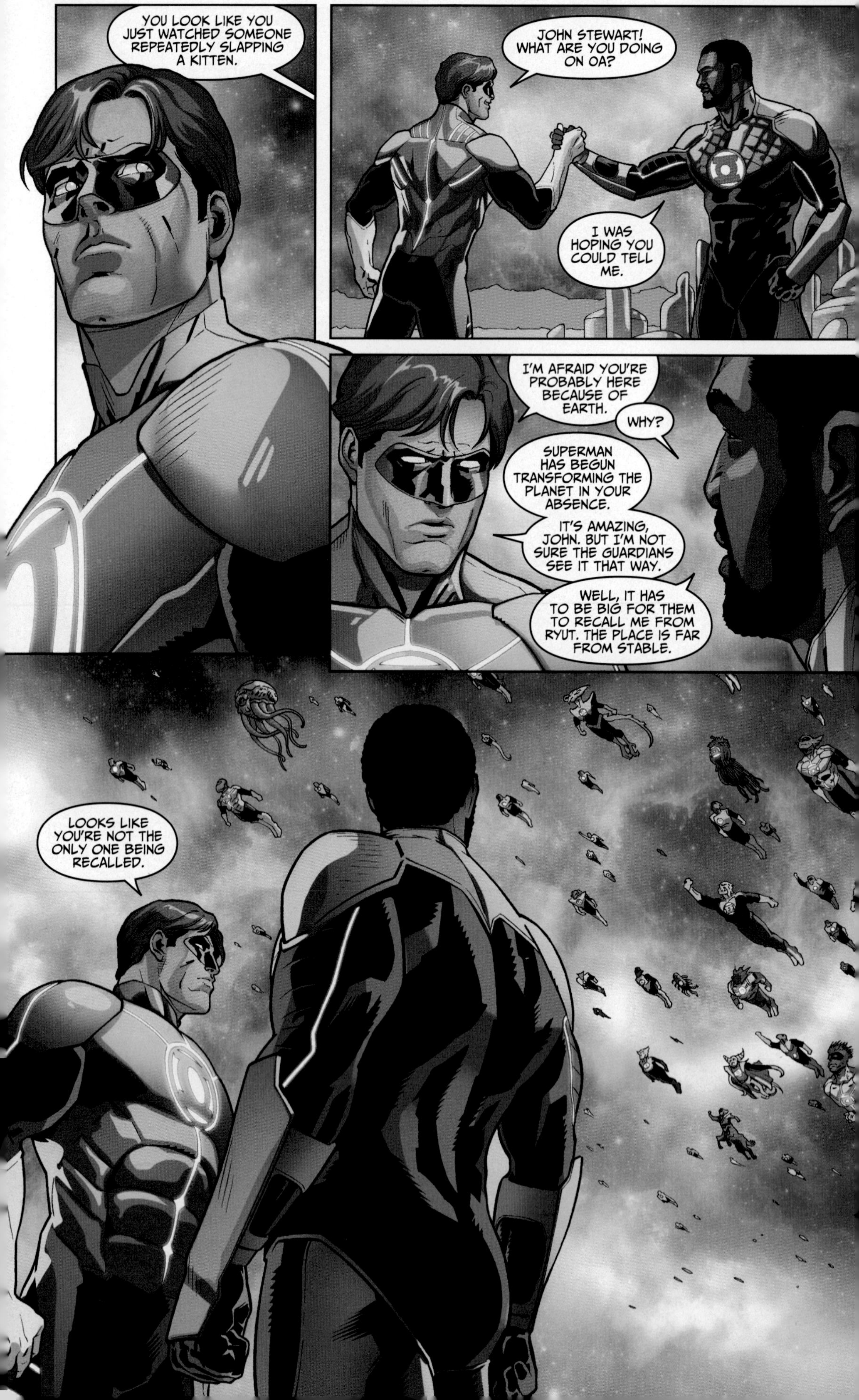
YOU LOOK LIKE YOU JUST WATCHED SOMEONE REPEATEDLY SLAPPING A KITTEN.
JOHN STEWART! WHAT ARE YOU DOING ON OA?
I WAS HOPING YOU COULD TELL ME.
I'M AFRAID YOU'RE PROBABLY HERE BECAUSE OF EARTH.
WHY?
SUPERMAN HAS BEGUN TRANSFORMING THE PLANET IN YOUR ABSENCE.
IT'S AMAZING, JOHN. BUT I'M NOT SURE THE GUARDIANS SEE IT THAT WAY.
WELL, IT HAS TO BE BIG FOR THEM TO RECALL ME FROM RYUT. THE PLACE IS FAR FROM STABLE.
LOOKS LIKE YOU'RE NOT THE ONLY ONE BEING RECALLED.

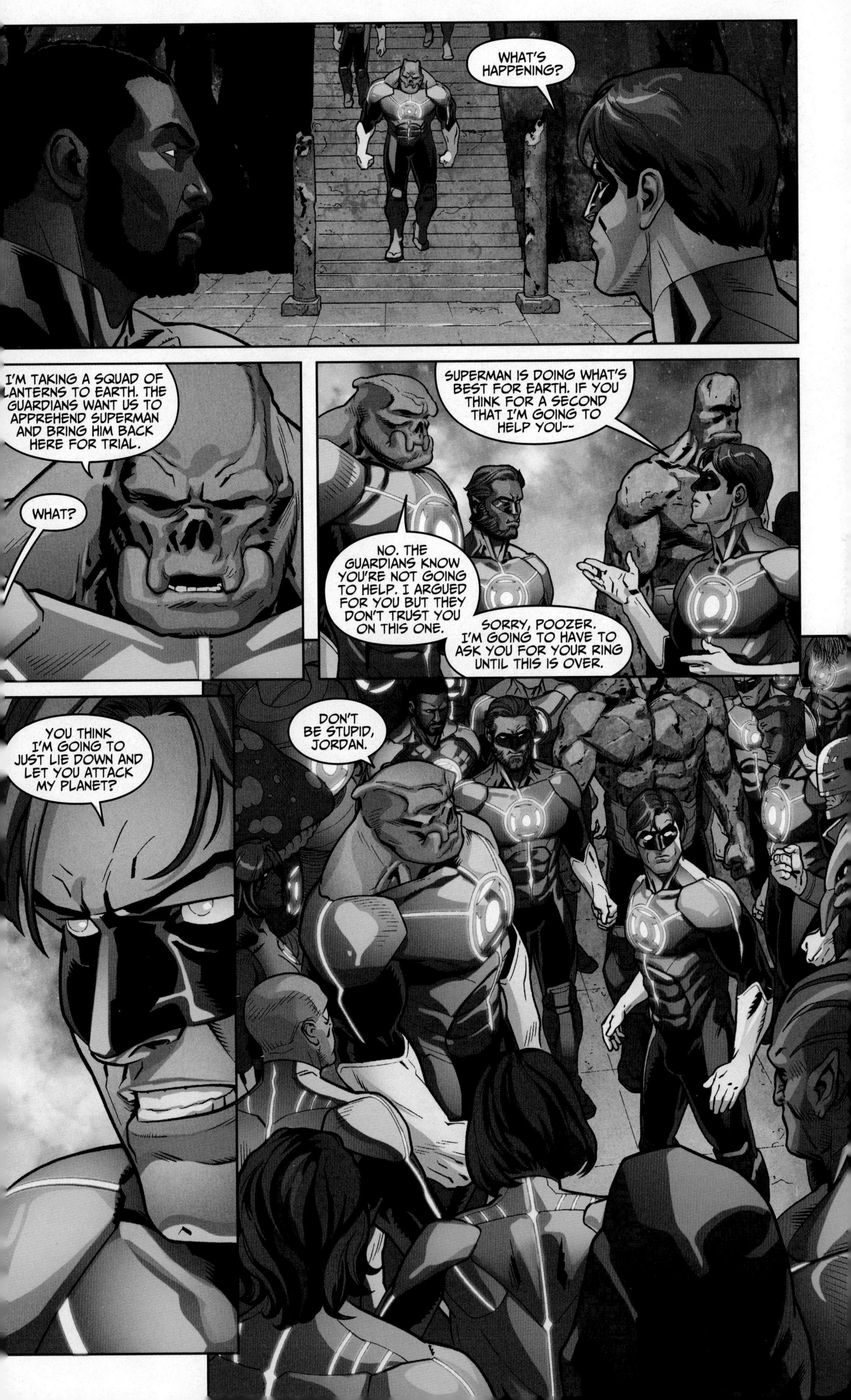
WHAT'S HAPPENING?
I'M TAKING A SQUAD OF LANTERNS TO EARTH. THE GUARDIANS WANT US TO APPREHEND SUPERMAN AND BRING HIM BACK HERE FOR TRIAL.
WHAT?
SUPERMAN IS DOING WHAT'S BEST FOR EARTH. IF YOU THINK FOR A SECOND THAT I'M GOING TO HELP YOU--
NO. THE GUARDIANS KNOW YOU'RE NOT GOING TO HELP. I ARGUED FOR YOU BUT THEY DON'T TRUST YOU ON THIS ONE.
SORRY, POOZER. I'M GOING TO HAVE TO ASK YOU FOR YOUR RING UNTIL THIS IS OVER.
YOU THINK I'M GOING TO JUST LIE DOWN AND LET YOU ATTACK MY PLANET?
DON'T BE STUPID, JORDAN.

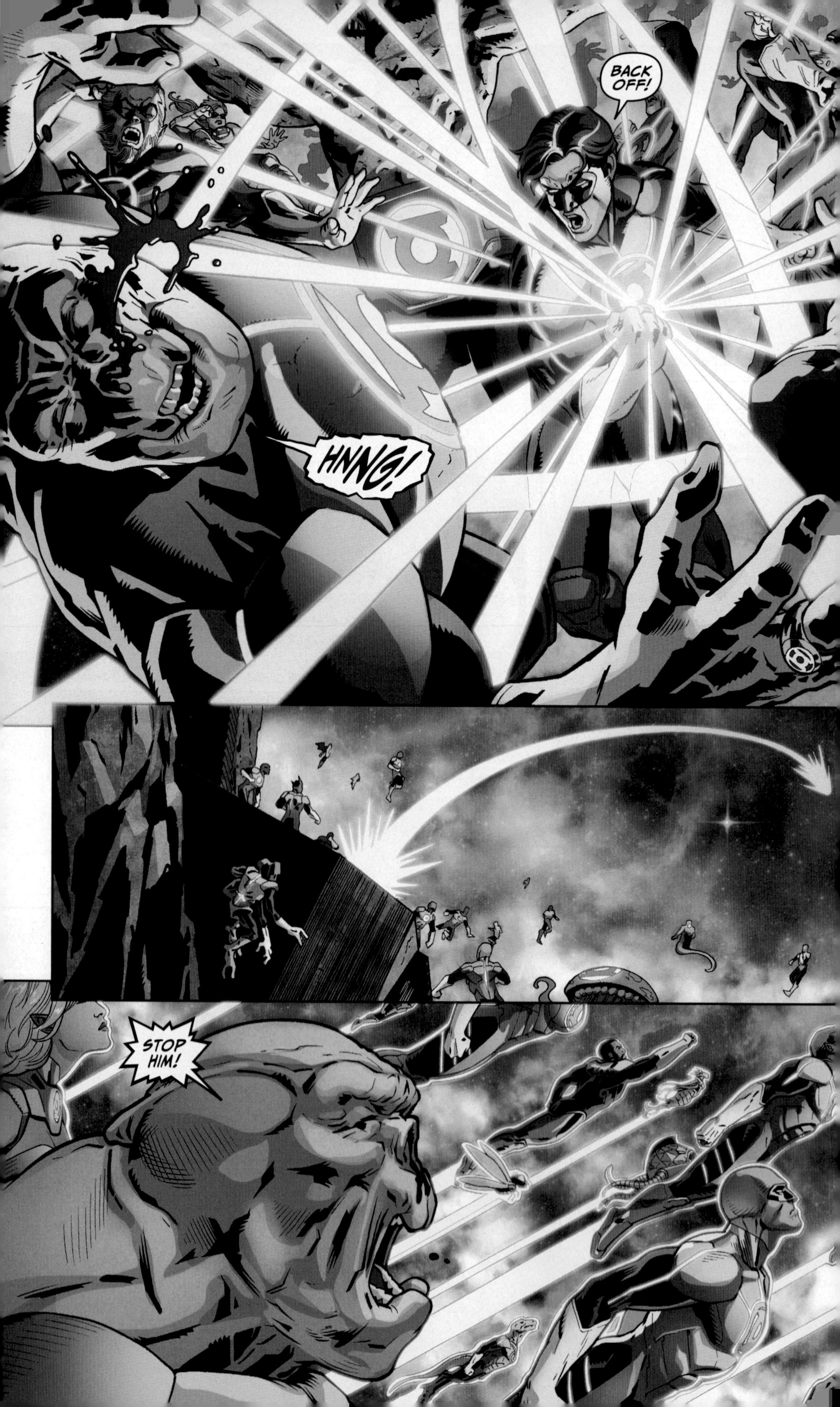
BACK OFF!
HNNG!
STOP HIM!

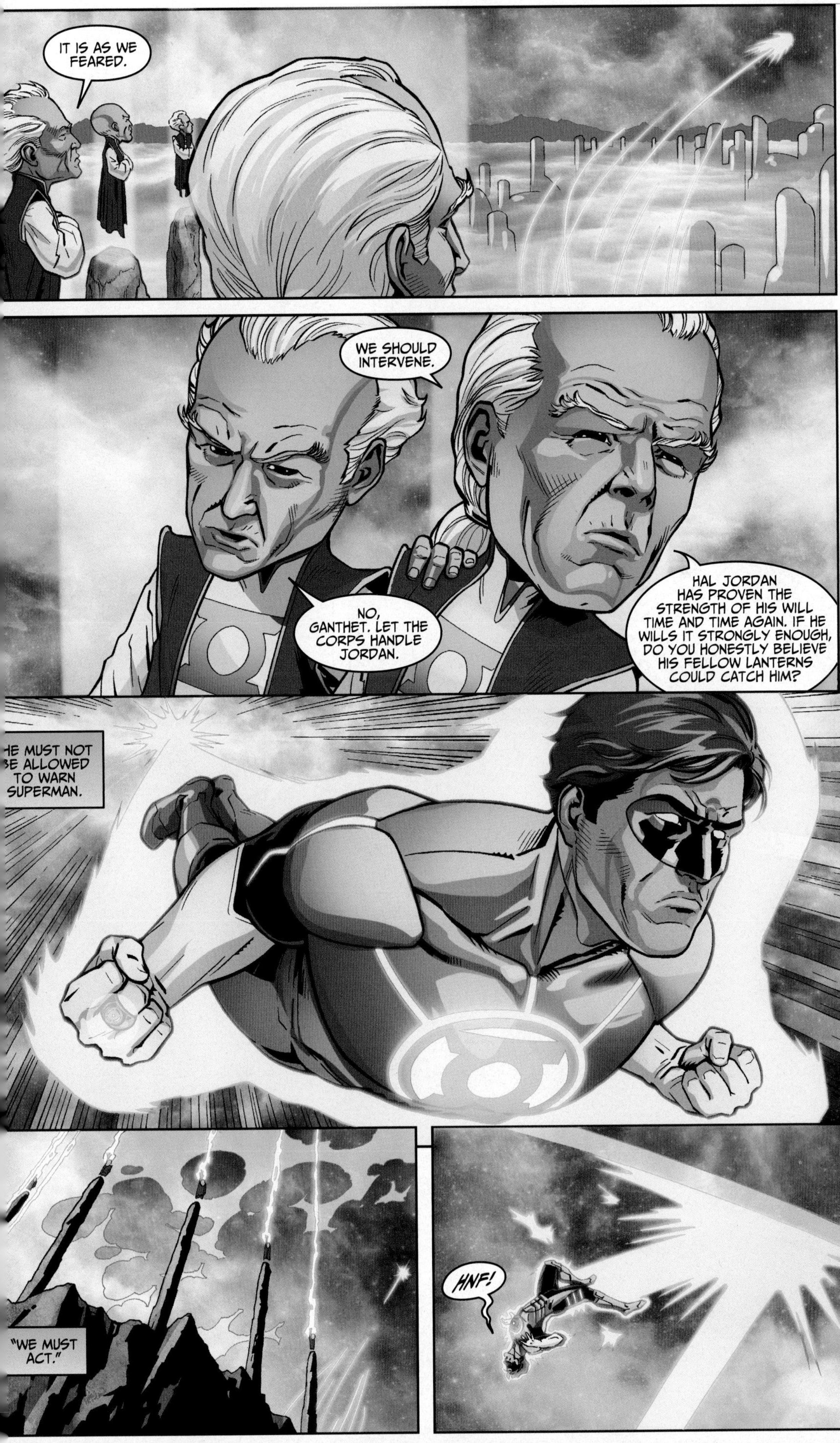
IT IS AS WE FEARED.
WE SHOULD INTERVENE.
NO, GANTHET. LET THE CORPS HANDLE JORDAN.
HAL JORDAN HAS PROVEN THE STRENGTH OF HIS WILL TIME AND TIME AGAIN. IF HE WILLS IT STRONGLY ENOUGH, DO YOU HONESTLY BELIEVE HIS FELLOW LANTERNS COULD CATCH HIM?
HE MUST NOT BE ALLOWED TO WARN SUPERMAN.
"WE MUST ACT."
HNF!

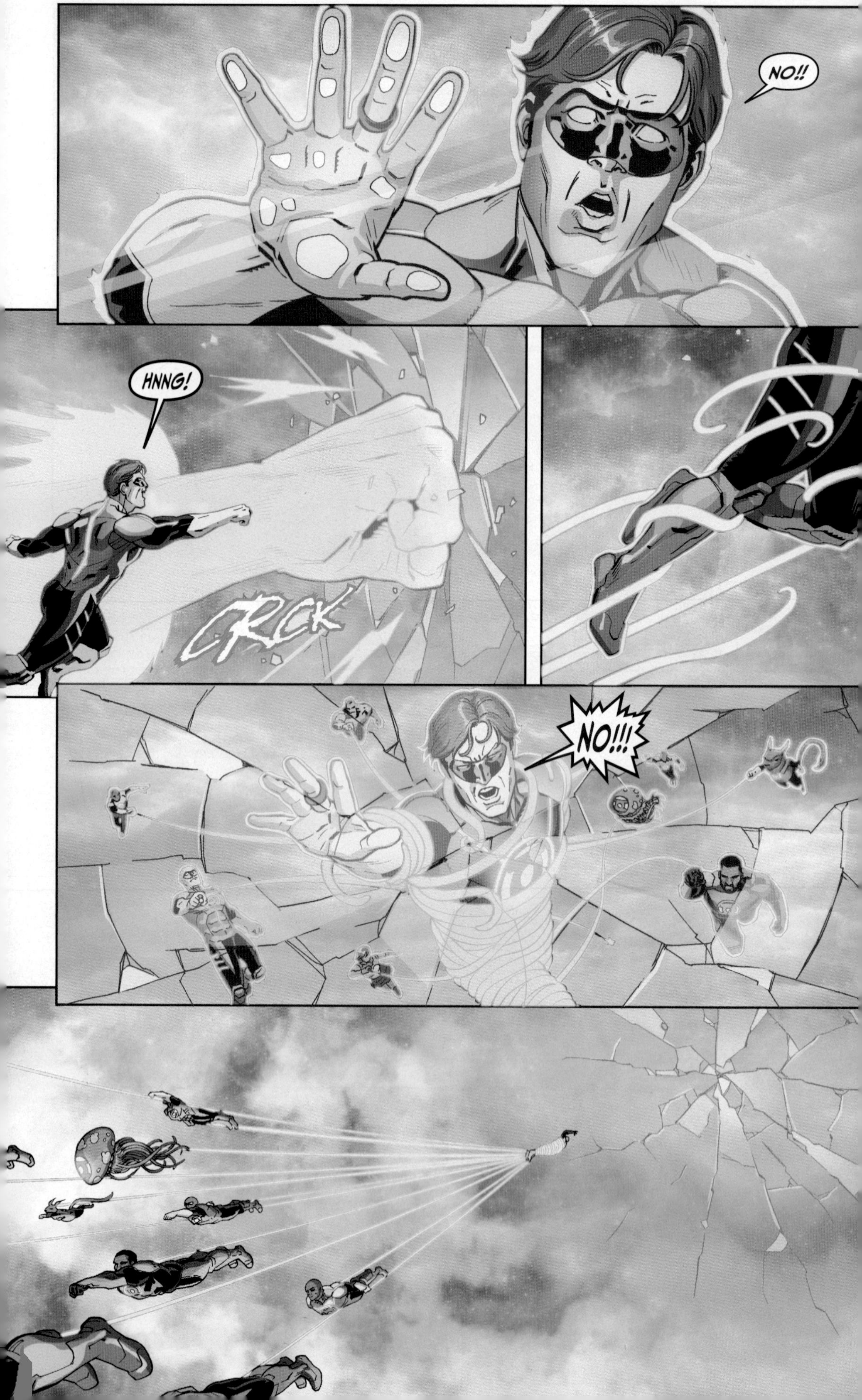
NO!!
HNNG!
CRCK
NO!!!

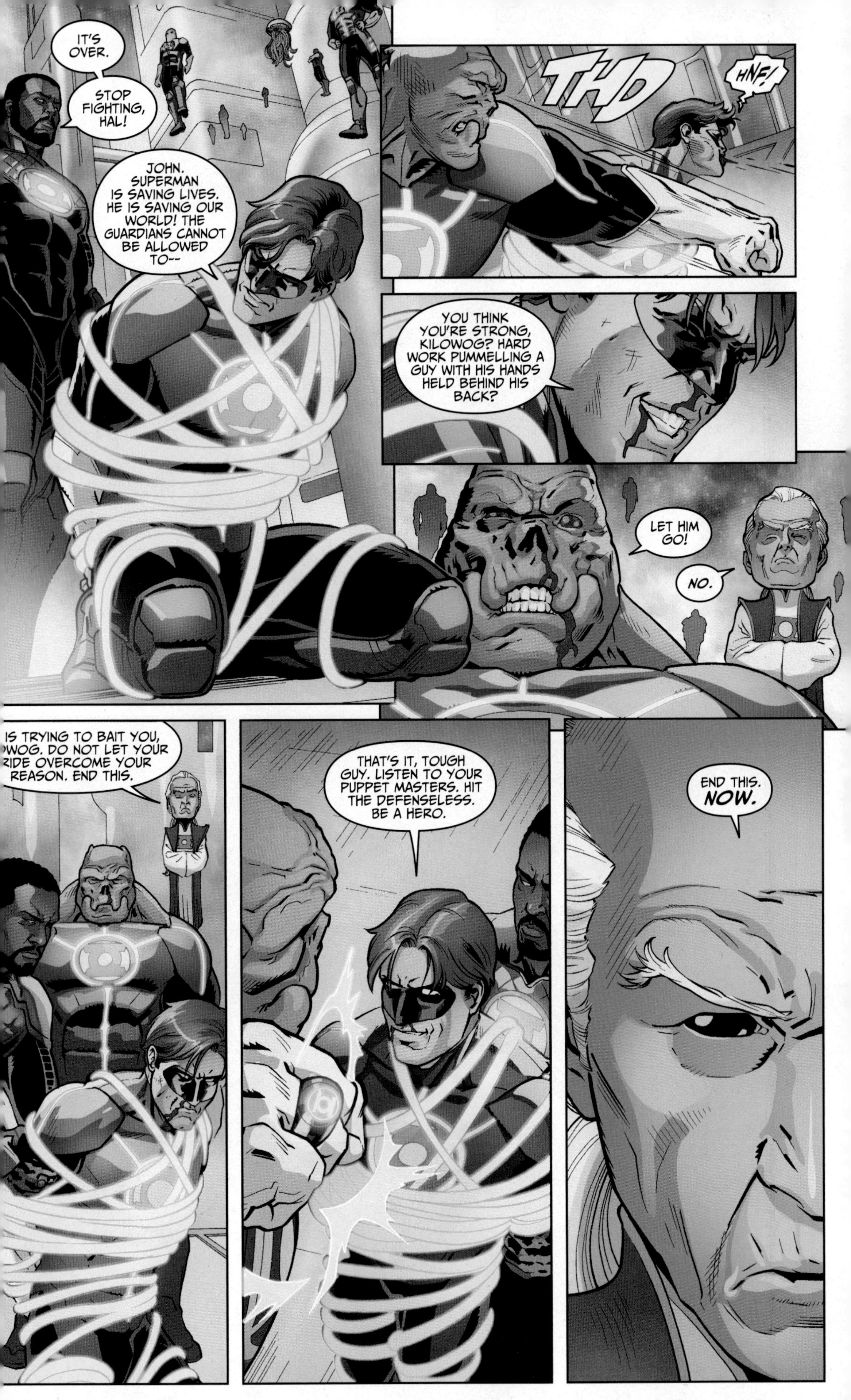
IT'S OVER.
STOP FIGHTING, HAL!
JOHN. SUPERMAN IS SAVING LIVES. HE IS SAVING OUR WORLD! THE GUARDIANS CANNOT BE ALLOWED TO--
THD
HNF!
YOU THINK YOU'RE STRONG, KILOWOG? HARD WORK PUMMELLING A GUY WITH HIS HANDS HELD BEHIND HIS BACK?
LET HIM GO!
NO.
IS TRYING TO BAIT YOU, OWOG. DO NOT LET YOUR RIDE OVERCOME YOUR REASON. END THIS.
THAT'S IT, TOUGH GUY. LISTEN TO YOUR PUPPET MASTERS. HIT THE DEFENSELESS. BE A HERO.
END THIS. NOW.

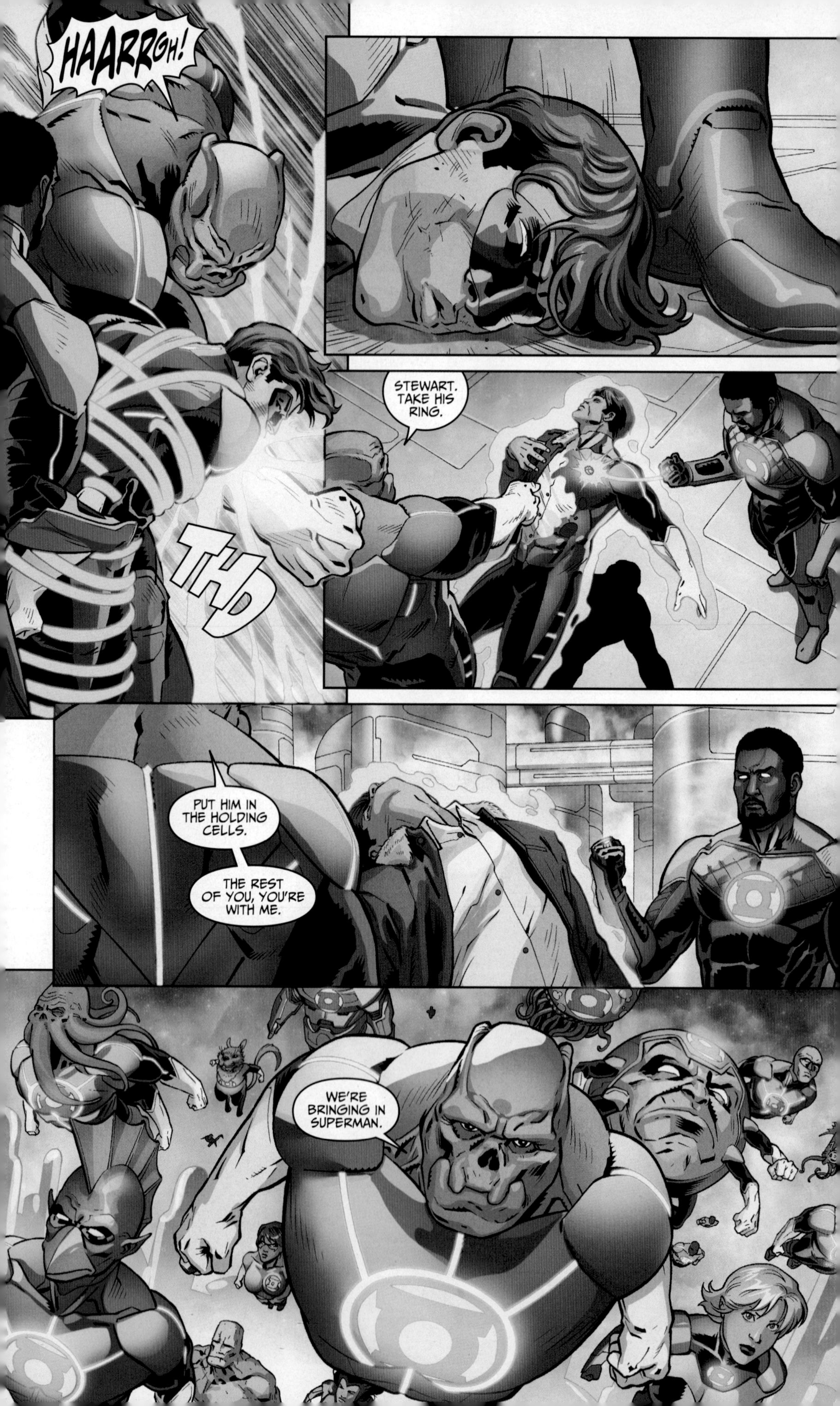
HAARRGH!
THD
STEWART. TAKE HIS RING.
PUT HIM IN THE HOLDING CELLS.
THE REST OF YOU, YOU'RE WITH ME.
WE'RE BRINGING IN SUPERMAN.

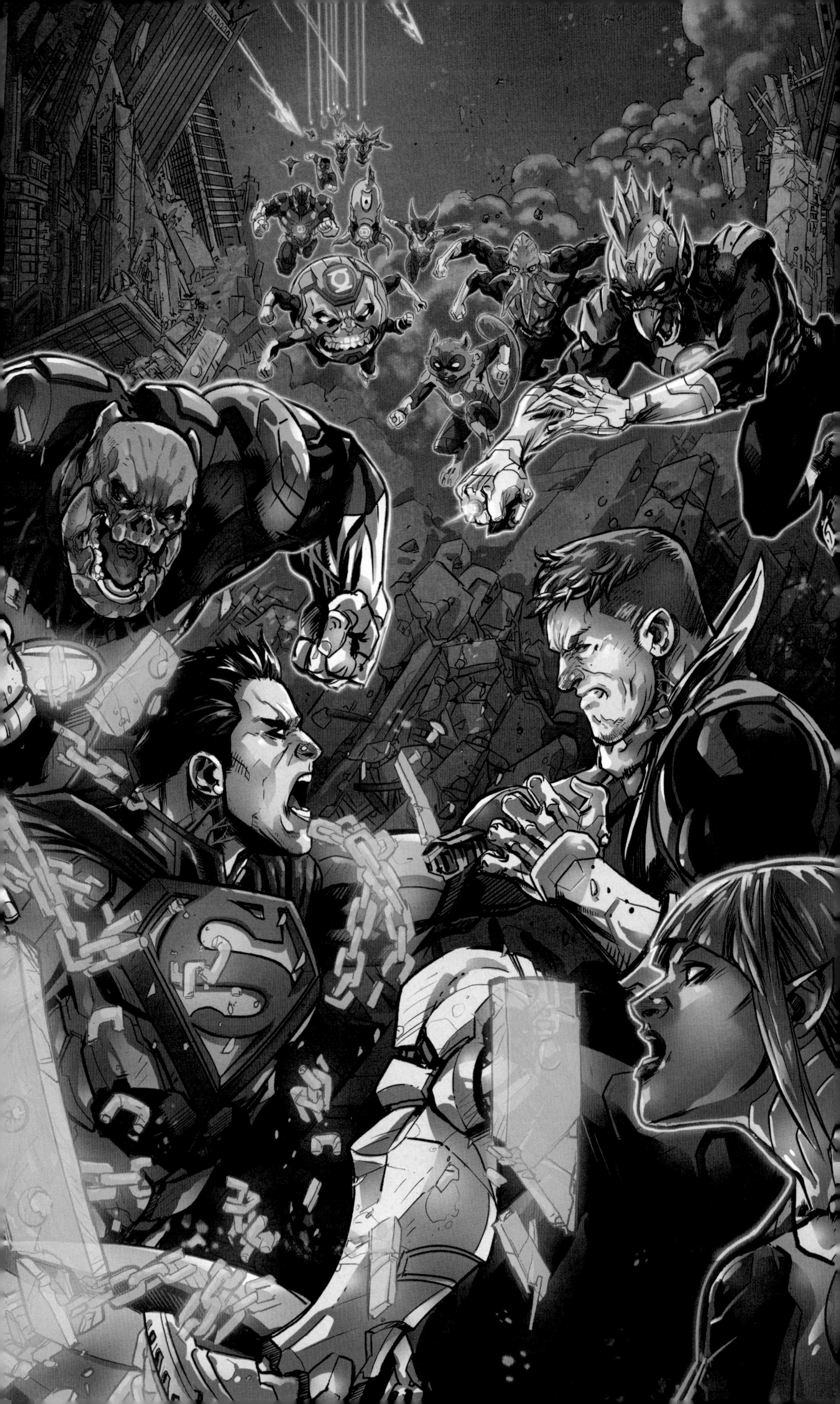

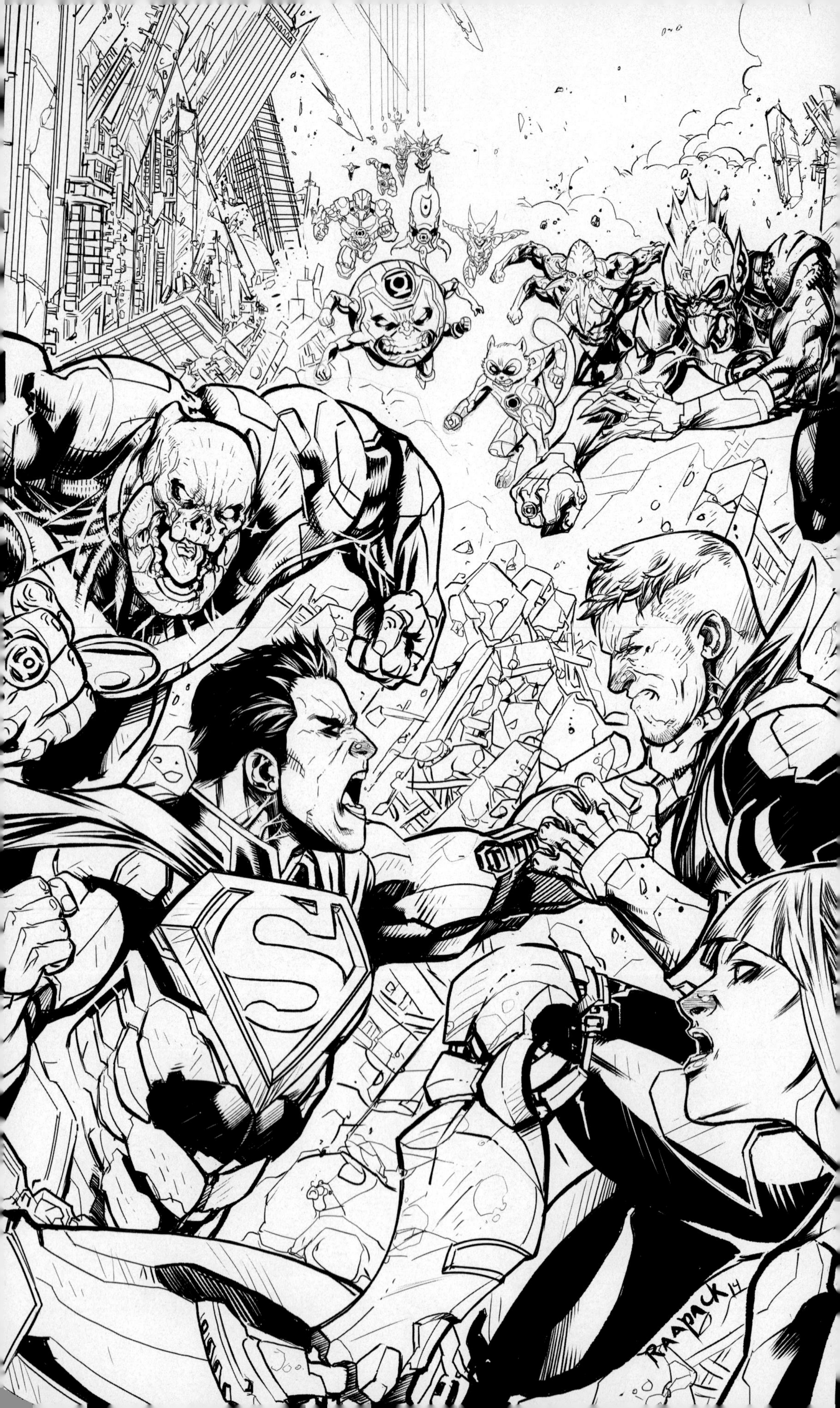
RAAPACK '14

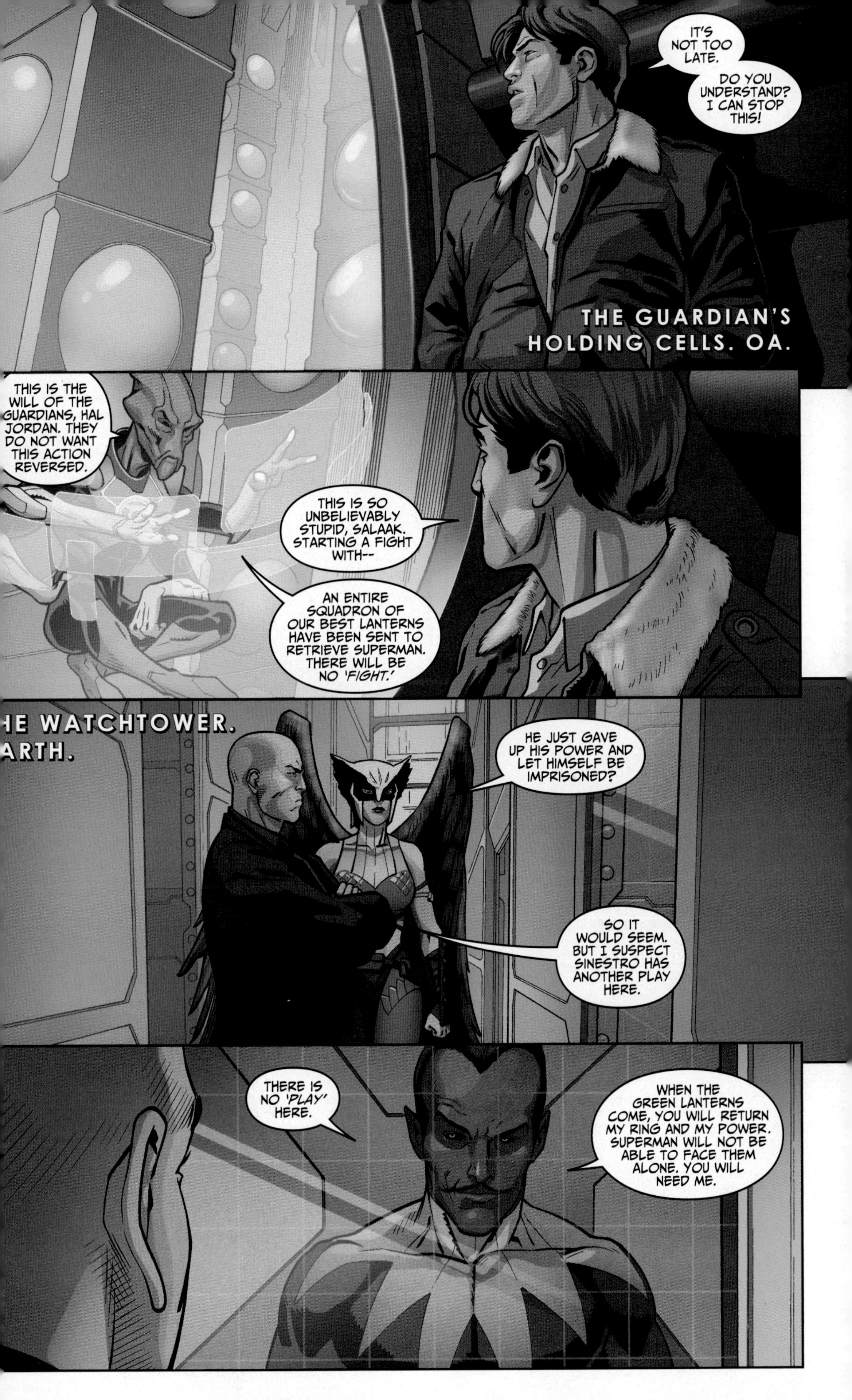
IT'S NOT TOO LATE.
DO YOU UNDERSTAND? I CAN STOP THIS!
THE GUARDIAN'S HOLDING CELLS. OA.
THIS IS THE WILL OF THE GUARDIANS, HAL JORDAN. THEY DO NOT WANT THIS ACTION REVERSED.
THIS IS SO UNBELIEVABLY STUPID, SALAAK. STARTING A FIGHT WITH--
AN ENTIRE SQUADRON OF OUR BEST LANTERNS HAVE BEEN SENT TO RETRIEVE SUPERMAN. THERE WILL BE NO 'FIGHT.'
HE WATCHTOWER. ARTH.
HE JUST GAVE UP HIS POWER AND LET HIMSELF BE IMPRISONED?
SO IT WOULD SEEM. BUT I SUSPECT SINESTRO HAS ANOTHER PLAY HERE.
THERE IS NO 'PLAY' HERE.
WHEN THE GREEN LANTERNS COME, YOU WILL RETURN MY RING AND MY POWER. SUPERMAN WILL NOT BE ABLE TO FACE THEM ALONE. YOU WILL NEED ME.

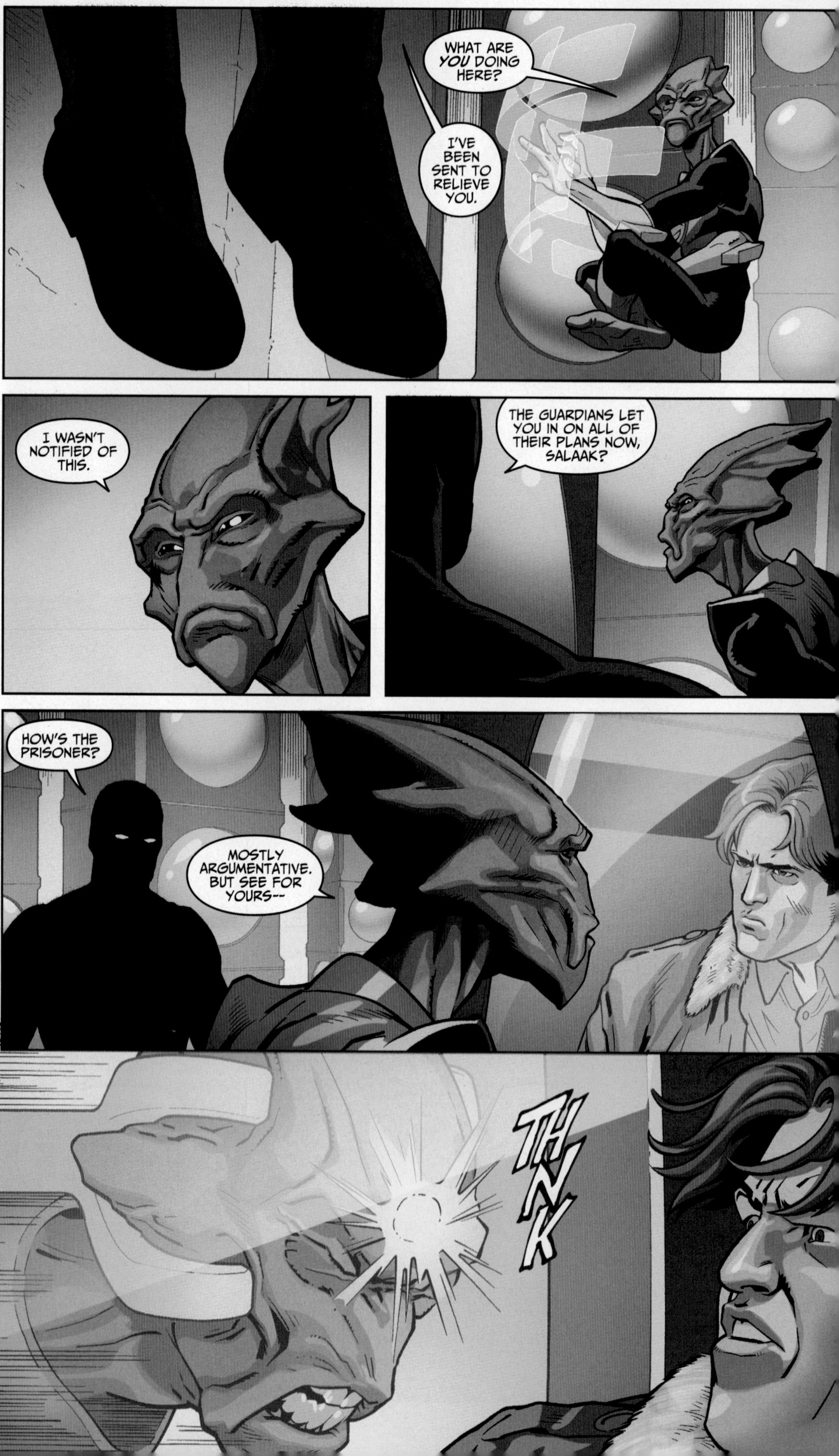
WHAT ARE YOU DOING HERE?
I'VE BEEN SENT TO RELIEVE YOU.
I WASN'T NOTIFIED OF THIS.
THE GUARDIANS LET YOU IN ON ALL OF THEIR PLANS NOW, SALAAK?
HOW'S THE PRISONER?
MOSTLY ARGUMENTATIVE. BUT SEE FOR YOURS--
THNK

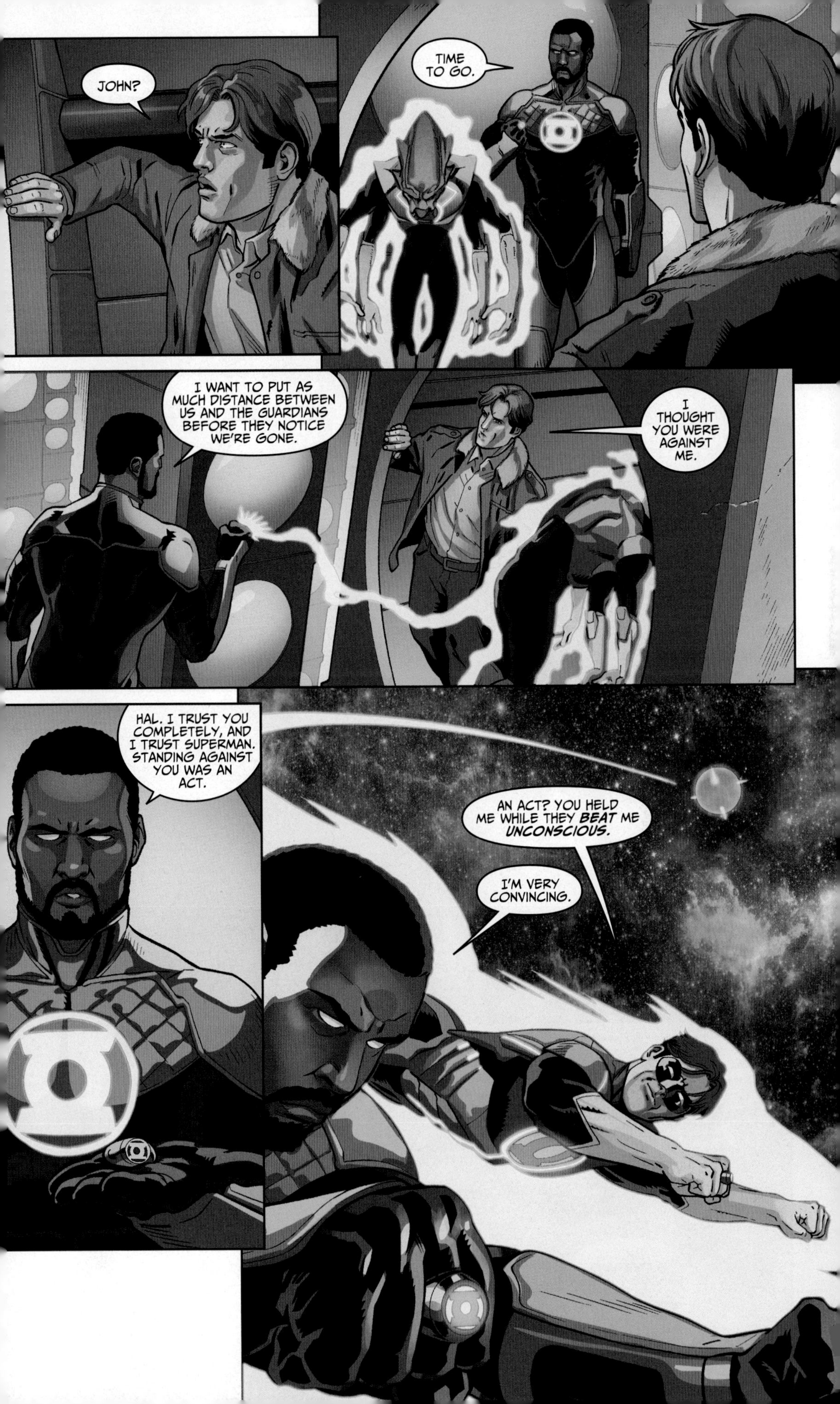
JOHN?
TIME TO GO.
I WANT TO PUT AS MUCH DISTANCE BETWEEN US AND THE GUARDIANS BEFORE THEY NOTICE WE'RE GONE.
I THOUGHT YOU WERE AGAINST ME.
HAL. I TRUST YOU COMPLETELY, AND I TRUST SUPERMAN. STANDING AGAINST YOU WAS AN ACT.
AN ACT? YOU HELD ME WHILE THEY *BEAT* ME *UNCONSCIOUS.*
I'M VERY CONVINCING.

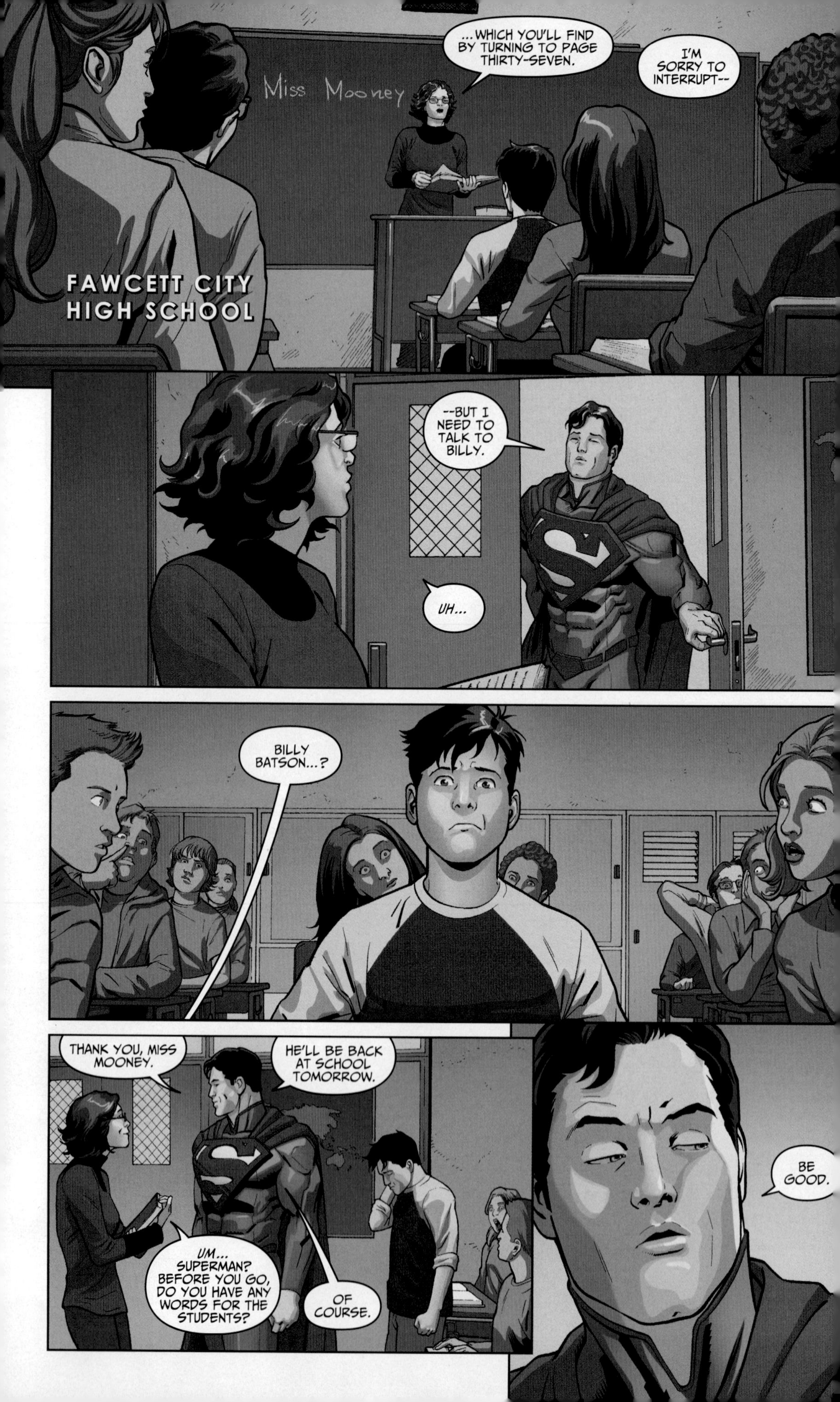
FAWCETT CITY HIGH SCHOOL
Miss Mooney
...WHICH YOU'LL FIND BY TURNING TO PAGE THIRTY-SEVEN.
I'M SORRY TO INTERRUPT--
--BUT I NEED TO TALK TO BILLY.
UH...
BILLY BATSON...?
THANK YOU, MISS MOONEY.
HE'LL BE BACK AT SCHOOL TOMORROW.
UM... SUPERMAN? BEFORE YOU GO, DO YOU HAVE ANY WORDS FOR THE STUDENTS?
OF COURSE.
BE GOOD.

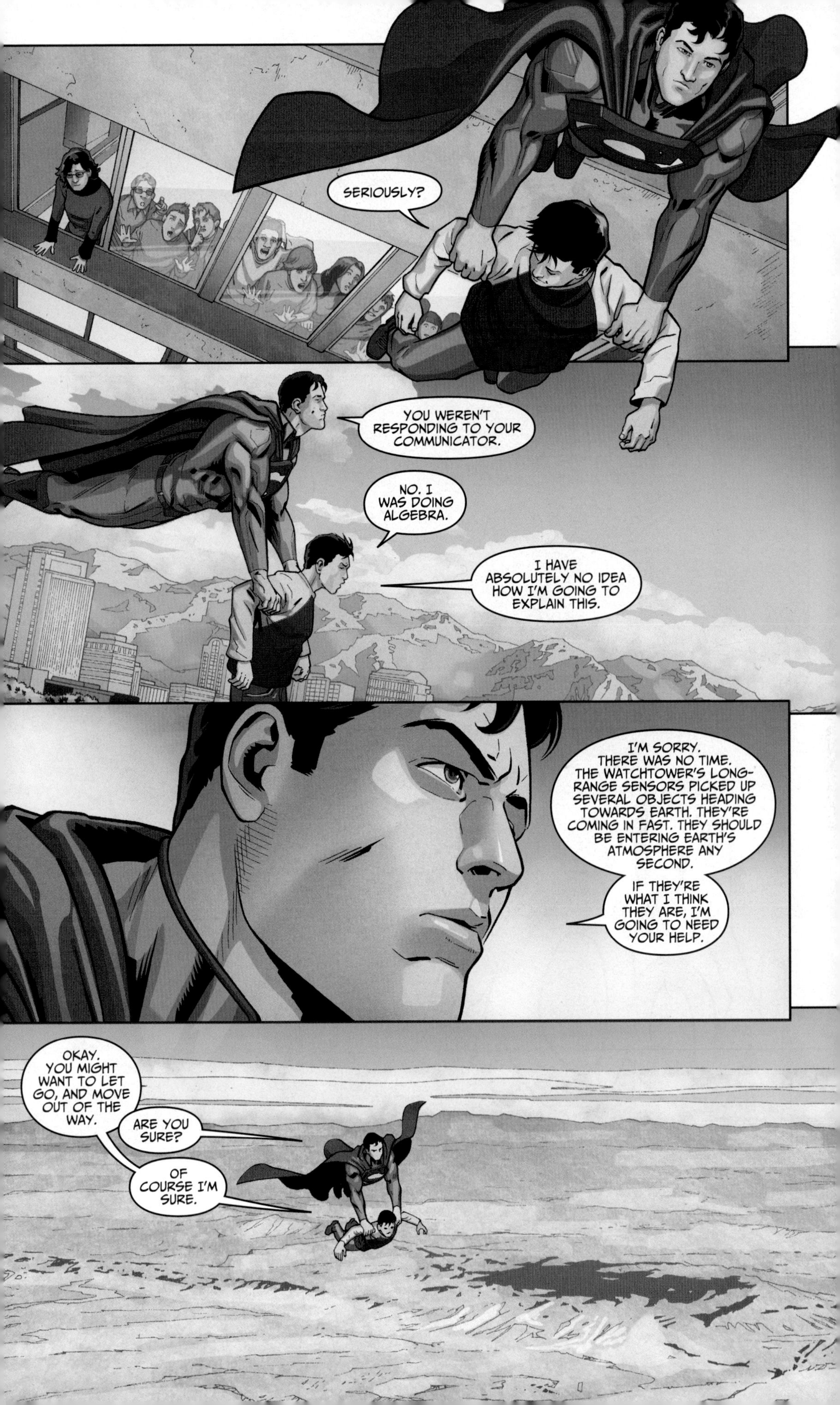

SERIOUSLY?
YOU WEREN'T RESPONDING TO YOUR COMMUNICATOR.
NO. I WAS DOING ALGEBRA.
I HAVE ABSOLUTELY NO IDEA HOW I'M GOING TO EXPLAIN THIS.
I'M SORRY. THERE WAS NO TIME. THE WATCHTOWER'S LONG-RANGE SENSORS PICKED UP SEVERAL OBJECTS HEADING TOWARDS EARTH. THEY'RE COMING IN FAST. THEY SHOULD BE ENTERING EARTH'S ATMOSPHERE ANY SECOND.
IF THEY'RE WHAT I THINK THEY ARE, I'M GOING TO NEED YOUR HELP.
OKAY. YOU MIGHT WANT TO LET GO, AND MOVE OUT OF THE WAY.
ARE YOU SURE?
OF COURSE I'M SURE.

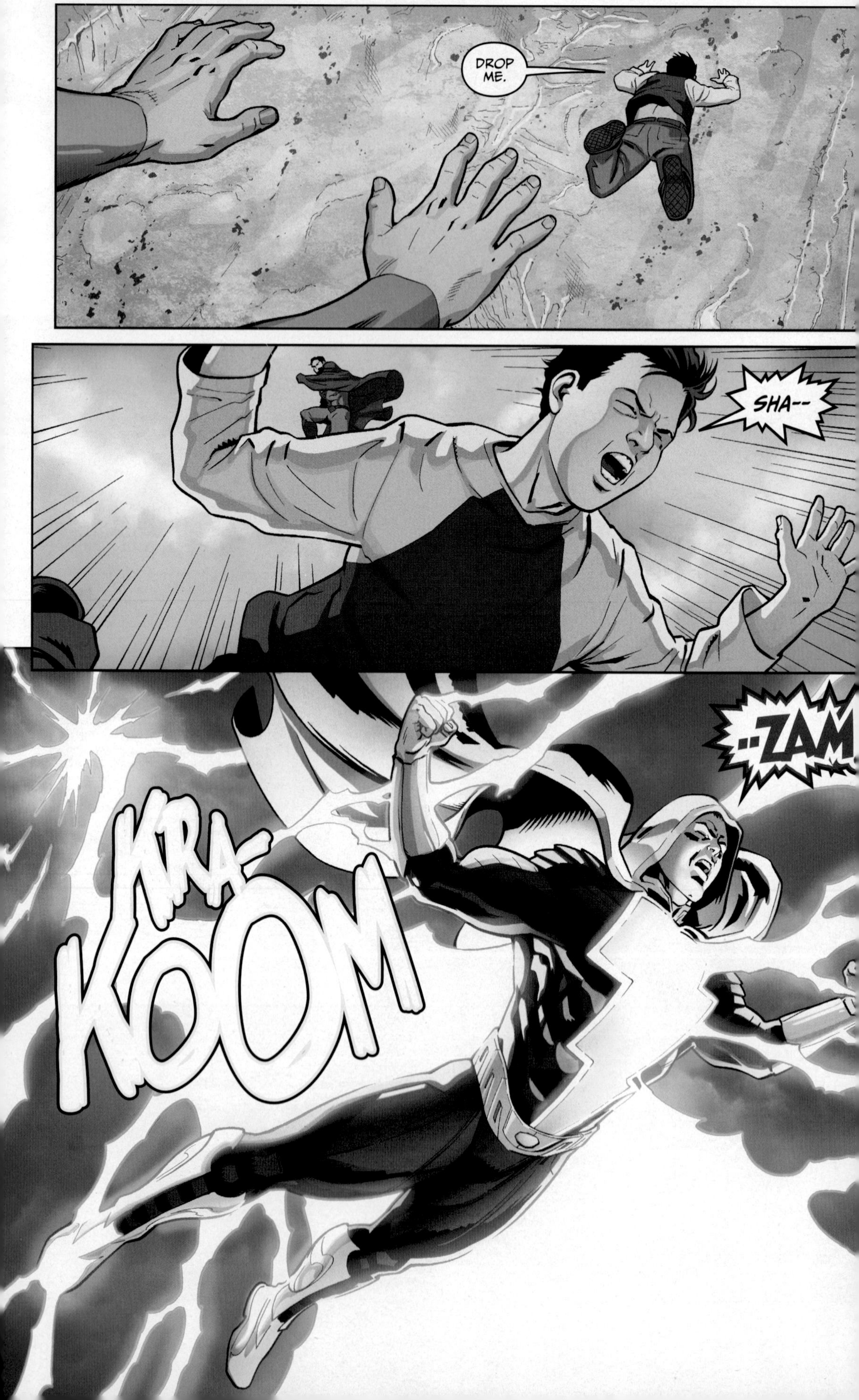
DROP ME.
SHA--
KRA-KOOM
..ZAM

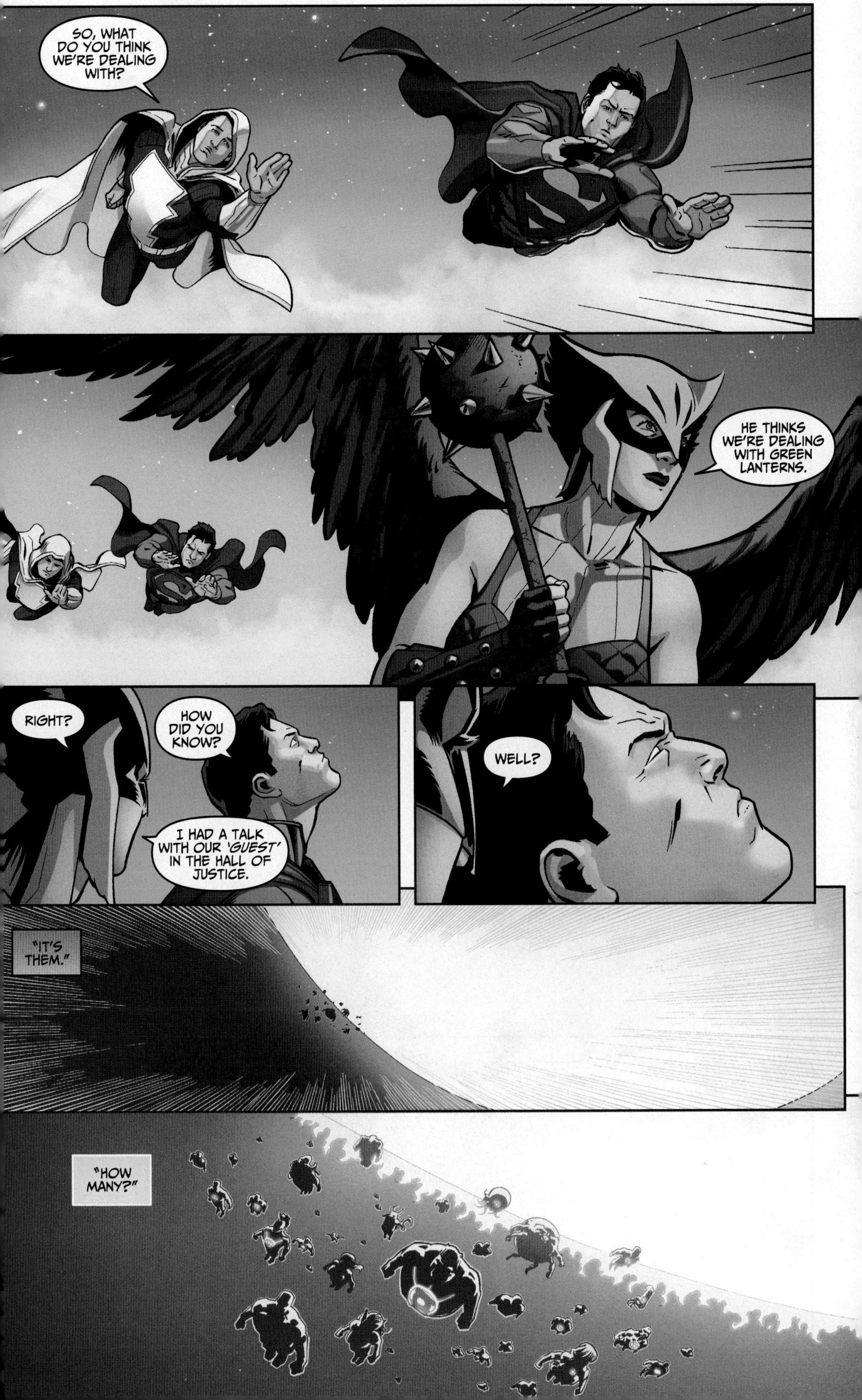
SO, WHAT DO YOU THINK WE'RE DEALING WITH?
HE THINKS WE'RE DEALING WITH GREEN LANTERNS.
RIGHT?
HOW DID YOU KNOW?
I HAD A TALK WITH OUR 'GUEST' IN THE HALL OF JUSTICE.
WELL?
"IT'S THEM."
"HOW MANY?"

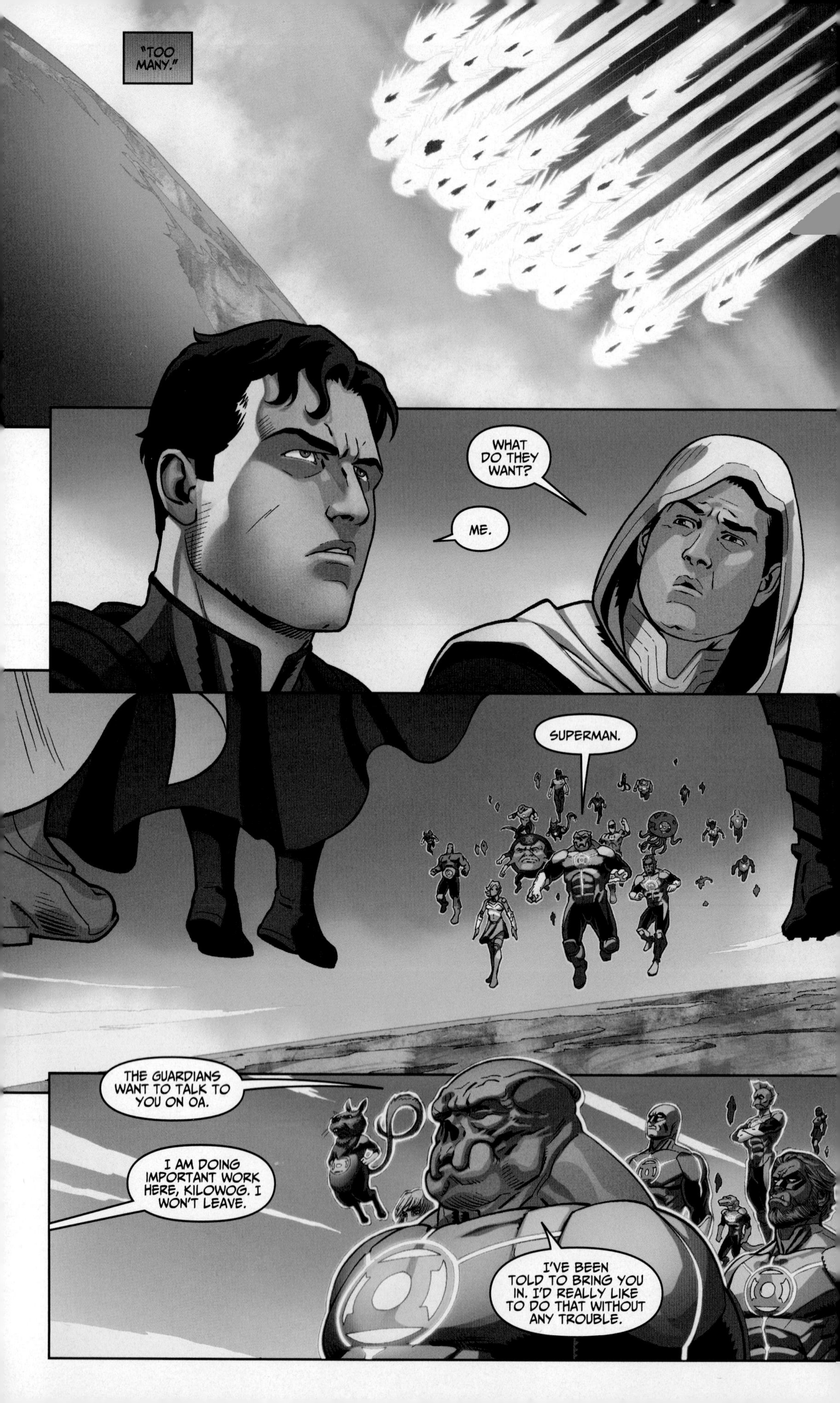
"TOO MANY."
WHAT DO THEY WANT?
ME.
SUPERMAN.
THE GUARDIANS WANT TO TALK TO YOU ON OA.
I AM DOING IMPORTANT WORK HERE, KILOWOG. I WON'T LEAVE.
I'VE BEEN TOLD TO BRING YOU IN. I'D REALLY LIKE TO DO THAT WITHOUT ANY TROUBLE.

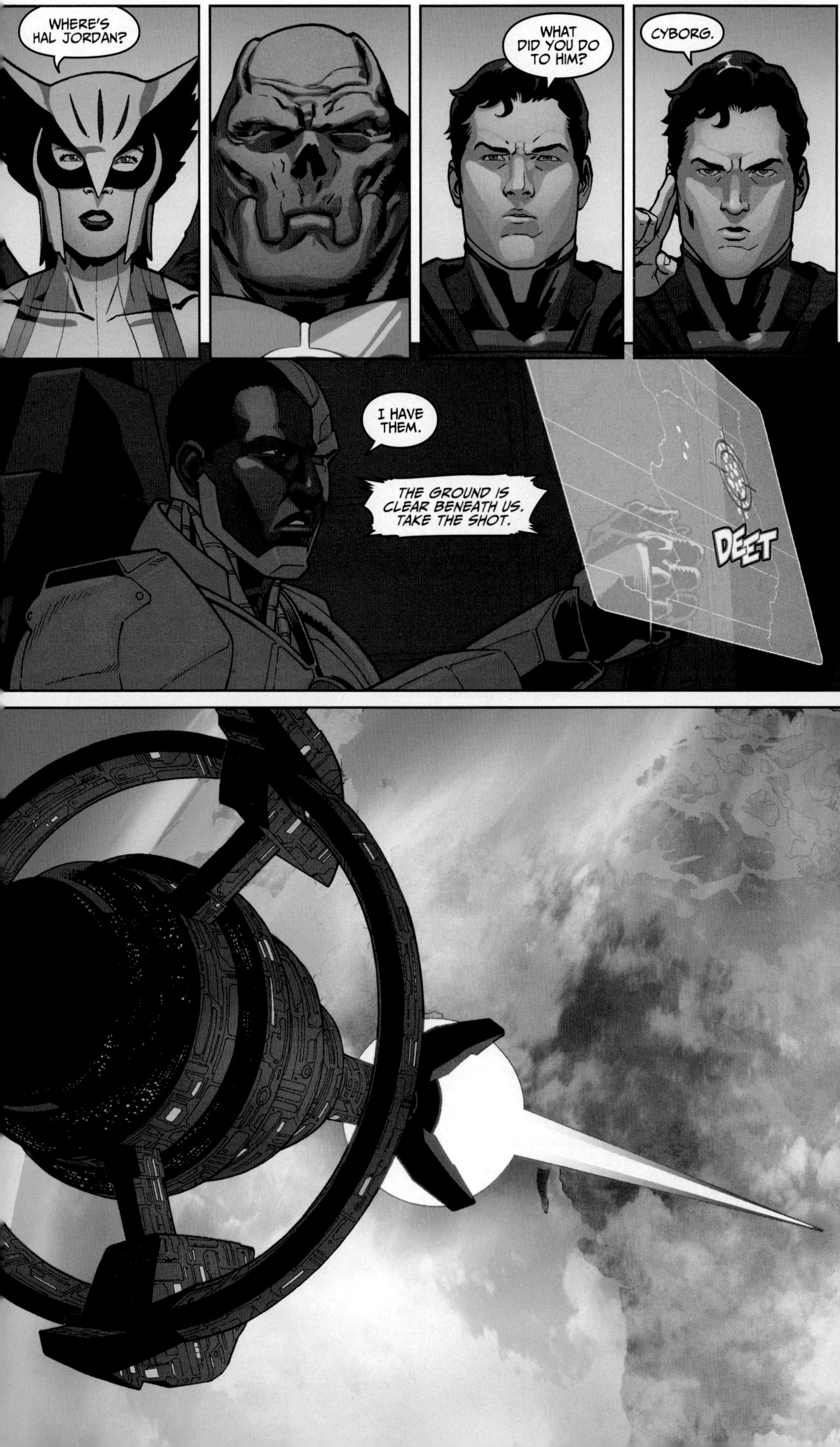
WHERE'S HAL JORDAN?
WHAT DID YOU DO TO HIM?
CYBORG.
I HAVE THEM.
THE GROUND IS CLEAR BENEATH US. TAKE THE SHOT.
DEET

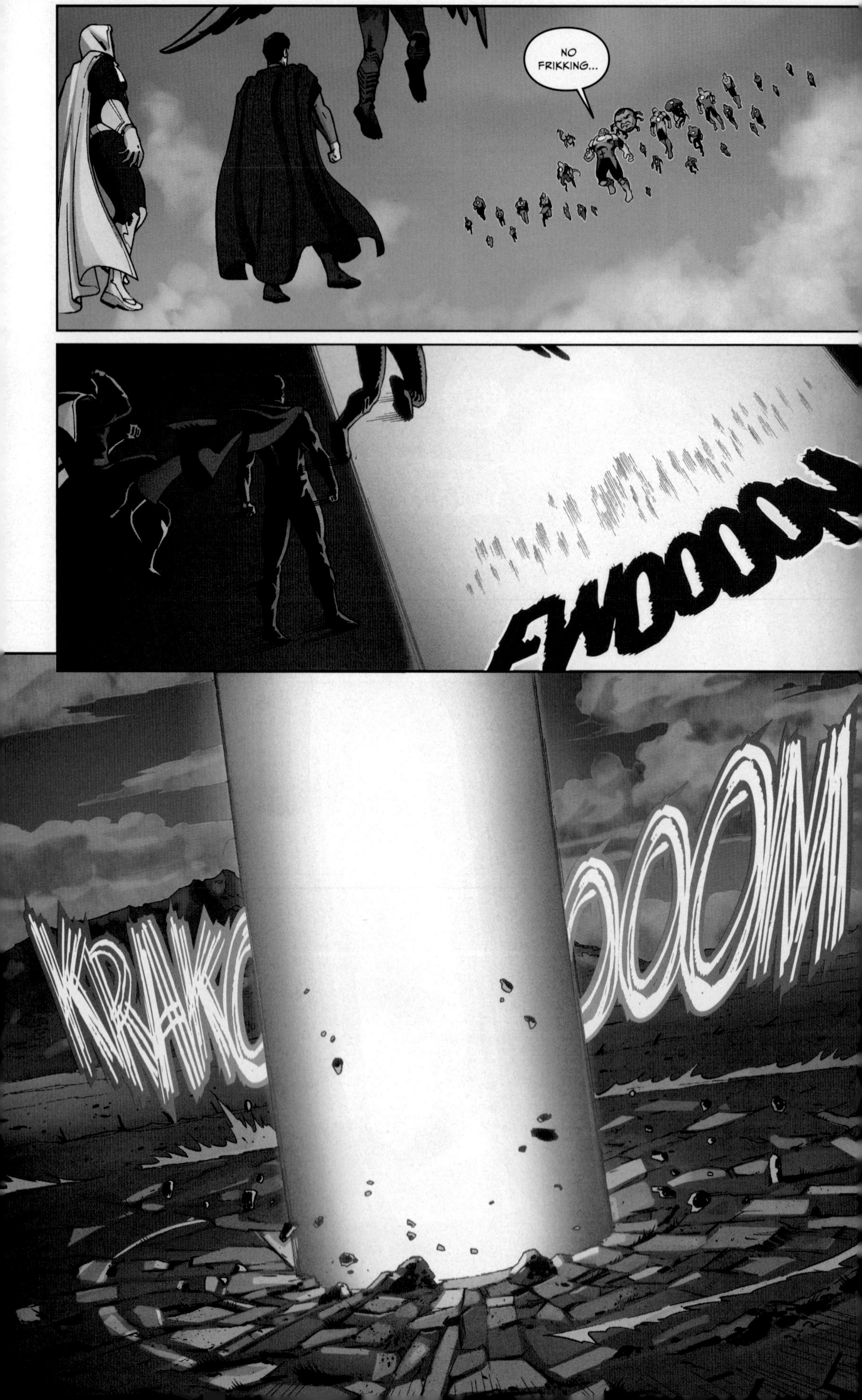

NO FRIKKING...
FWOOOO
KRAKO
OOOM

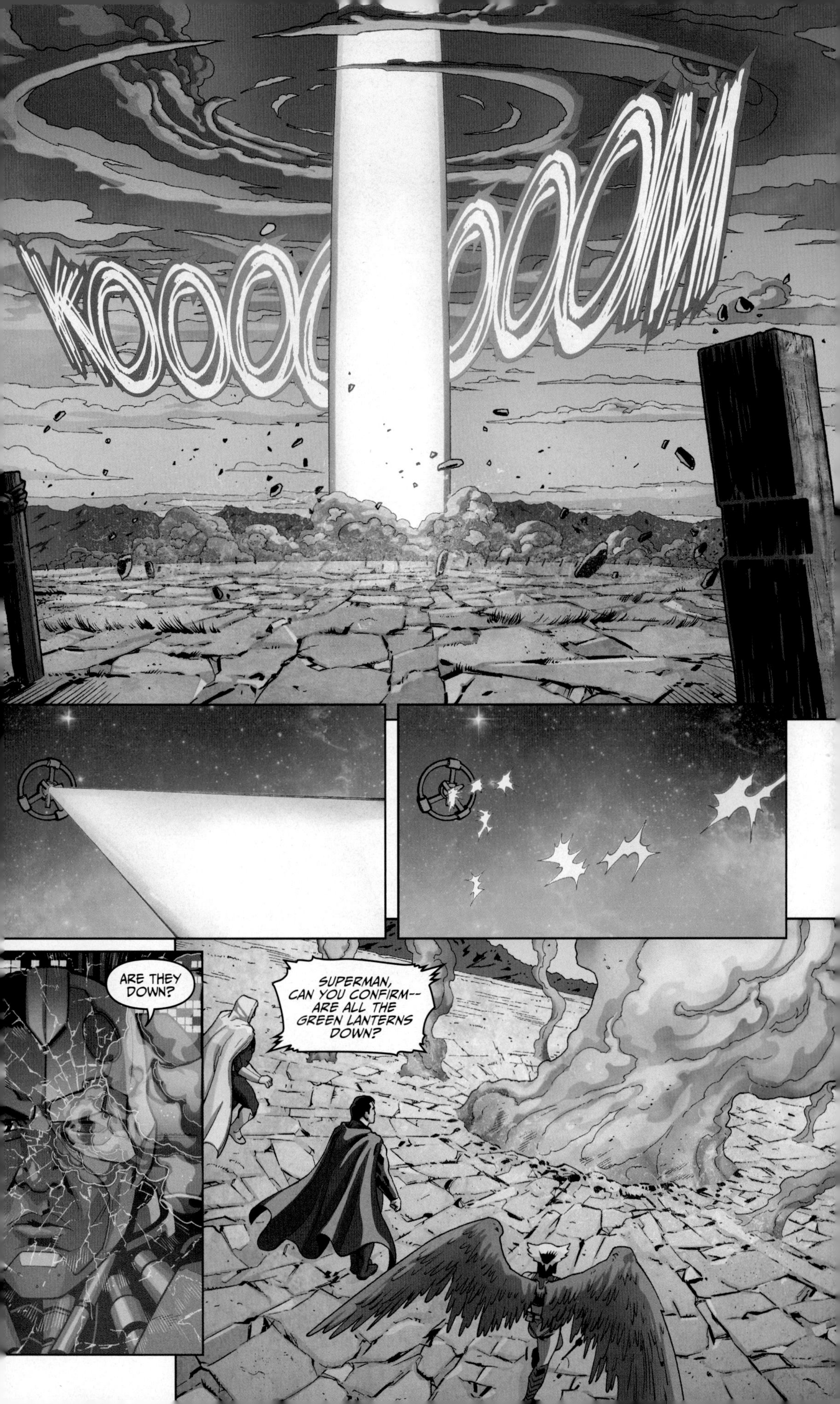
KOOOOOOOOM
ARE THEY DOWN?
SUPERMAN, CAN YOU CONFIRM-- ARE ALL THE GREEN LANTERNS DOWN?

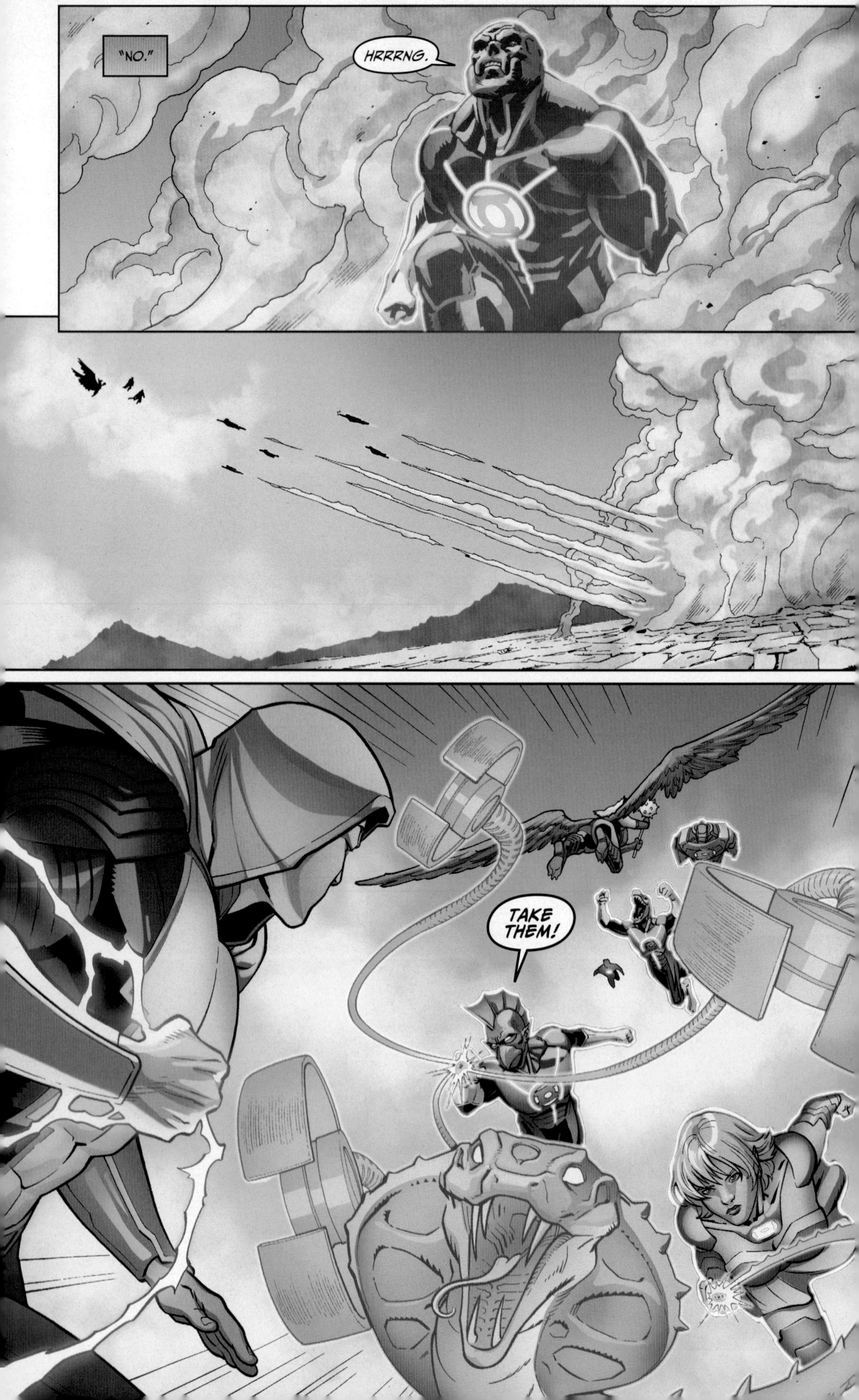
"NO."
HRRRNG.
TAKE THEM!

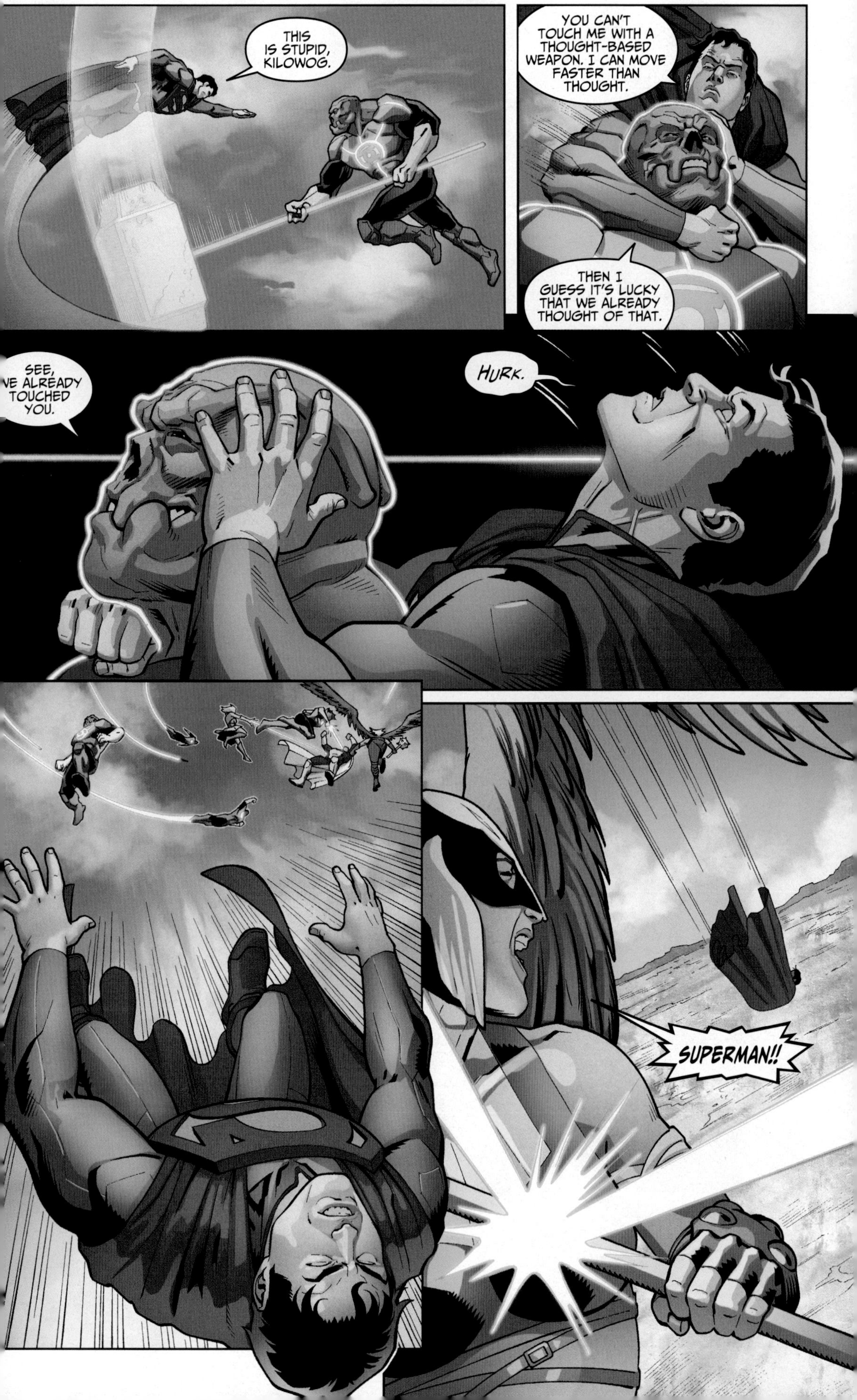

THIS IS STUPID, KILOWOG.
YOU CAN'T TOUCH ME WITH A THOUGHT-BASED WEAPON. I CAN MOVE FASTER THAN THOUGHT.
THEN I GUESS IT'S LUCKY THAT WE ALREADY THOUGHT OF THAT.
SEE, WE ALREADY TOUCHED YOU.
HURK.
SUPERMAN!!

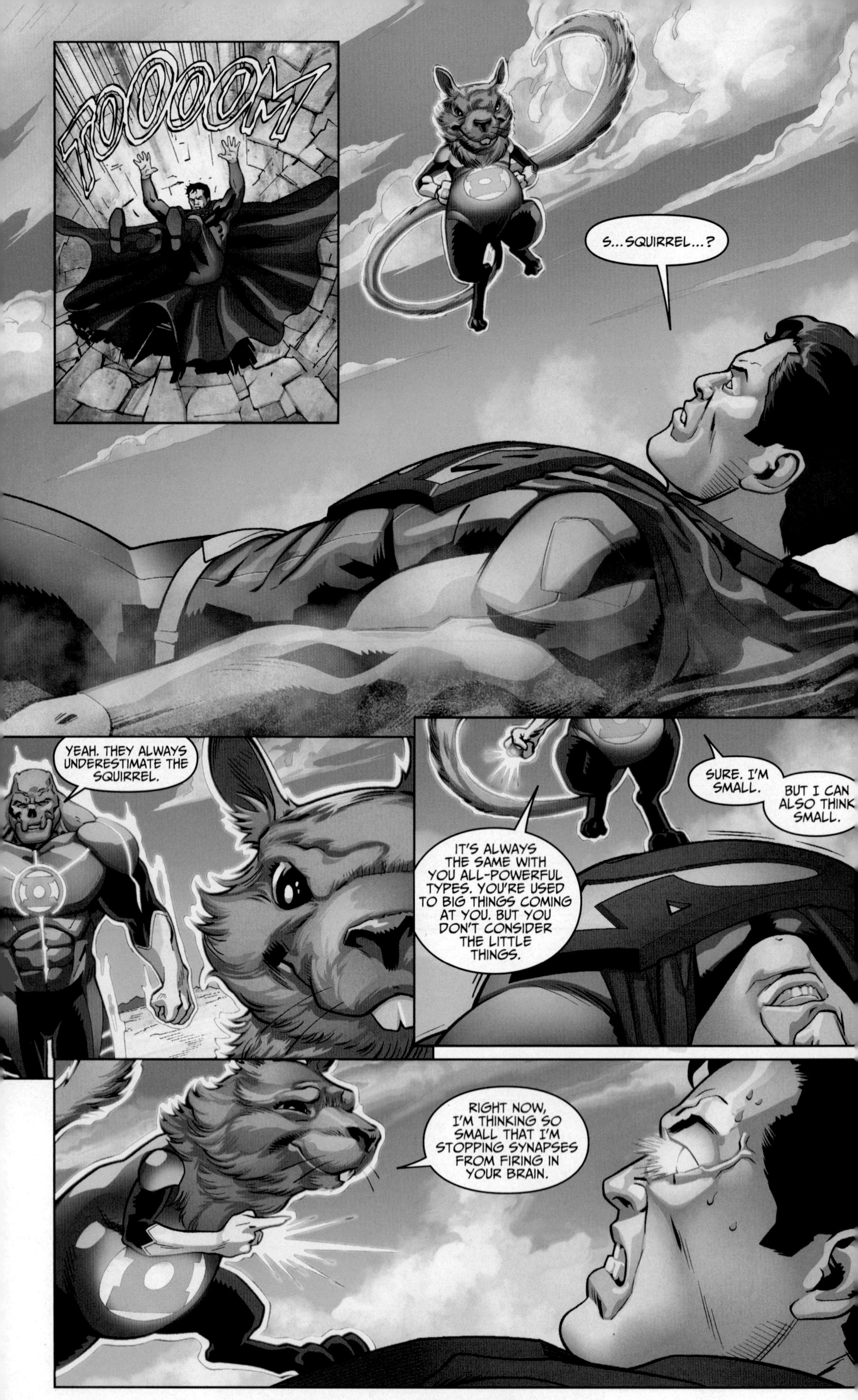
ZOOOOOM
S...SQUIRREL...?
YEAH. THEY ALWAYS UNDERESTIMATE THE SQUIRREL.
SURE. I'M SMALL.
BUT I CAN ALSO THINK SMALL.
IT'S ALWAYS THE SAME WITH YOU ALL-POWERFUL TYPES. YOU'RE USED TO BIG THINGS COMING AT YOU. BUT YOU DON'T CONSIDER THE LITTLE THINGS.
RIGHT NOW, I'M THINKING SO SMALL THAT I'M STOPPING SYNAPSES FROM FIRING IN YOUR BRAIN.

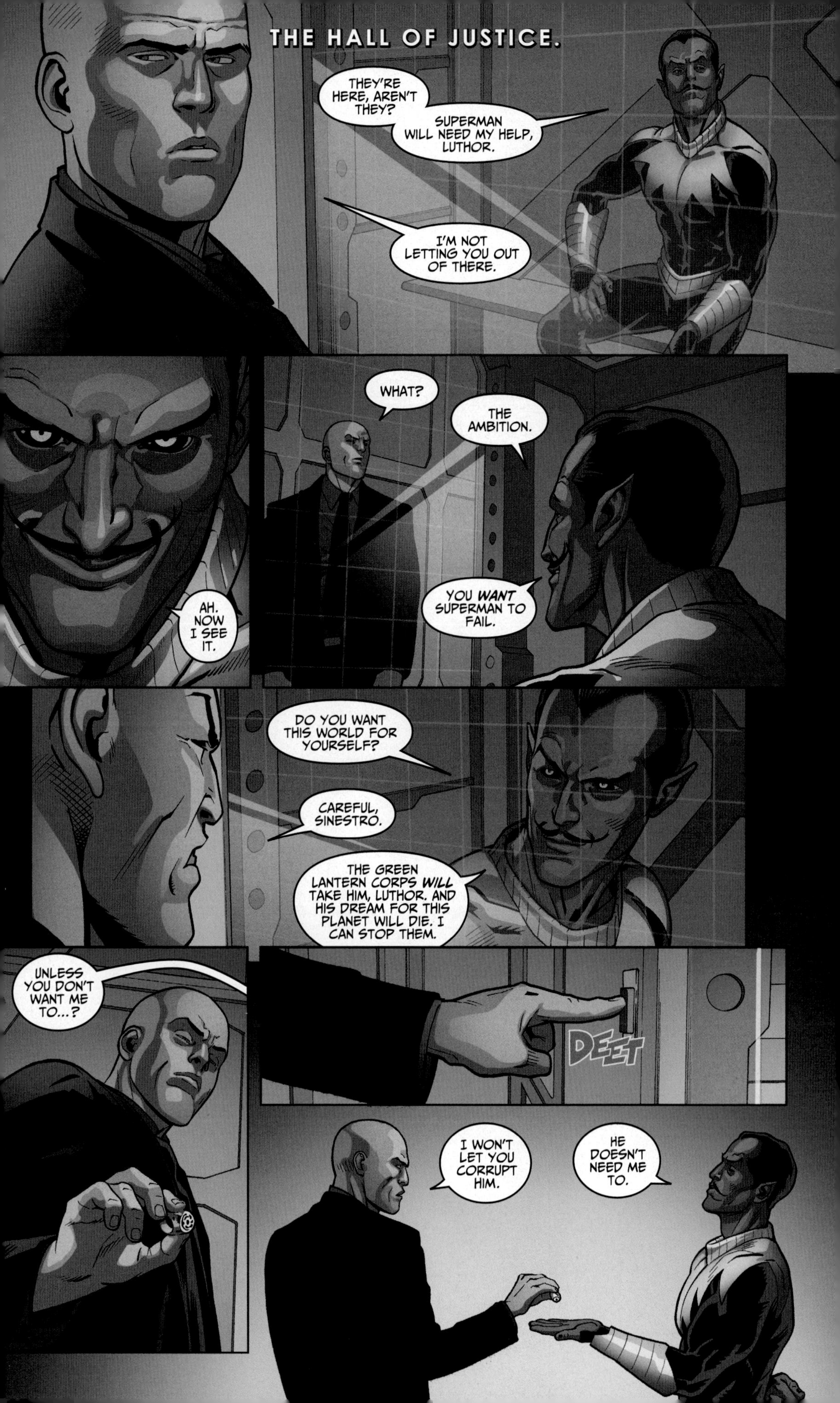
THE HALL OF JUSTICE.
THEY'RE HERE, AREN'T THEY?
SUPERMAN WILL NEED MY HELP, LUTHOR.
I'M NOT LETTING YOU OUT OF THERE.
AH. NOW I SEE IT.
WHAT?
THE AMBITION.
YOU WANT SUPERMAN TO FAIL.
DO YOU WANT THIS WORLD FOR YOURSELF?
CAREFUL, SINESTRO.
THE GREEN LANTERN CORPS WILL TAKE HIM, LUTHOR. AND HIS DREAM FOR THIS PLANET WILL DIE. I CAN STOP THEM.
UNLESS YOU DON'T WANT ME TO...?
DEET
I WON'T LET YOU CORRUPT HIM.
HE DOESN'T NEED ME TO.

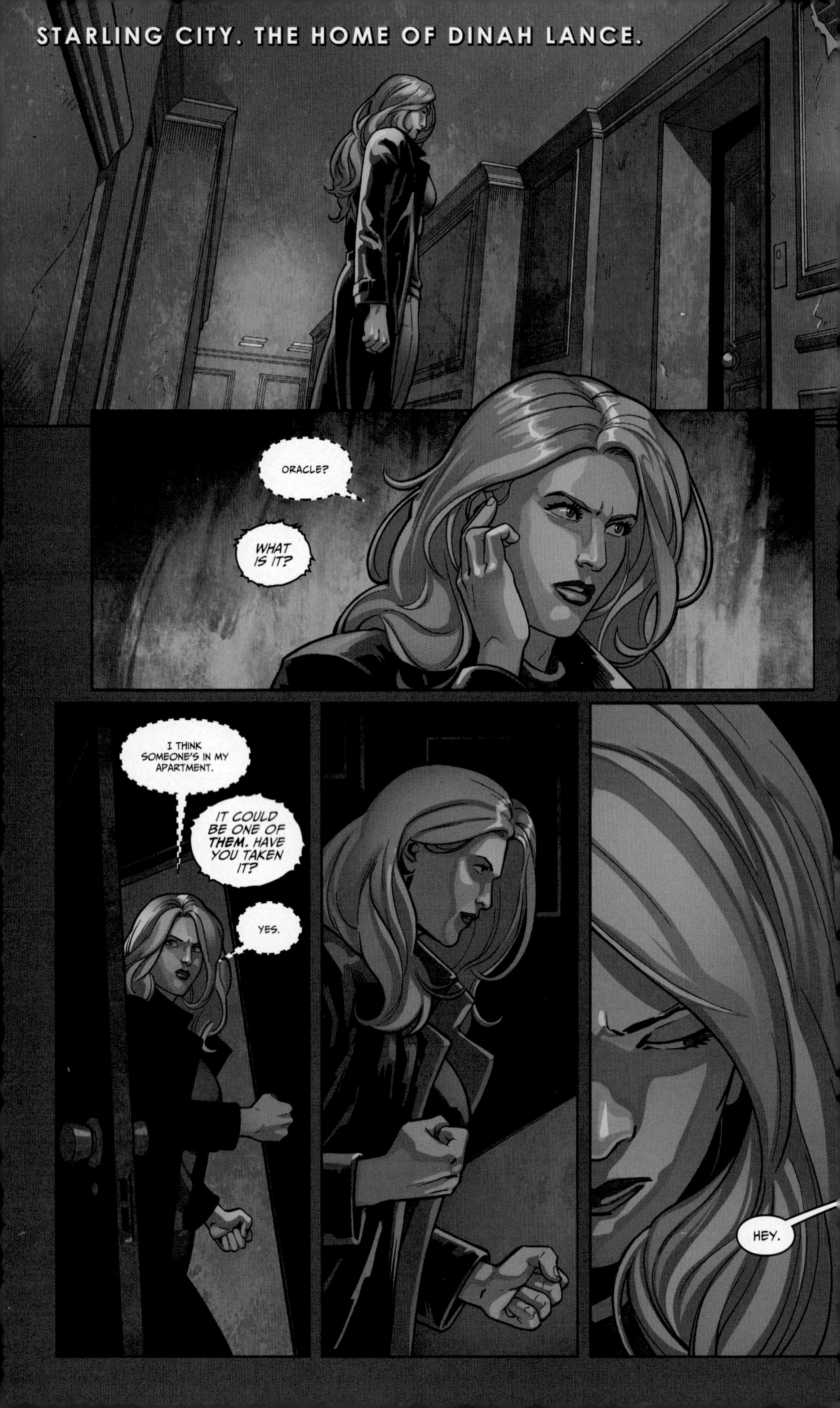

STARLING CITY. THE HOME OF DINAH LANCE.
ORACLE?
WHAT IS IT?
I THINK SOMEONE'S IN MY APARTMENT.
IT COULD BE ONE OF THEM. HAVE YOU TAKEN IT?
YES.
HEY.

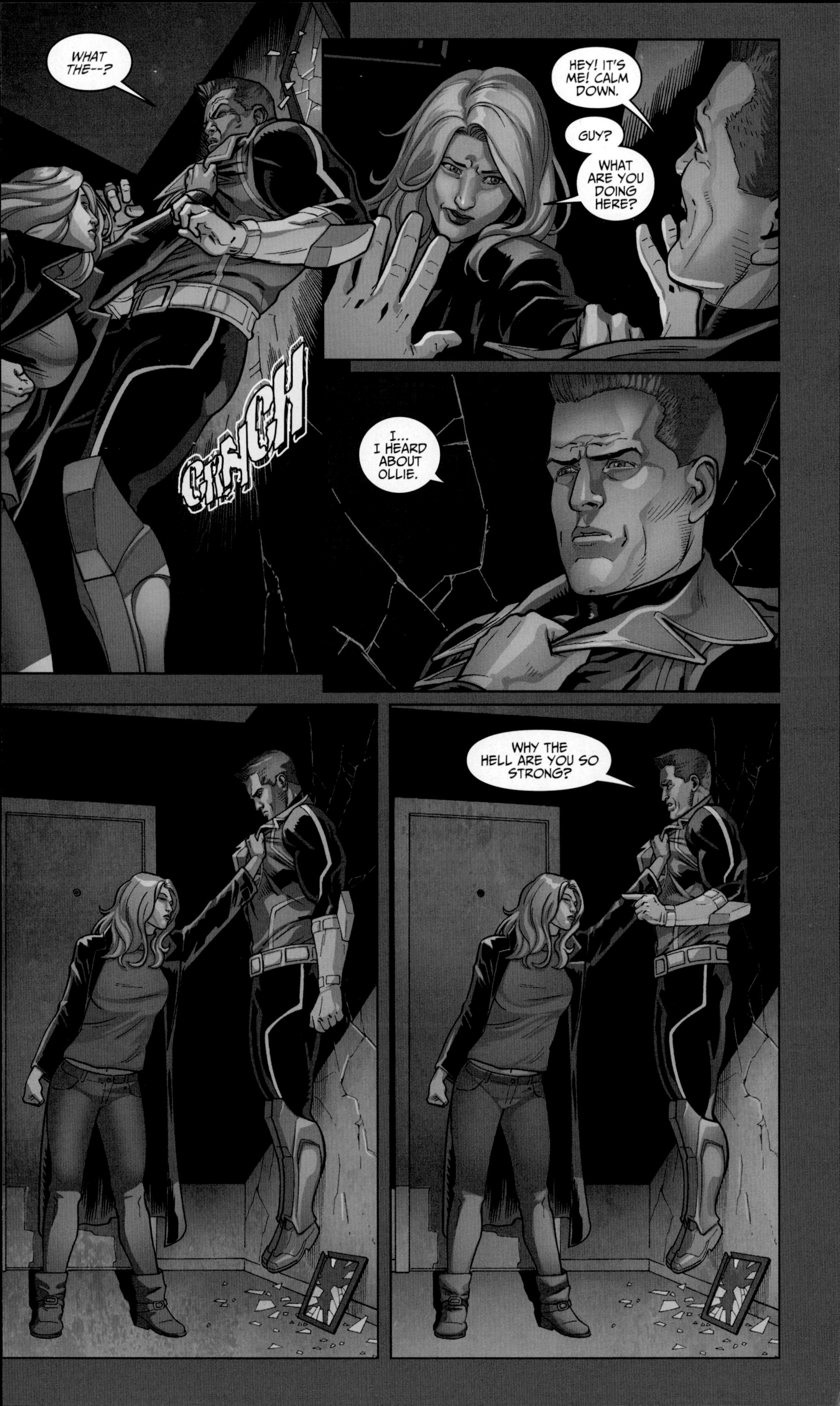
WHAT THE--?
CRNCH
HEY! IT'S ME! CALM DOWN.
GUY?
WHAT ARE YOU DOING HERE?
I... I HEARD ABOUT OLLIE.
WHY THE HELL ARE YOU SO STRONG?

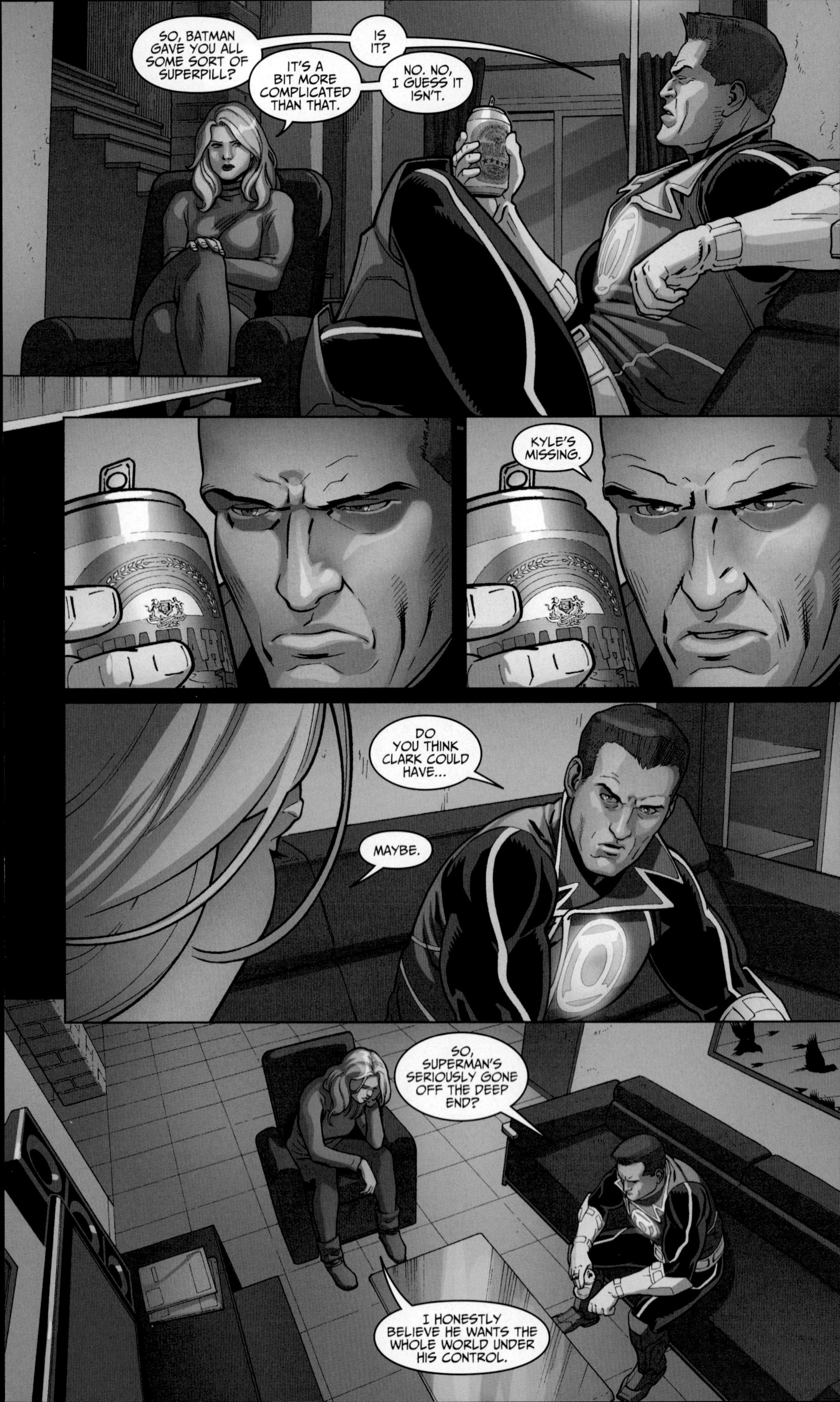

SO, BATMAN GAVE YOU ALL SOME SORT OF SUPERPILL?
IS IT?
IT'S A BIT MORE COMPLICATED THAN THAT.
NO. NO, I GUESS IT ISN'T.
KYLE'S MISSING.
DO YOU THINK CLARK COULD HAVE...
MAYBE.
SO, SUPERMAN'S SERIOUSLY GONE OFF THE DEEP END?
I HONESTLY BELIEVE HE WANTS THE WHOLE WORLD UNDER HIS CONTROL.

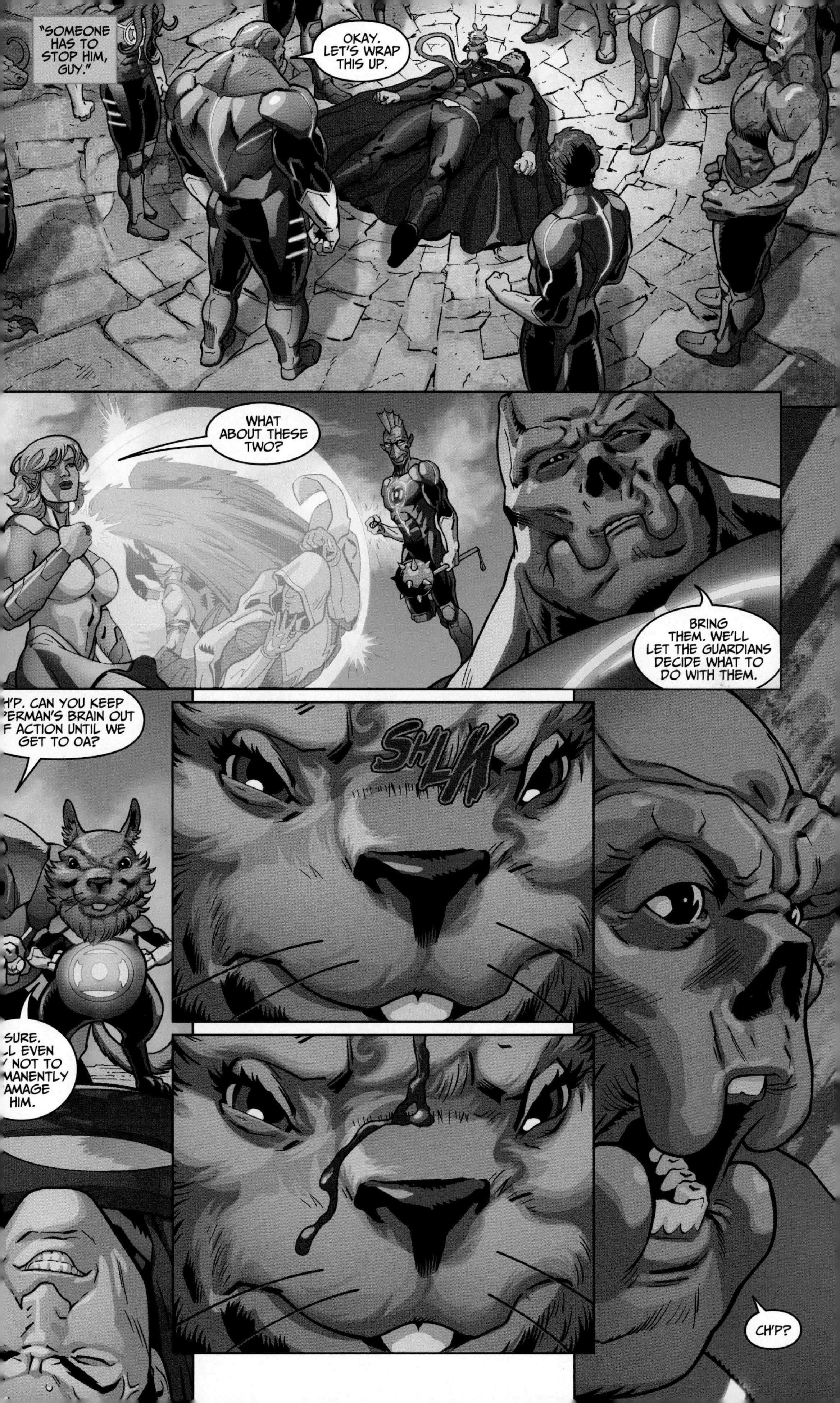
"SOMEONE HAS TO STOP HIM, GUY."
OKAY. LET'S WRAP THIS UP.
WHAT ABOUT THESE TWO?
BRING THEM. WE'LL LET THE GUARDIANS DECIDE WHAT TO DO WITH THEM.
H'P. CAN YOU KEEP PERMAN'S BRAIN OUT F ACTION UNTIL WE GET TO OA?
SHLK
SURE. L EVEN NOT TO MANENTLY AMAGE HIM.
CH'P?

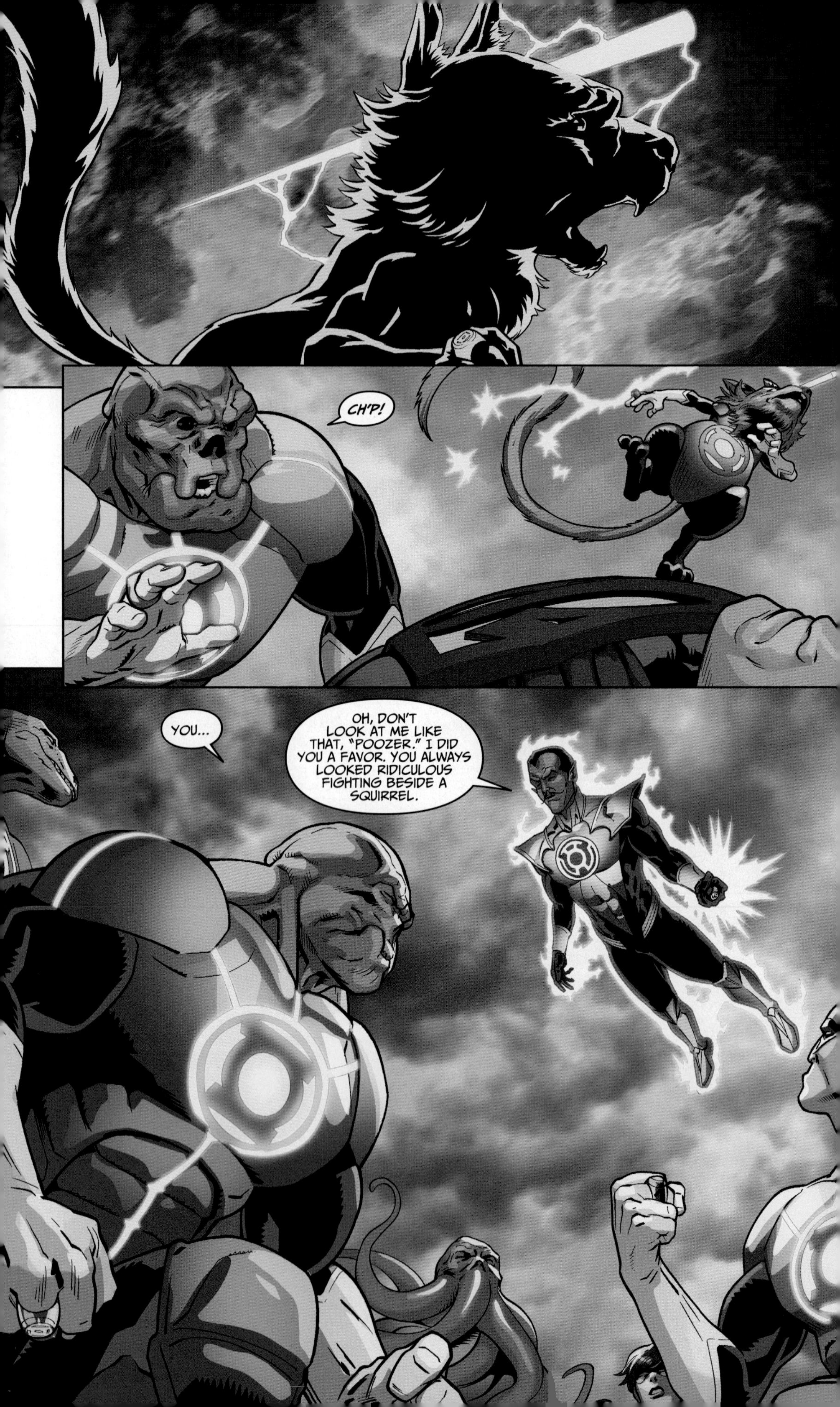
CH'P!
YOU...
OH, DON'T LOOK AT ME LIKE THAT, "POOZER." I DID YOU A FAVOR. YOU ALWAYS LOOKED RIDICULOUS FIGHTING BESIDE A SQUIRREL.

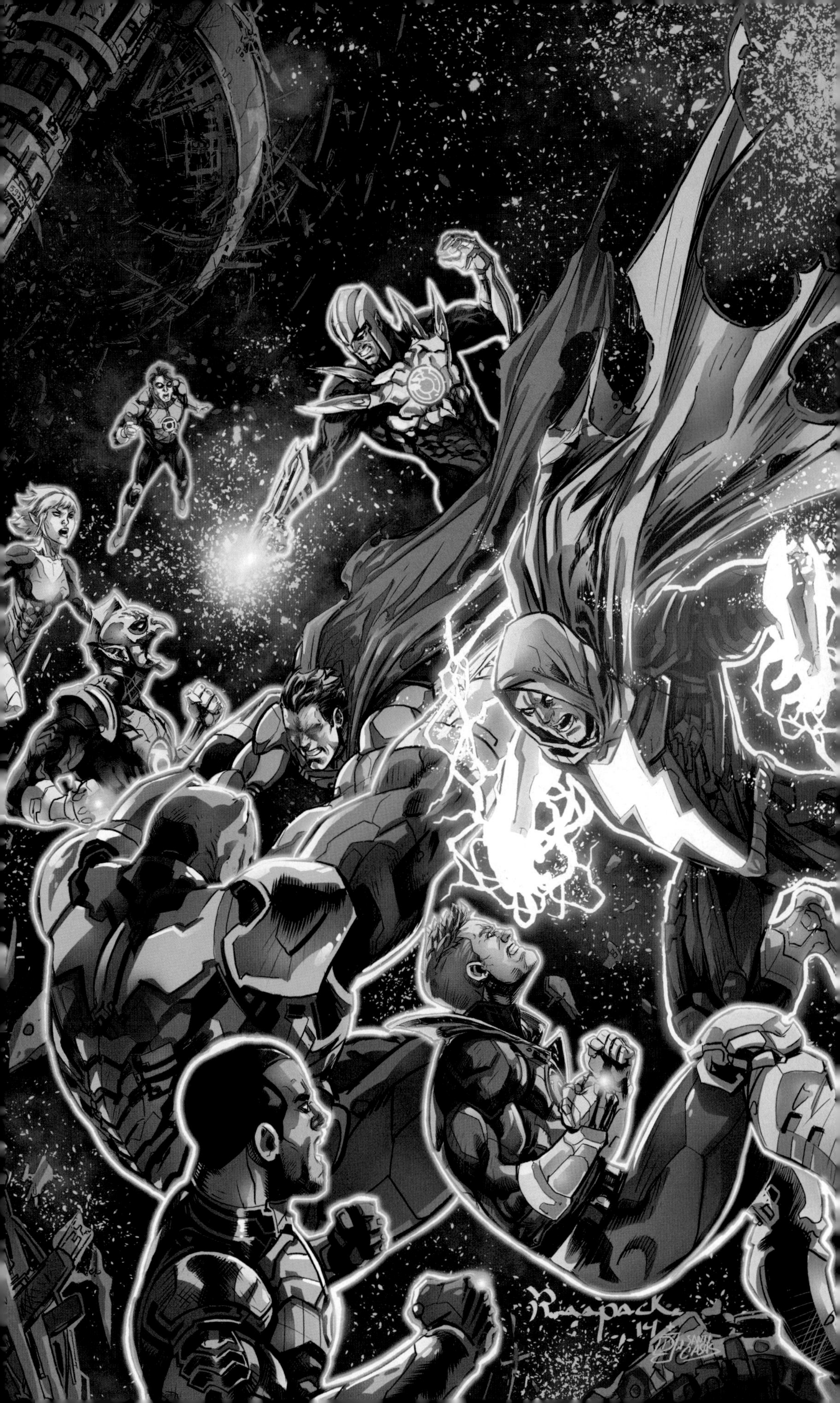

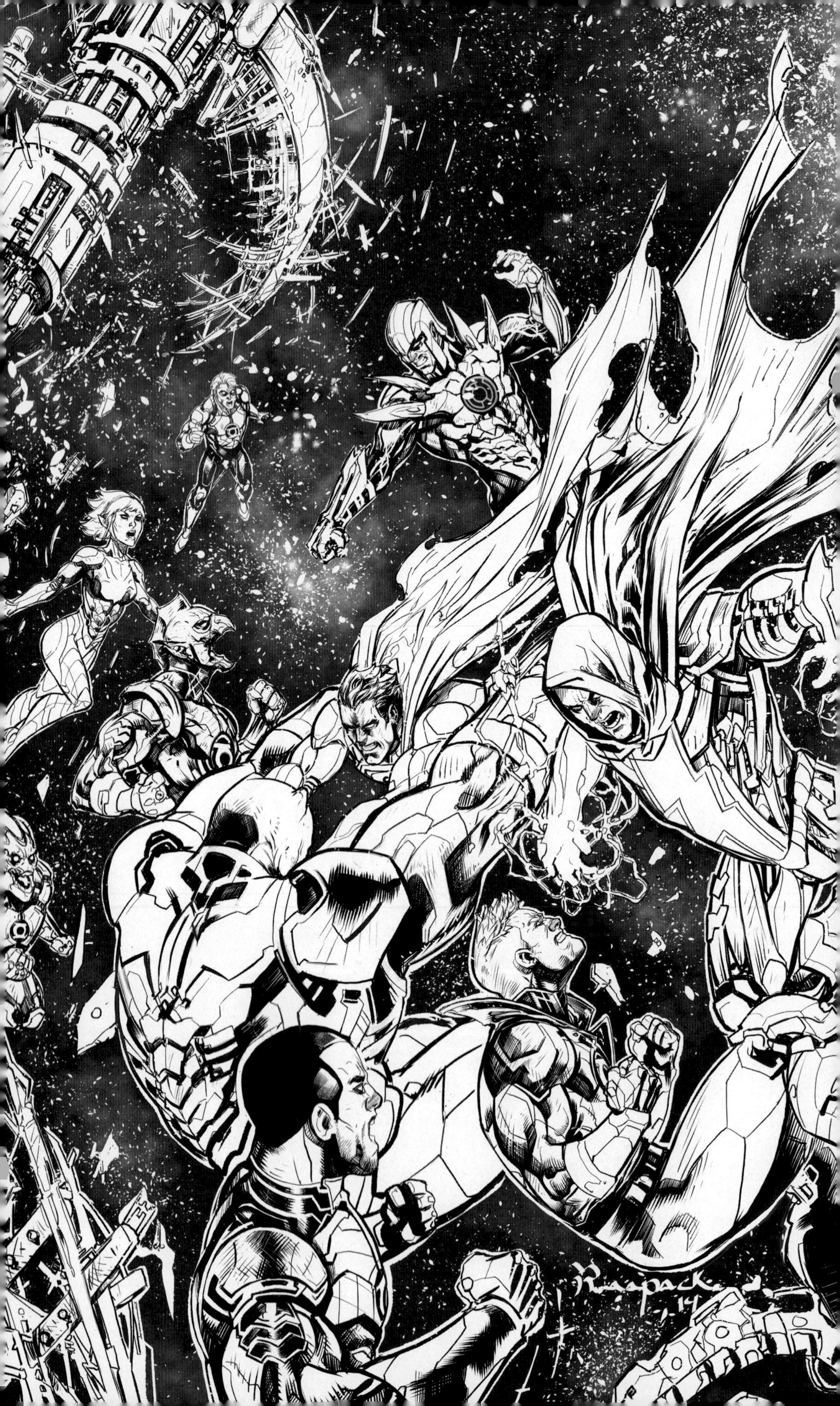
Raapack
'14

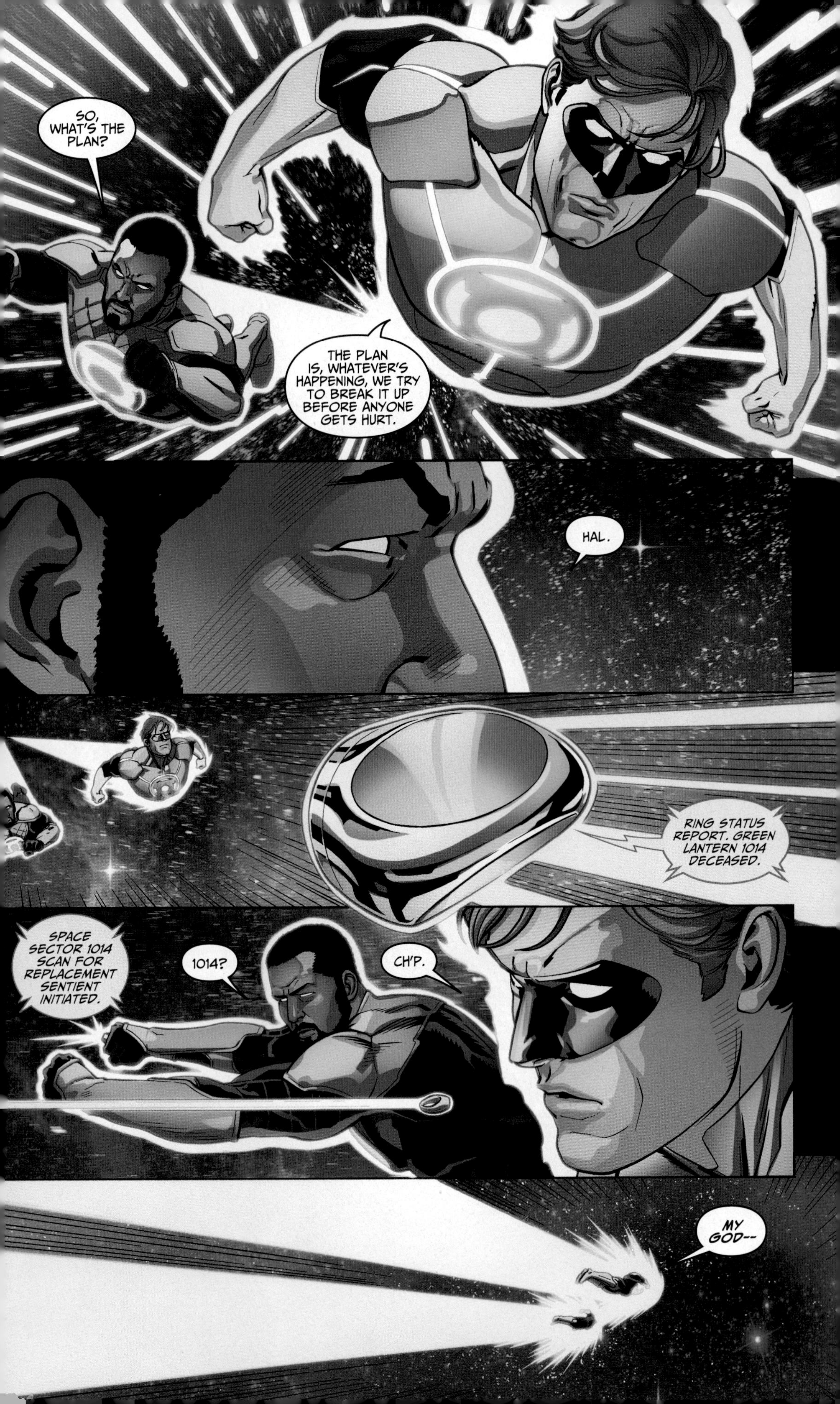
SO, WHAT'S THE PLAN?
THE PLAN IS, WHATEVER'S HAPPENING, WE TRY TO BREAK IT UP BEFORE ANYONE GETS HURT.
HAL.
RING STATUS REPORT. GREEN LANTERN 1014 DECEASED.
SPACE SECTOR 1014 SCAN FOR REPLACEMENT SENTIENT INITIATED.
1014?
CH'P.
MY GOD--

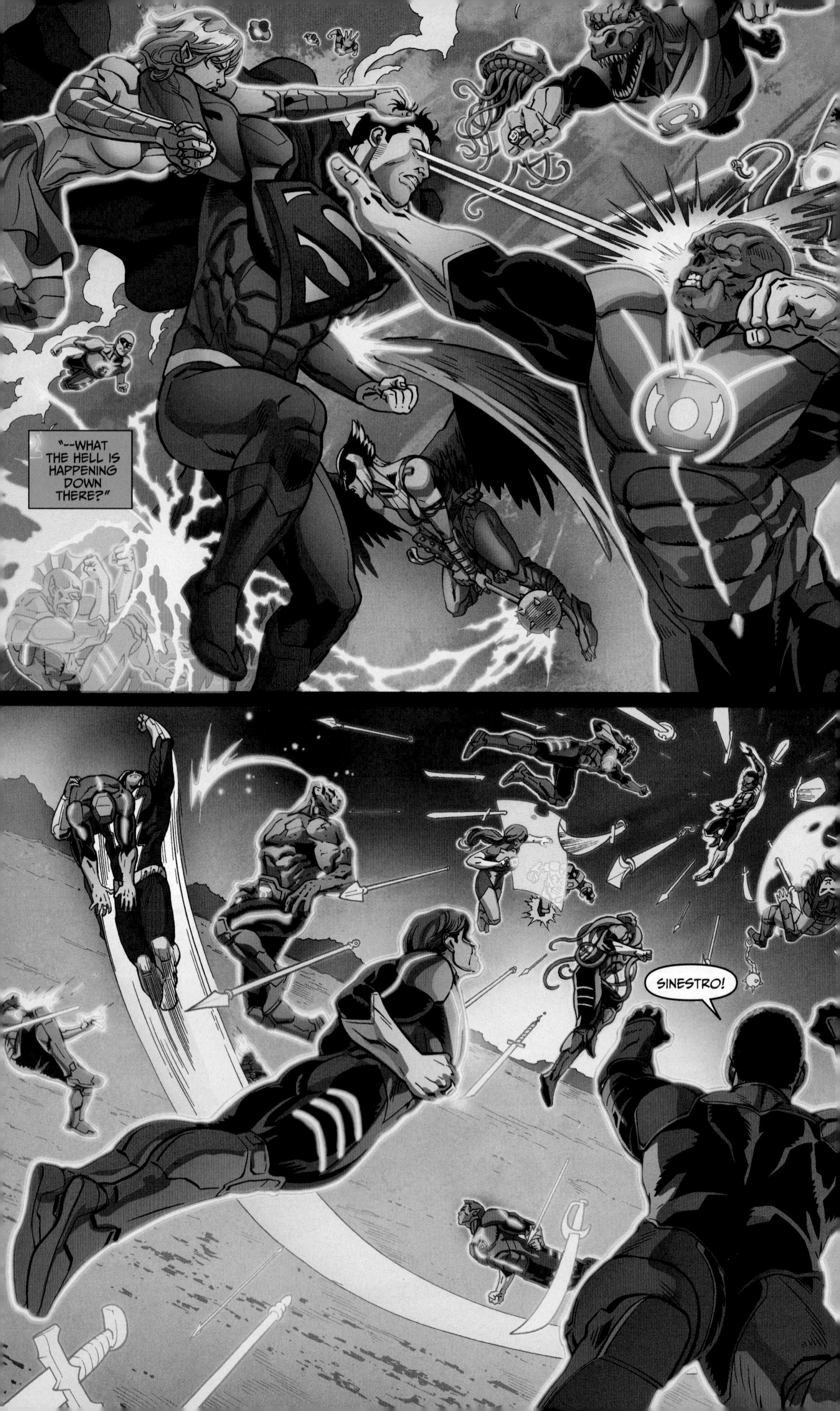
"--WHAT THE HELL IS HAPPENING DOWN THERE?"
SINESTRO!

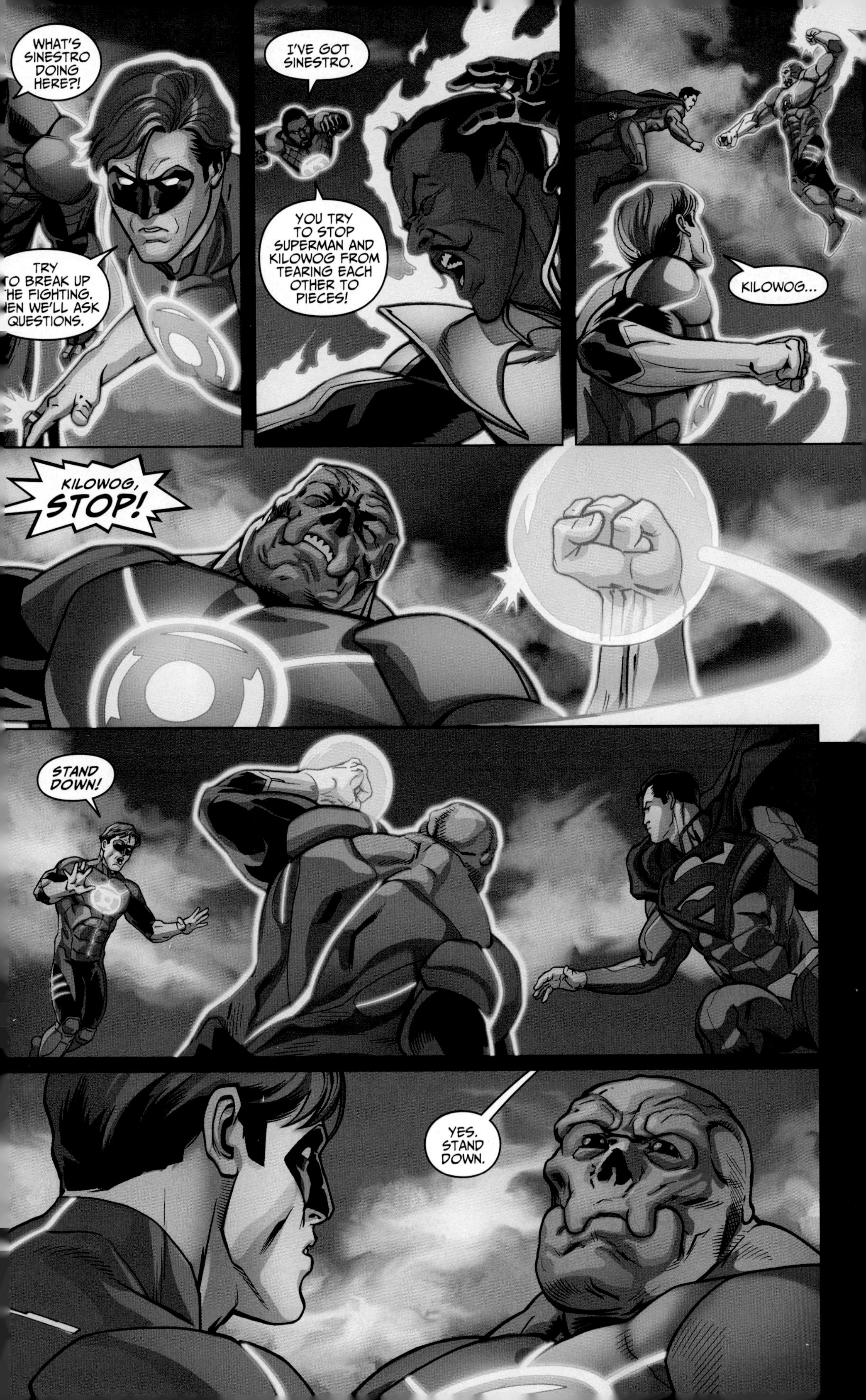
WHAT'S SINESTRO DOING HERE?!
TRY TO BREAK UP HE FIGHTING. IEN WE'LL ASK QUESTIONS.
I'VE GOT SINESTRO.
YOU TRY TO STOP SUPERMAN AND KILOWOG FROM TEARING EACH OTHER TO PIECES!
KILOWOG...
KILOWOG, STOP!
STAND DOWN!
YES. STAND DOWN.

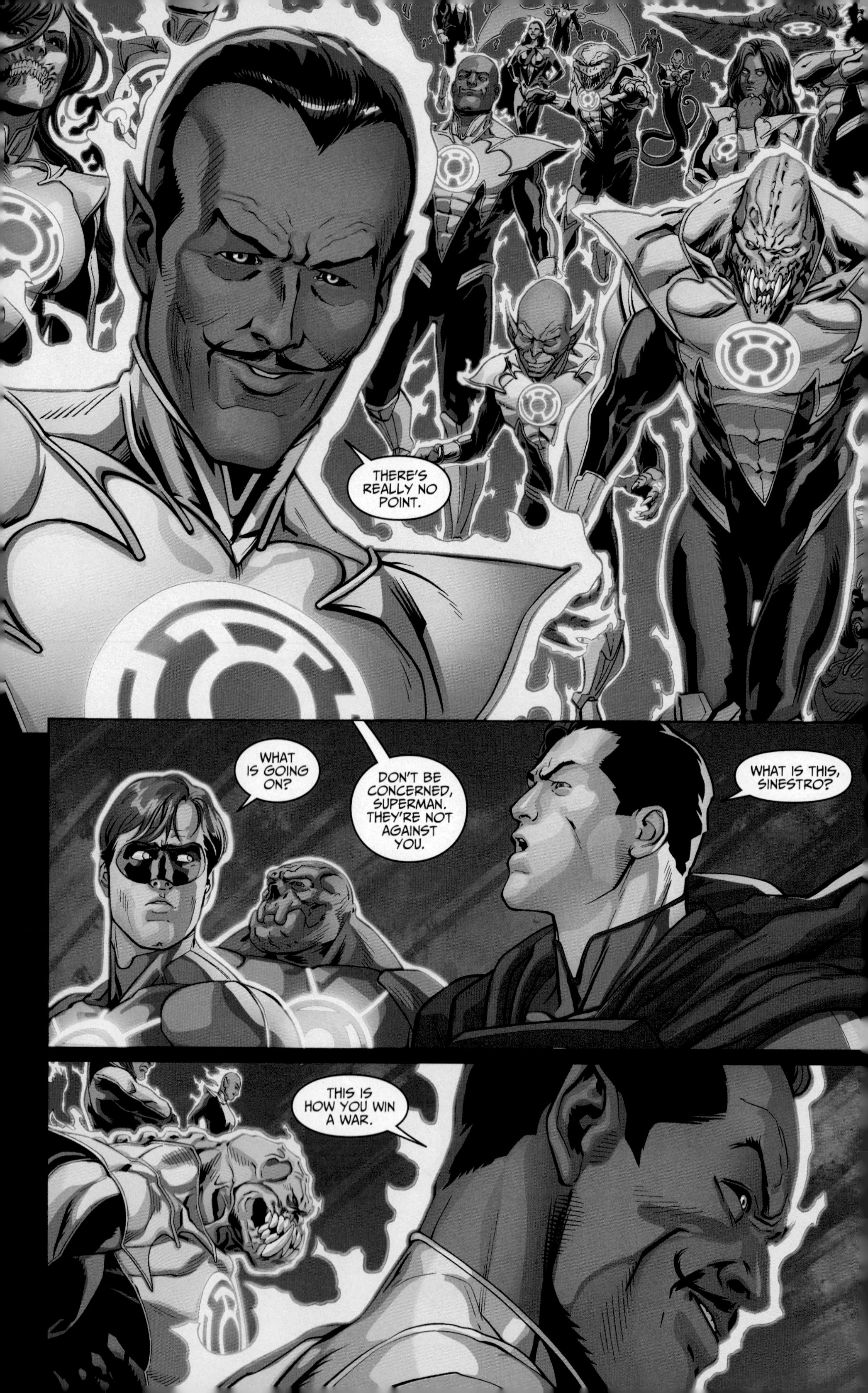
THERE'S REALLY NO POINT.
WHAT IS GOING ON?
DON'T BE CONCERNED, SUPERMAN. THEY'RE NOT AGAINST YOU.
WHAT IS THIS, SINESTRO?
THIS IS HOW YOU WIN A WAR.

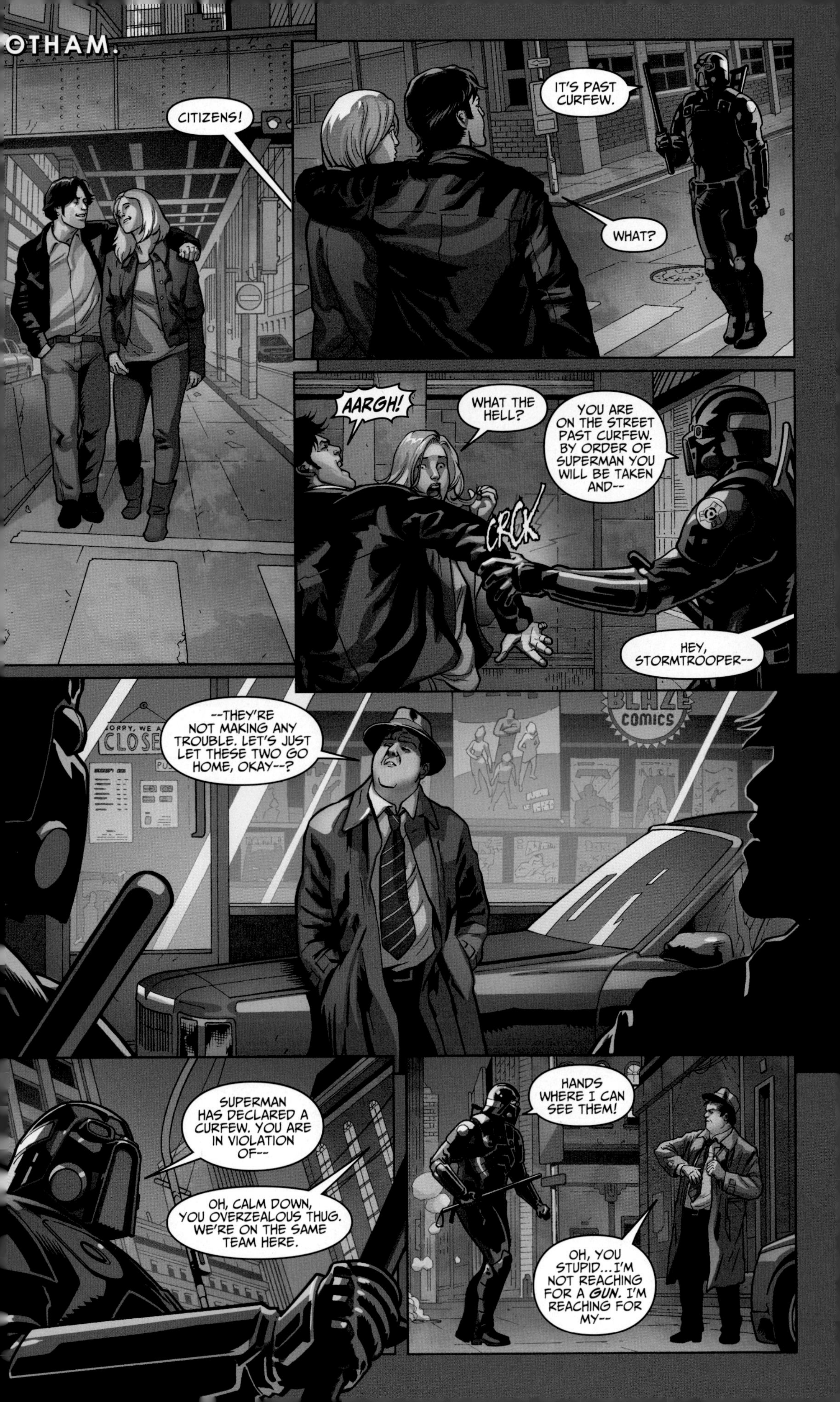
GOTHAM.
CITIZENS!
IT'S PAST CURFEW.
WHAT?
AARGH!
WHAT THE HELL?
YOU ARE ON THE STREET PAST CURFEW. BY ORDER OF SUPERMAN YOU WILL BE TAKEN AND--
CRCK
HEY, STORMTROOPER--
--THEY'RE NOT MAKING ANY TROUBLE. LET'S JUST LET THESE TWO GO HOME, OKAY--?
CLOSE
COMICS
SUPERMAN HAS DECLARED A CURFEW. YOU ARE IN VIOLATION OF--
OH, CALM DOWN, YOU OVERZEALOUS THUG. WE'RE ON THE SAME TEAM HERE.
HANDS WHERE I CAN SEE THEM!
OH, YOU STUPID...I'M NOT REACHING FOR A GUN. I'M REACHING FOR MY--

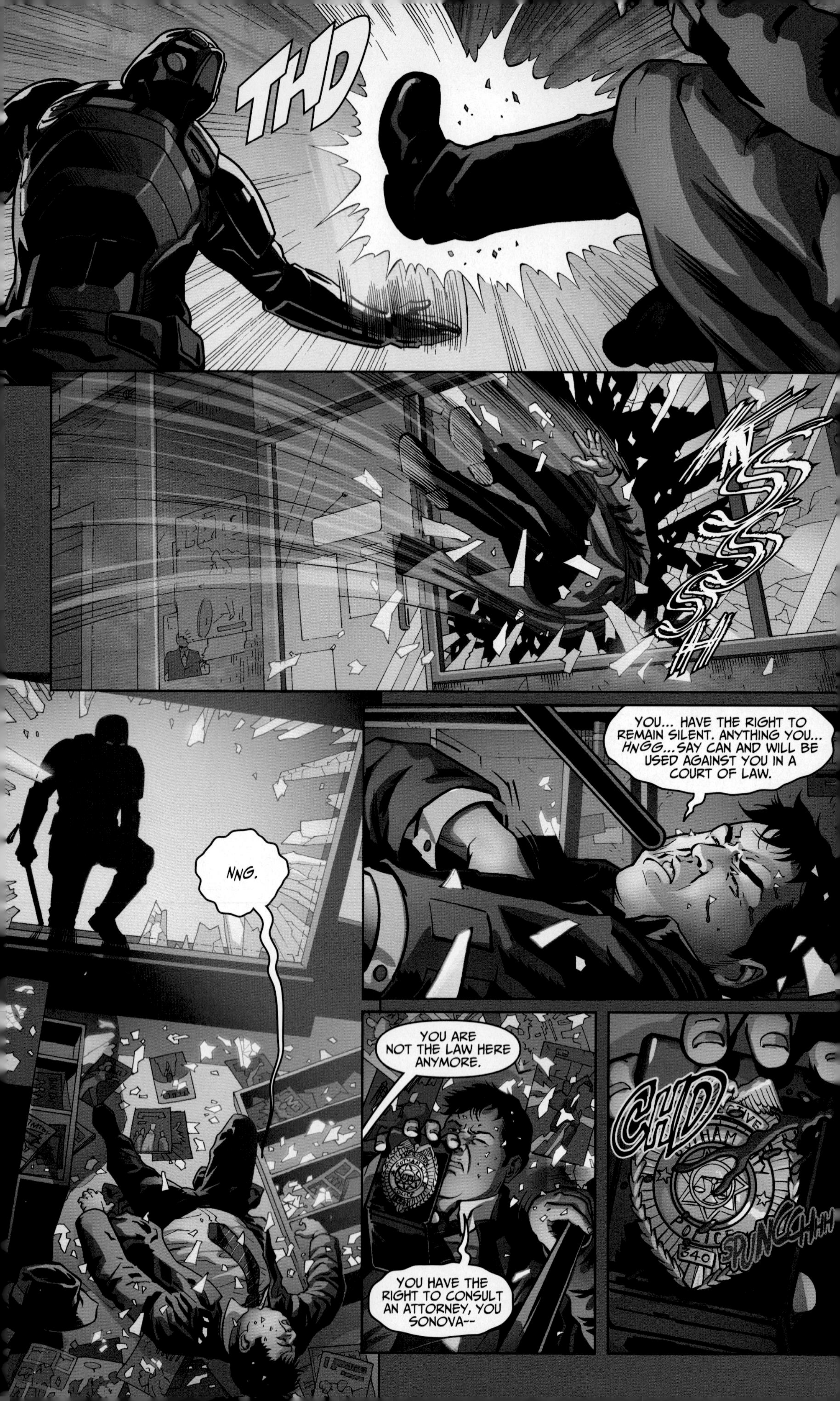
THD
KSSSSH
NNG.
YOU... HAVE THE RIGHT TO REMAIN SILENT. ANYTHING YOU... HNGG...SAY CAN AND WILL BE USED AGAINST YOU IN A COURT OF LAW.
YOU ARE NOT THE LAW HERE ANYMORE.
YOU HAVE THE RIGHT TO CONSULT AN ATTORNEY, YOU SONOVA--
CHD
SPUNCHHH
340

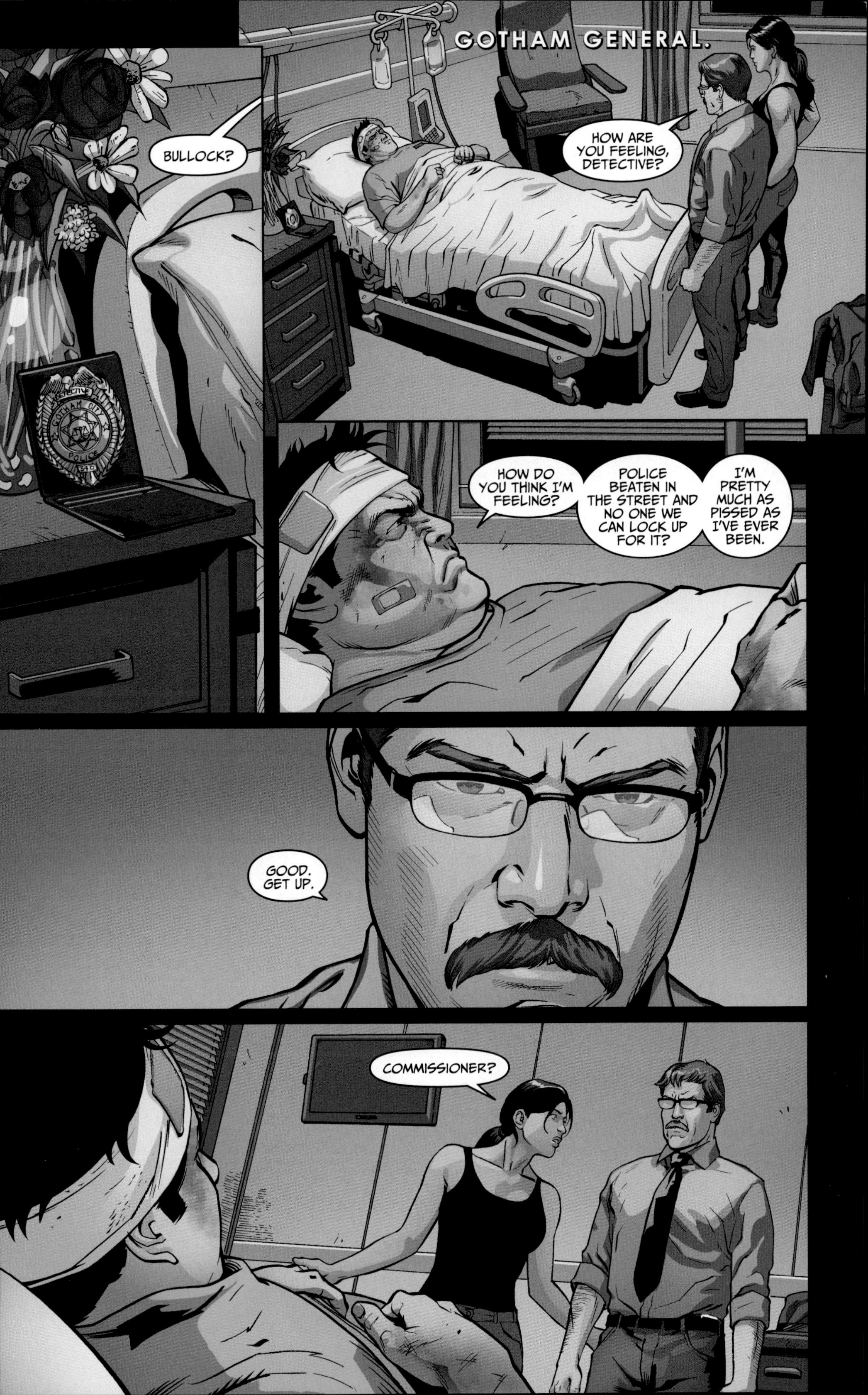
GOTHAM GENERAL.
BULLOCK?
HOW ARE YOU FEELING, DETECTIVE?
DETECTIVE
GOTHAM CITY
POLICE
HOW DO YOU THINK I'M FEELING?
POLICE BEATEN IN THE STREET AND NO ONE WE CAN LOCK UP FOR IT?
I'M PRETTY MUCH AS PISSED AS I'VE EVER BEEN.
GOOD. GET UP.
COMMISSIONER?

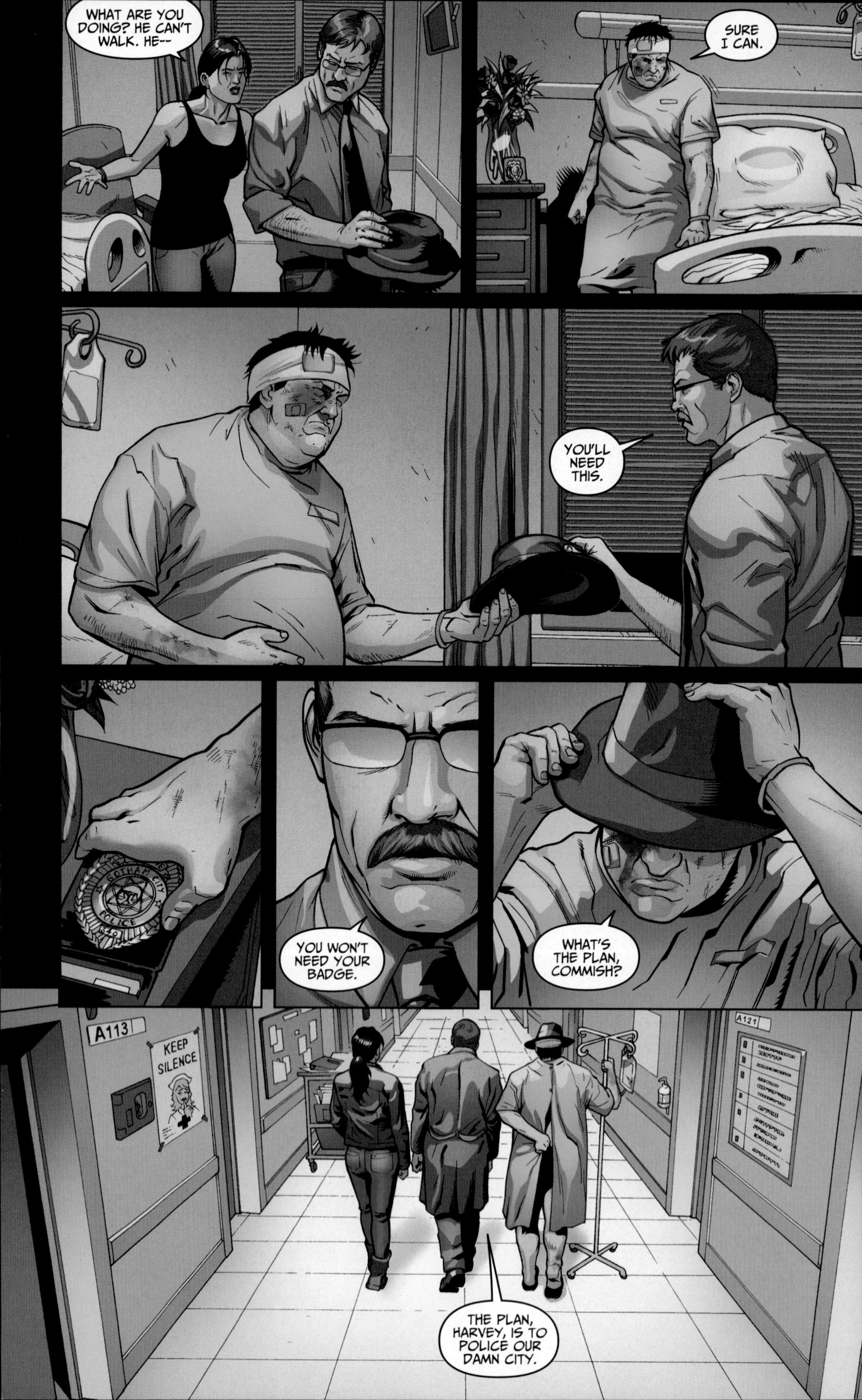
WHAT ARE YOU DOING? HE CAN'T WALK. HE--
SURE I CAN.
YOU'LL NEED THIS.
GOTHAM CITY POLICE
YOU WON'T NEED YOUR BADGE.
WHAT'S THE PLAN, COMMISH?
A113
KEEP SILENCE
A121
THE PLAN, HARVEY, IS TO POLICE OUR DAMN CITY.

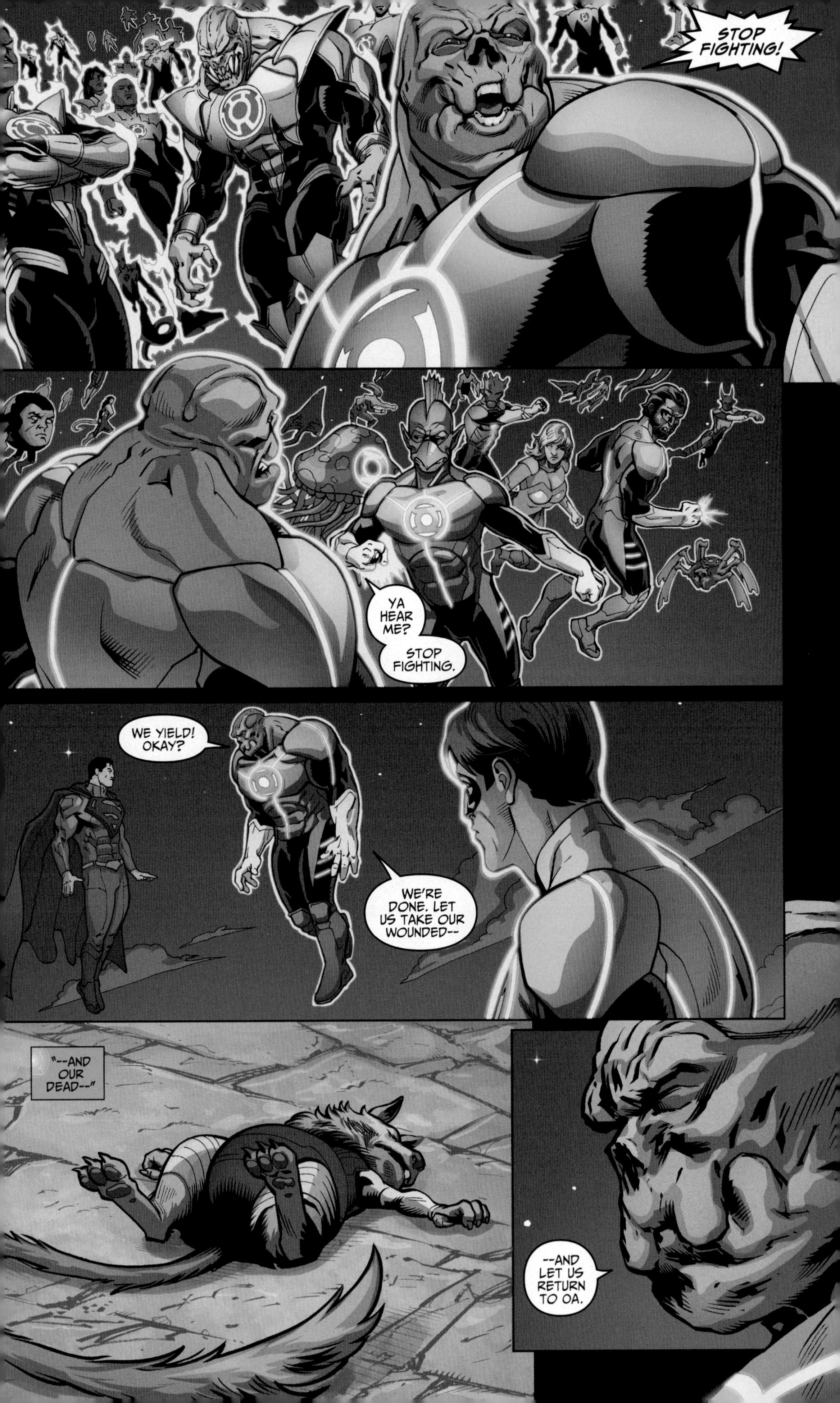
STOP FIGHTING!
YA HEAR ME?
STOP FIGHTING.
WE YIELD! OKAY?
WE'RE DONE. LET US TAKE OUR WOUNDED--
"--AND OUR DEAD--"
--AND LET US RETURN TO OA.

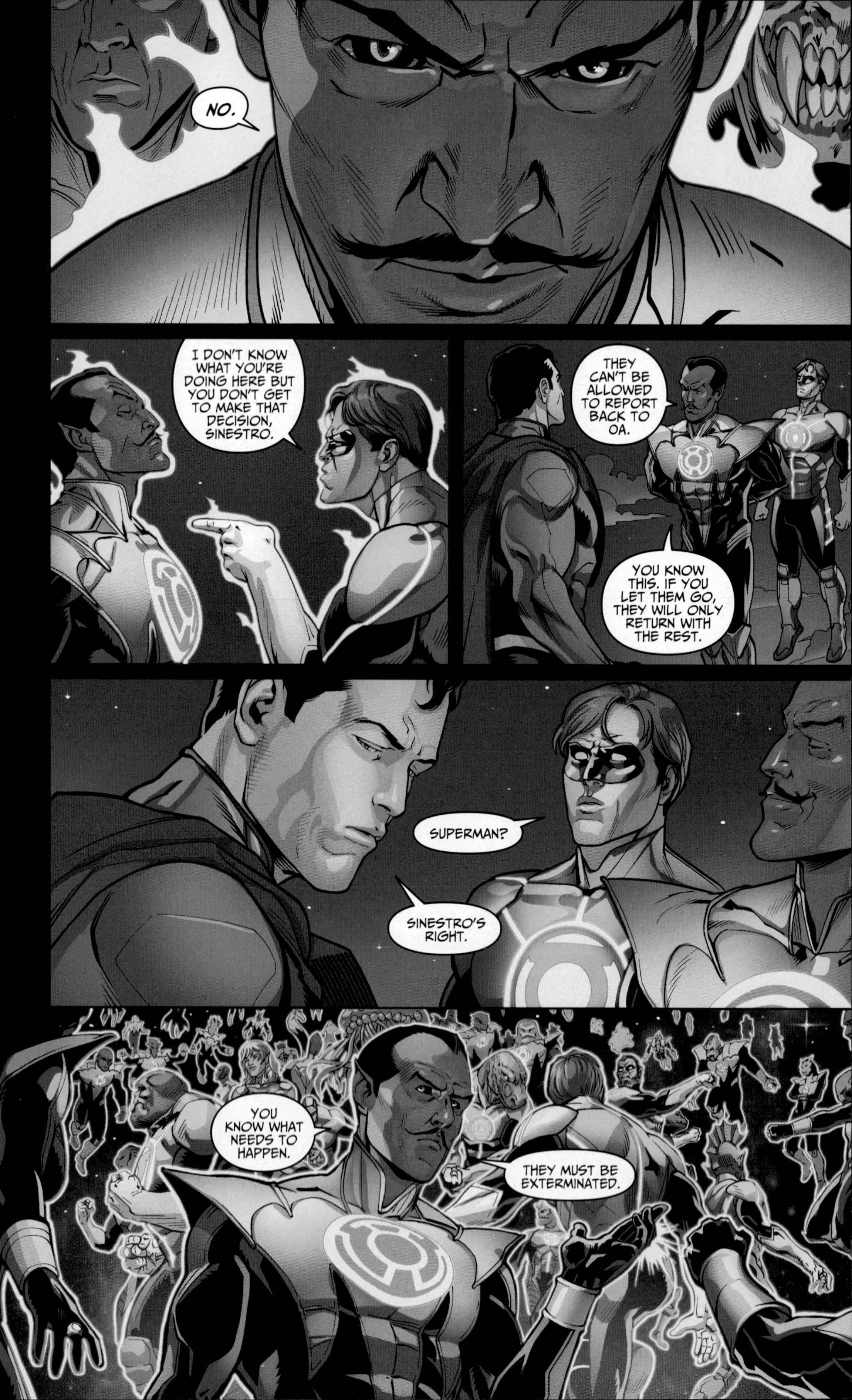
NO.
I DON'T KNOW WHAT YOU'RE DOING HERE BUT YOU DON'T GET TO MAKE THAT DECISION, SINESTRO.
THEY CAN'T BE ALLOWED TO REPORT BACK TO OA.
YOU KNOW THIS. IF YOU LET THEM GO, THEY WILL ONLY RETURN WITH THE REST.
SUPERMAN?
SINESTRO'S RIGHT.
YOU KNOW WHAT NEEDS TO HAPPEN.
THEY MUST BE EXTERMINATED.

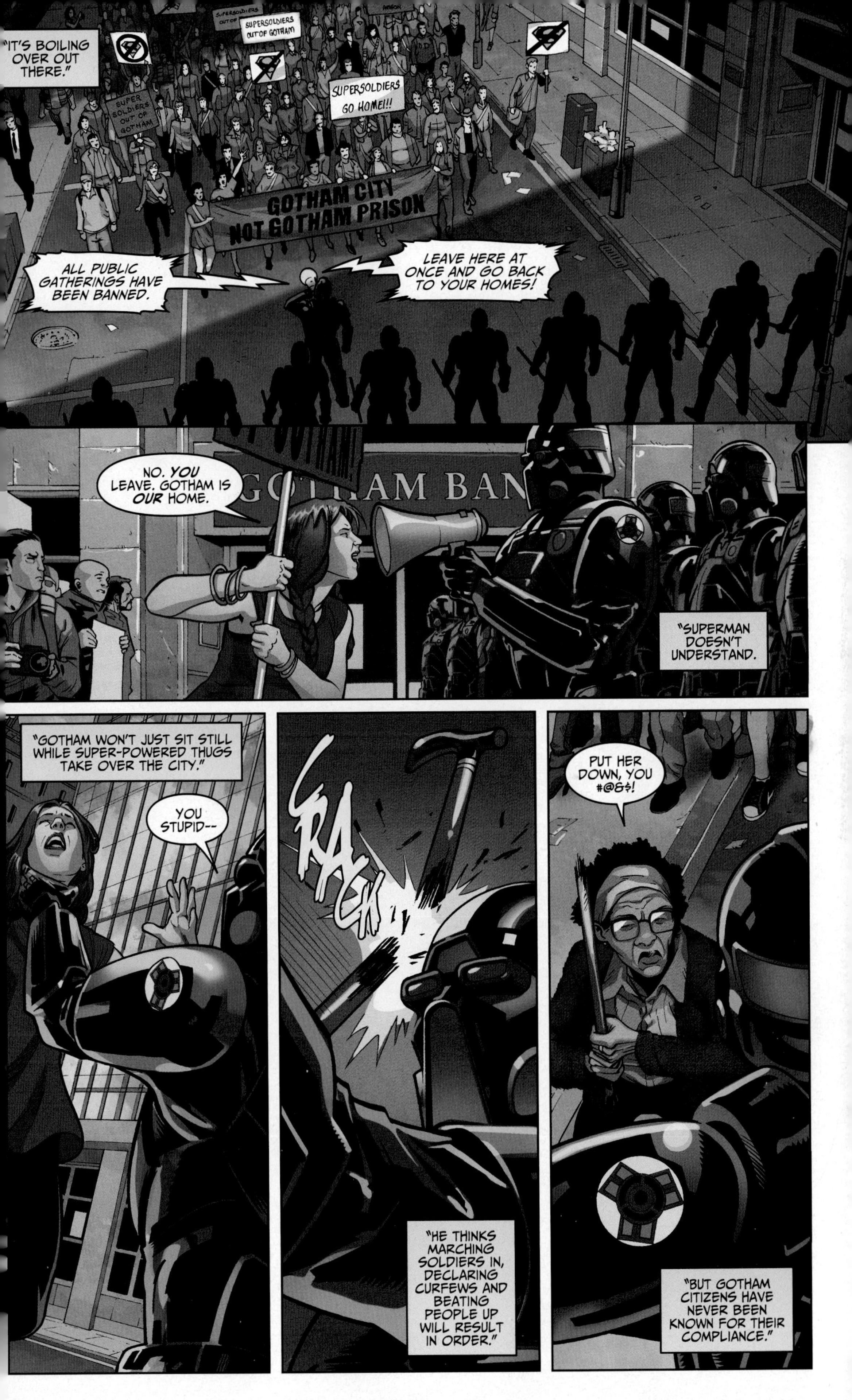

"IT'S BOILING OVER OUT THERE."
SUPERSOLDIERS OUT OF GOTHAM
SUPER SOLDIERS OUT OF GOTHAM
SUPERSOLDIERS GO HOME!!!
GOTHAM CITY NOT GOTHAM PRISON
ALL PUBLIC GATHERINGS HAVE BEEN BANNED.
LEAVE HERE AT ONCE AND GO BACK TO YOUR HOMES!
GOTHAM BAN
NO. *YOU* LEAVE. GOTHAM IS *OUR* HOME.
"SUPERMAN DOESN'T UNDERSTAND.
"GOTHAM WON'T JUST SIT STILL WHILE SUPER-POWERED THUGS TAKE OVER THE CITY."
YOU STUPID--
CRACK
"HE THINKS MARCHING SOLDIERS IN, DECLARING CURFEWS AND BEATING PEOPLE UP WILL RESULT IN ORDER."
PUT HER DOWN, YOU #@&$!
"BUT GOTHAM CITIZENS HAVE NEVER BEEN KNOWN FOR THEIR COMPLIANCE."

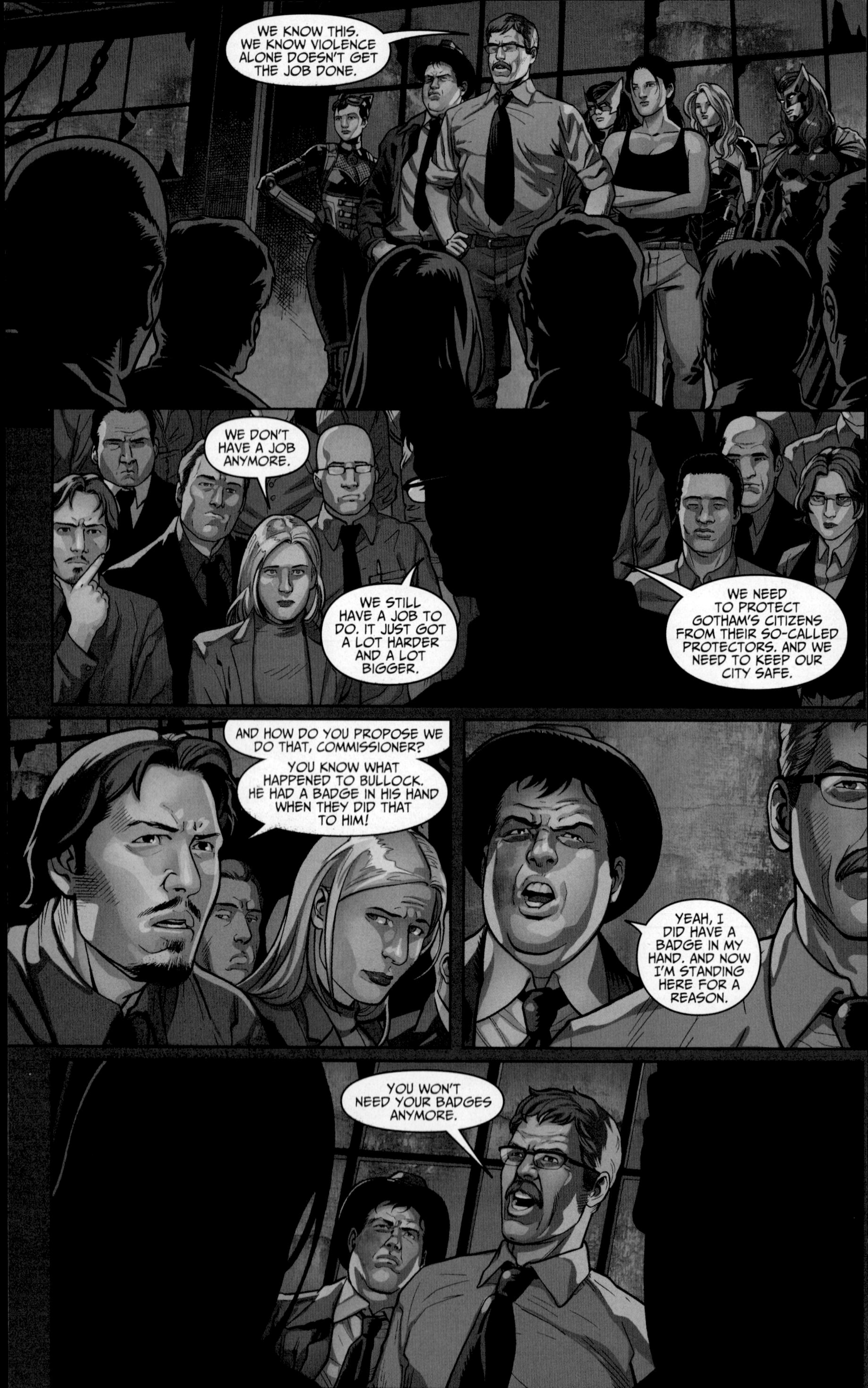
WE KNOW THIS. WE KNOW VIOLENCE ALONE DOESN'T GET THE JOB DONE.
WE DON'T HAVE A JOB ANYMORE.
WE STILL HAVE A JOB TO DO. IT JUST GOT A LOT HARDER AND A LOT BIGGER.
WE NEED TO PROTECT GOTHAM'S CITIZENS FROM THEIR SO-CALLED PROTECTORS. AND WE NEED TO KEEP OUR CITY SAFE.
AND HOW DO YOU PROPOSE WE DO THAT, COMMISSIONER?
YOU KNOW WHAT HAPPENED TO BULLOCK. HE HAD A BADGE IN HIS HAND WHEN THEY DID THAT TO HIM!
YEAH, I DID HAVE A BADGE IN MY HAND. AND NOW I'M STANDING HERE FOR A REASON.
YOU WON'T NEED YOUR BADGES ANYMORE.

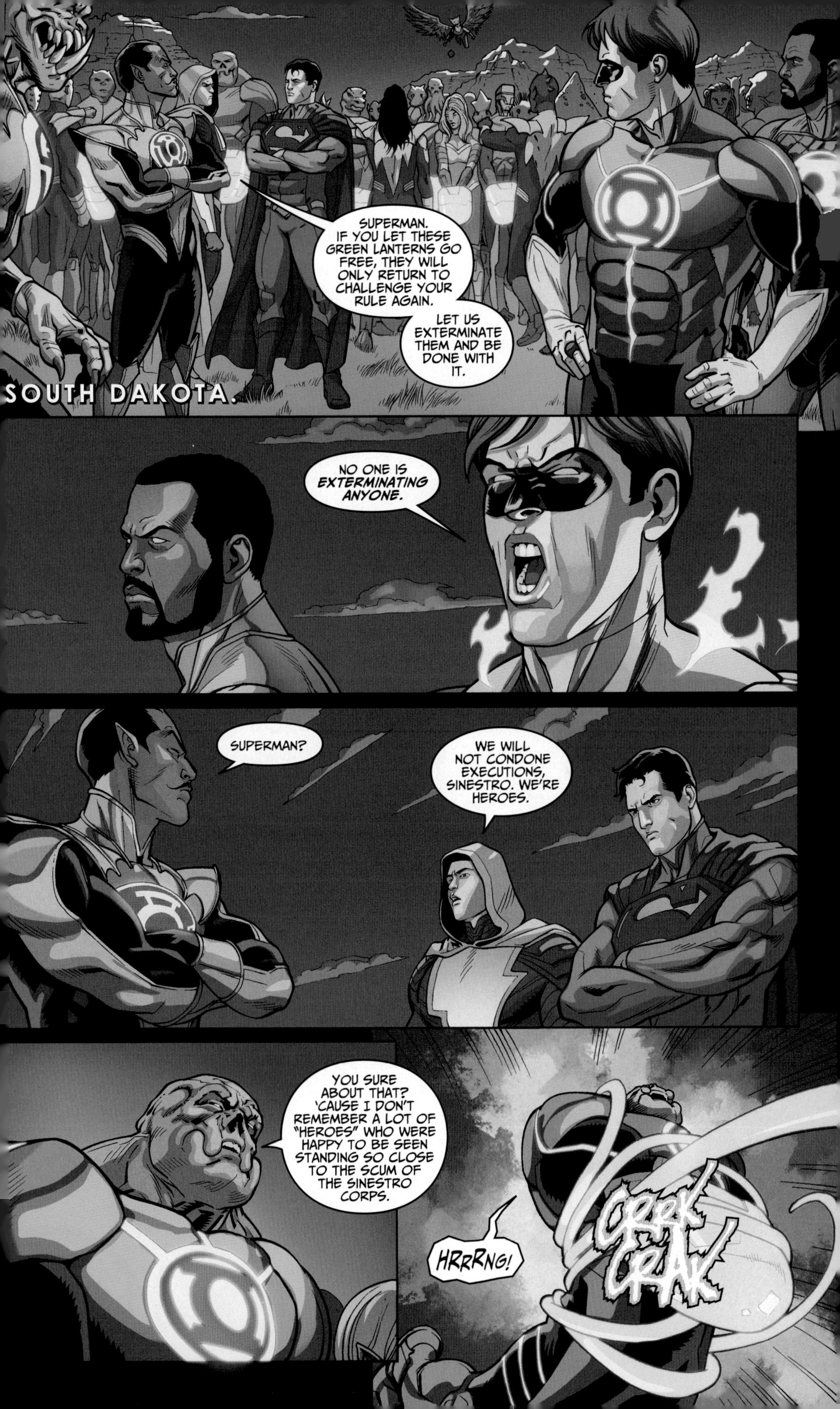

SOUTH DAKOTA.
SUPERMAN. IF YOU LET THESE GREEN LANTERNS GO FREE, THEY WILL ONLY RETURN TO CHALLENGE YOUR RULE AGAIN.
LET US EXTERMINATE THEM AND BE DONE WITH IT.
NO ONE IS *EXTERMINATING ANYONE.*
SUPERMAN?
WE WILL NOT CONDONE EXECUTIONS, SINESTRO. WE'RE HEROES.
YOU SURE ABOUT THAT? 'CAUSE I DON'T REMEMBER A LOT OF "HEROES" WHO WERE HAPPY TO BE SEEN STANDING SO CLOSE TO THE SCUM OF THE SINESTRO CORPS.
HRRRNG!
CRRK CRAK

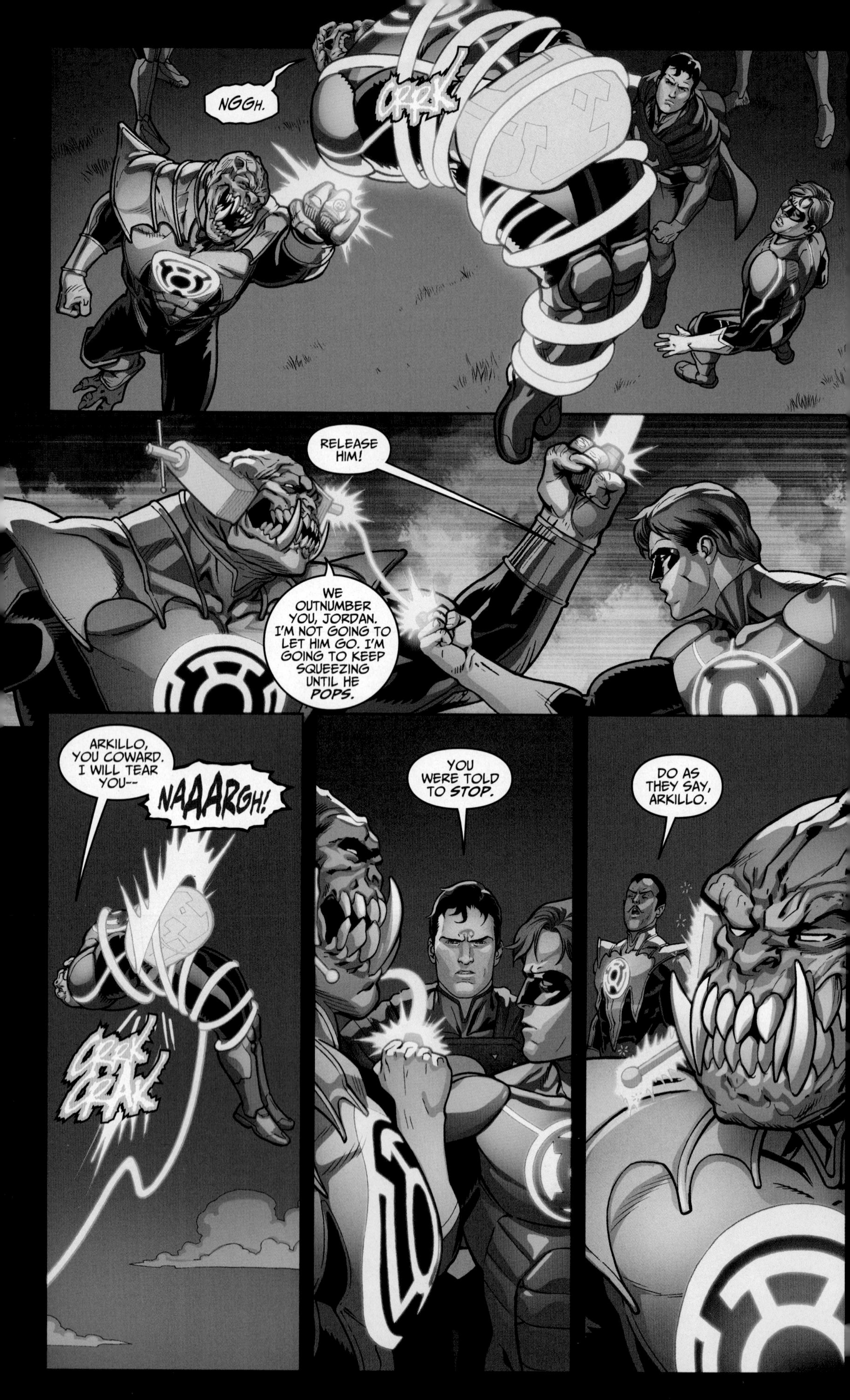
NGGH.
CRRK
RELEASE HIM!
WE OUTNUMBER YOU, JORDAN. I'M NOT GOING TO LET HIM GO. I'M GOING TO KEEP SQUEEZING UNTIL HE POPS.
ARKILLO, YOU COWARD. I WILL TEAR YOU--
NAAARGH!
CRRK CRAK
YOU WERE TOLD TO STOP.
DO AS THEY SAY, ARKILLO.

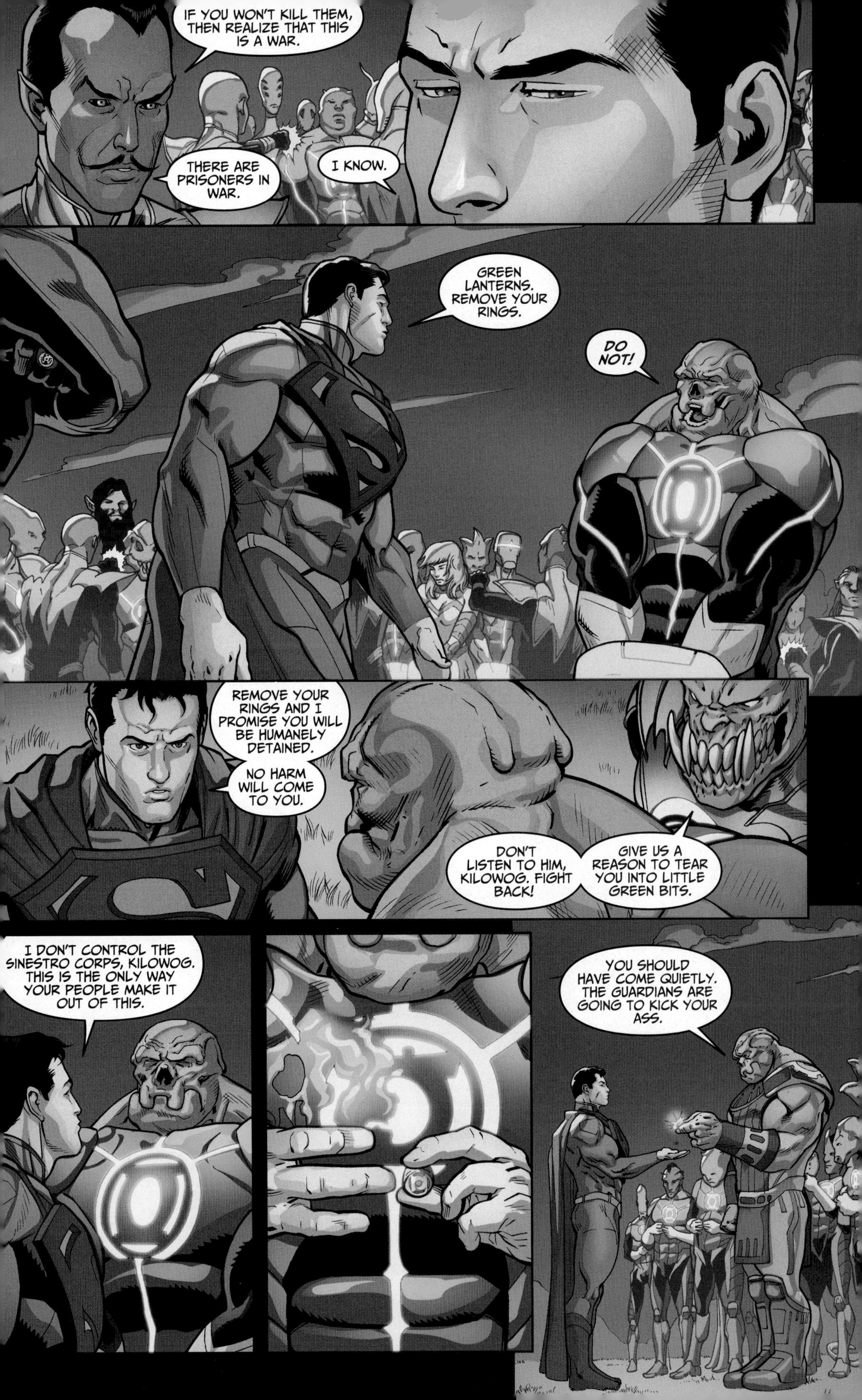
IF YOU WON'T KILL THEM, THEN REALIZE THAT THIS IS A WAR.
THERE ARE PRISONERS IN WAR.
I KNOW.
GREEN LANTERNS. REMOVE YOUR RINGS.
DO NOT!
REMOVE YOUR RINGS AND I PROMISE YOU WILL BE HUMANELY DETAINED.
NO HARM WILL COME TO YOU.
DON'T LISTEN TO HIM, KILOWOG. FIGHT BACK!
GIVE US A REASON TO TEAR YOU INTO LITTLE GREEN BITS.
I DON'T CONTROL THE SINESTRO CORPS, KILOWOG. THIS IS THE ONLY WAY YOUR PEOPLE MAKE IT OUT OF THIS.
YOU SHOULD HAVE COME QUIETLY. THE GUARDIANS ARE GOING TO KICK YOUR ASS.

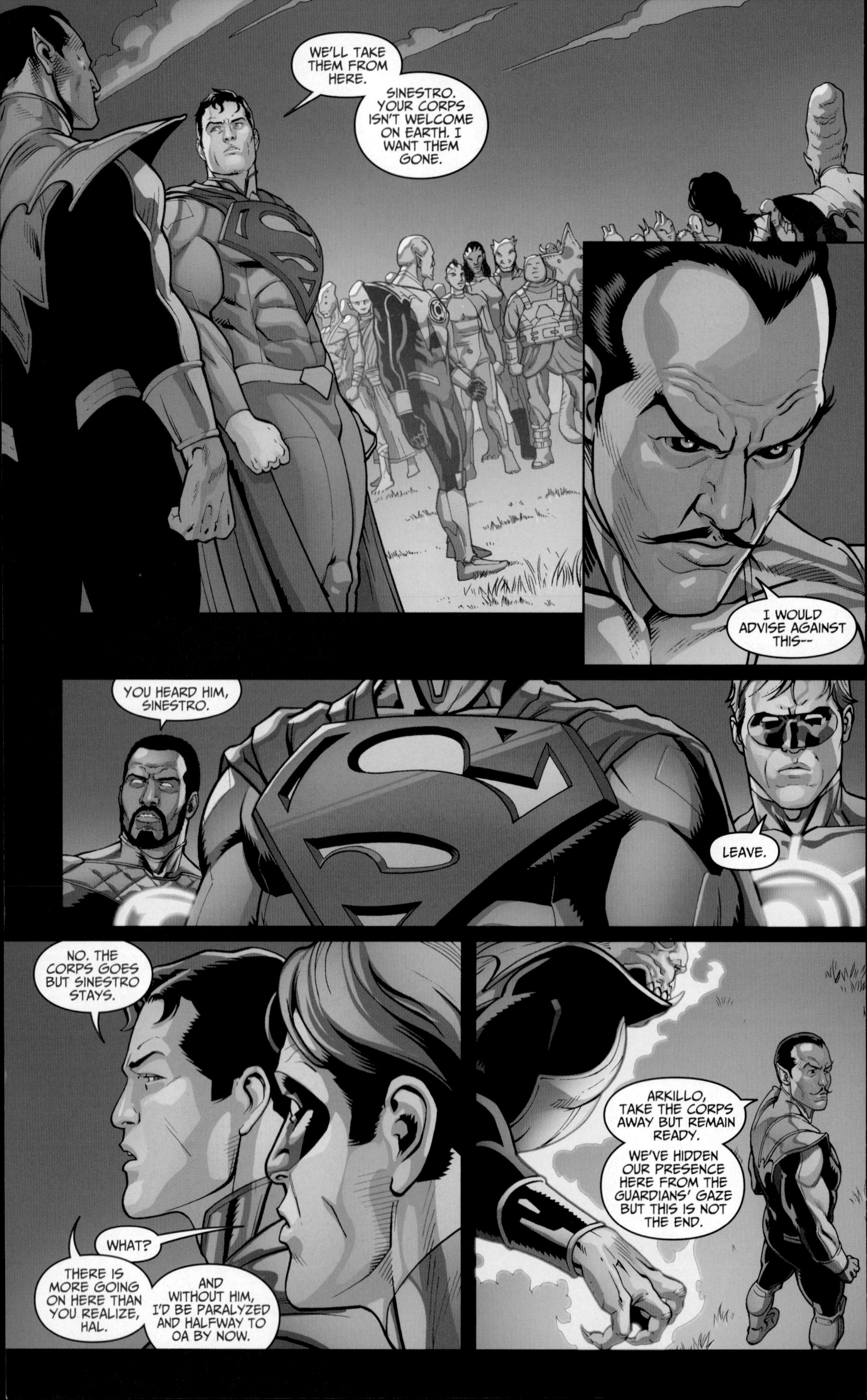

WE'LL TAKE THEM FROM HERE.
SINESTRO. YOUR CORPS ISN'T WELCOME ON EARTH. I WANT THEM GONE.
I WOULD ADVISE AGAINST THIS--
YOU HEARD HIM, SINESTRO.
LEAVE.
NO. THE CORPS GOES BUT SINESTRO STAYS.
WHAT?
THERE IS MORE GOING ON HERE THAN YOU REALIZE, HAL.
AND WITHOUT HIM, I'D BE PARALYZED AND HALFWAY TO OA BY NOW.
ARKILLO, TAKE THE CORPS AWAY BUT REMAIN READY.
WE'VE HIDDEN OUR PRESENCE HERE FROM THE GUARDIANS' GAZE BUT THIS IS NOT THE END.

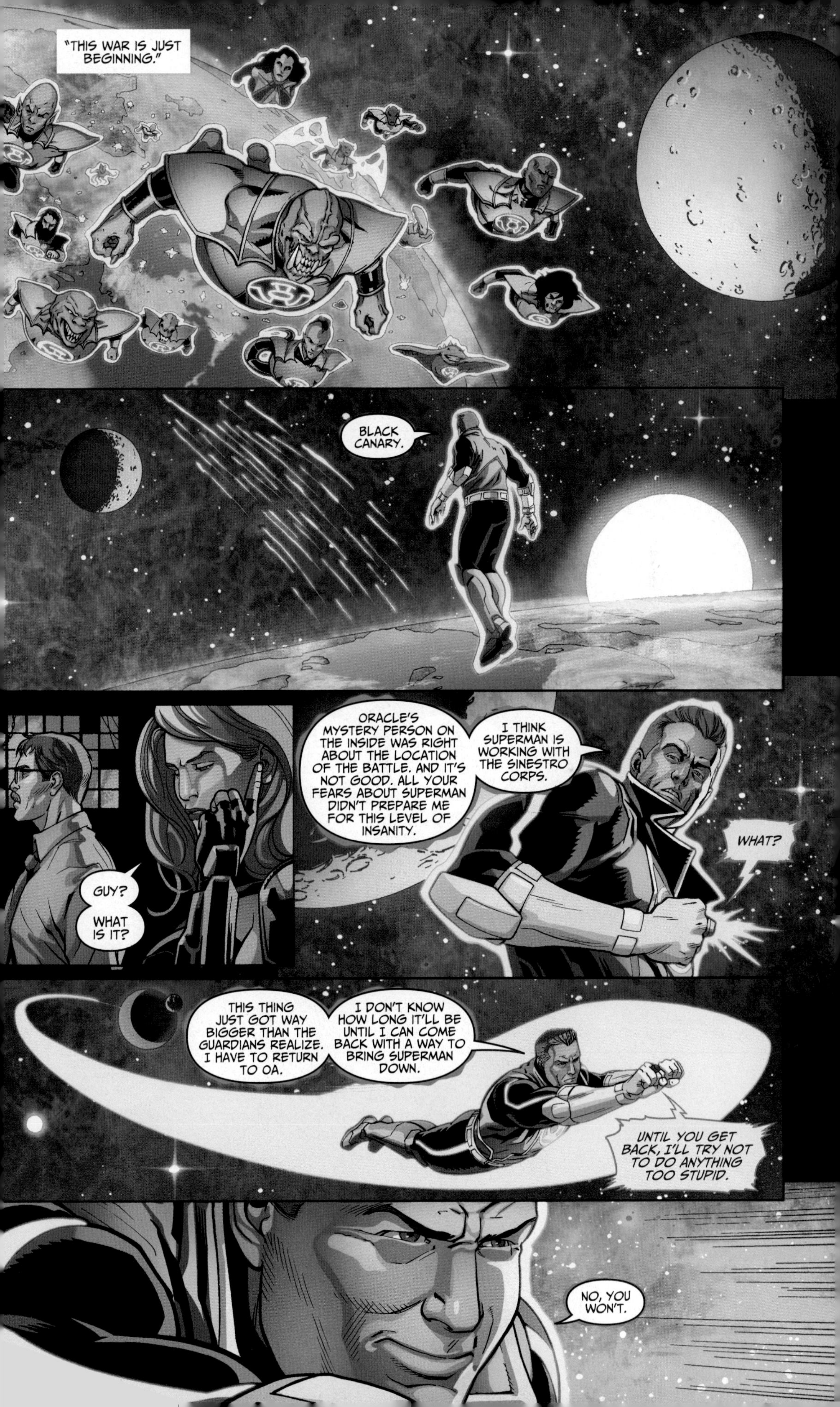
"THIS WAR IS JUST BEGINNING."
BLACK CANARY.
ORACLE'S MYSTERY PERSON ON THE INSIDE WAS RIGHT ABOUT THE LOCATION OF THE BATTLE. AND IT'S NOT GOOD. ALL YOUR FEARS ABOUT SUPERMAN DIDN'T PREPARE ME FOR THIS LEVEL OF INSANITY.
I THINK SUPERMAN IS WORKING WITH THE SINESTRO CORPS.
GUY?
WHAT IS IT?
WHAT?
THIS THING JUST GOT WAY BIGGER THAN THE GUARDIANS REALIZE. I HAVE TO RETURN TO OA.
I DON'T KNOW HOW LONG IT'LL BE UNTIL I CAN COME BACK WITH A WAY TO BRING SUPERMAN DOWN.
UNTIL YOU GET BACK, I'LL TRY NOT TO DO ANYTHING TOO STUPID.
NO, YOU WON'T.

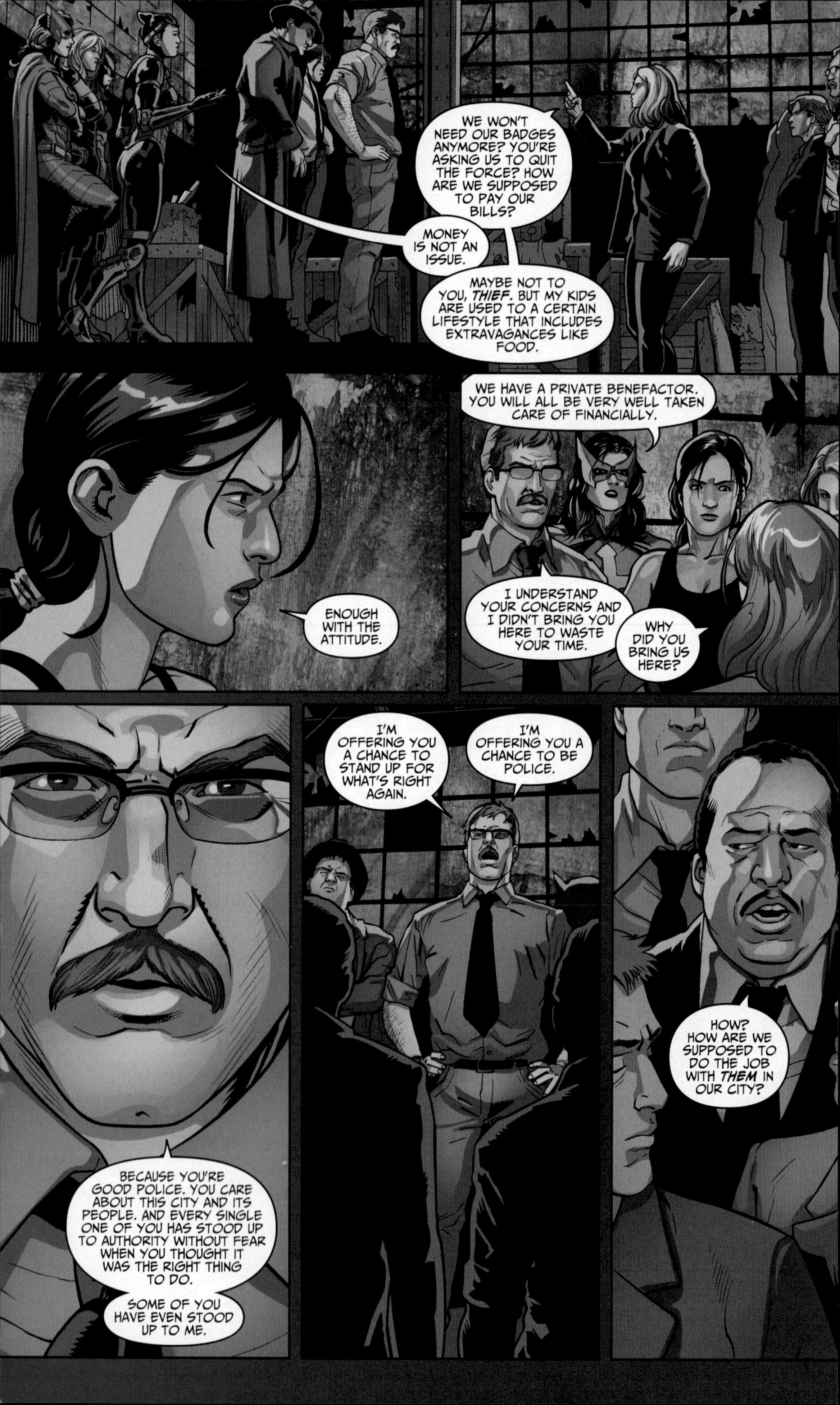
WE WON'T NEED OUR BADGES ANYMORE? YOU'RE ASKING US TO QUIT THE FORCE? HOW ARE WE SUPPOSED TO PAY OUR BILLS?
MONEY IS NOT AN ISSUE.
MAYBE NOT TO YOU, *THIEF.* BUT MY KIDS ARE USED TO A CERTAIN LIFESTYLE THAT INCLUDES EXTRAVAGANCES LIKE FOOD.
ENOUGH WITH THE ATTITUDE.
WE HAVE A PRIVATE BENEFACTOR. YOU WILL ALL BE VERY WELL TAKEN CARE OF FINANCIALLY.
I UNDERSTAND YOUR CONCERNS AND I DIDN'T BRING YOU HERE TO WASTE YOUR TIME.
WHY DID YOU BRING US HERE?
BECAUSE YOU'RE GOOD POLICE. YOU CARE ABOUT THIS CITY AND ITS PEOPLE. AND EVERY SINGLE ONE OF YOU HAS STOOD UP TO AUTHORITY WITHOUT FEAR WHEN YOU THOUGHT IT WAS THE RIGHT THING TO DO.
SOME OF YOU HAVE EVEN STOOD UP TO ME.
I'M OFFERING YOU A CHANCE TO STAND UP FOR WHAT'S RIGHT AGAIN.
I'M OFFERING YOU A CHANCE TO BE POLICE.
HOW? HOW ARE WE SUPPOSED TO DO THE JOB WITH *THEM* IN OUR CITY?

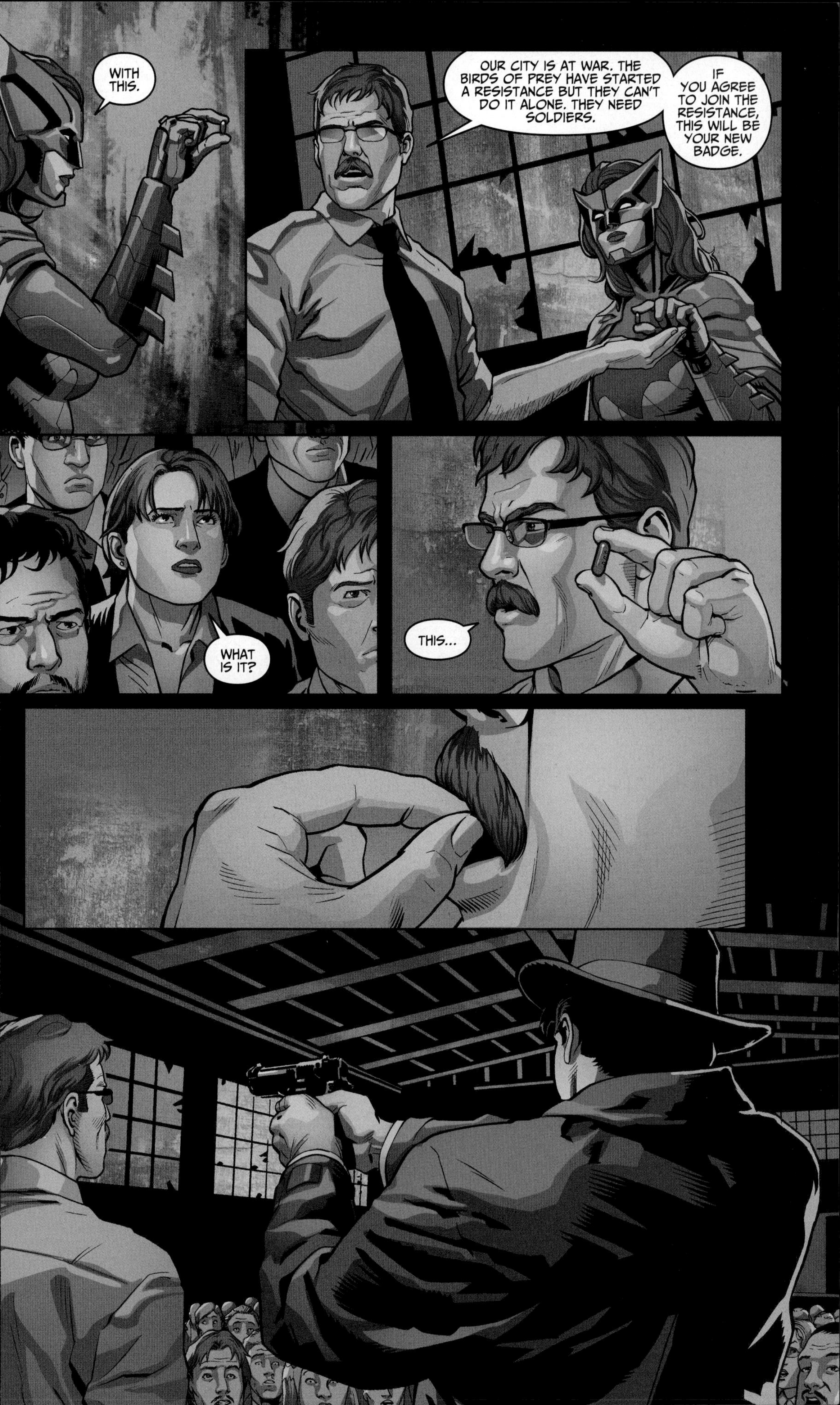
WITH THIS.
OUR CITY IS AT WAR. THE BIRDS OF PREY HAVE STARTED A RESISTANCE BUT THEY CAN'T DO IT ALONE. THEY NEED SOLDIERS.
IF YOU AGREE TO JOIN THE RESISTANCE, THIS WILL BE YOUR NEW BADGE.
WHAT IS IT?
THIS...

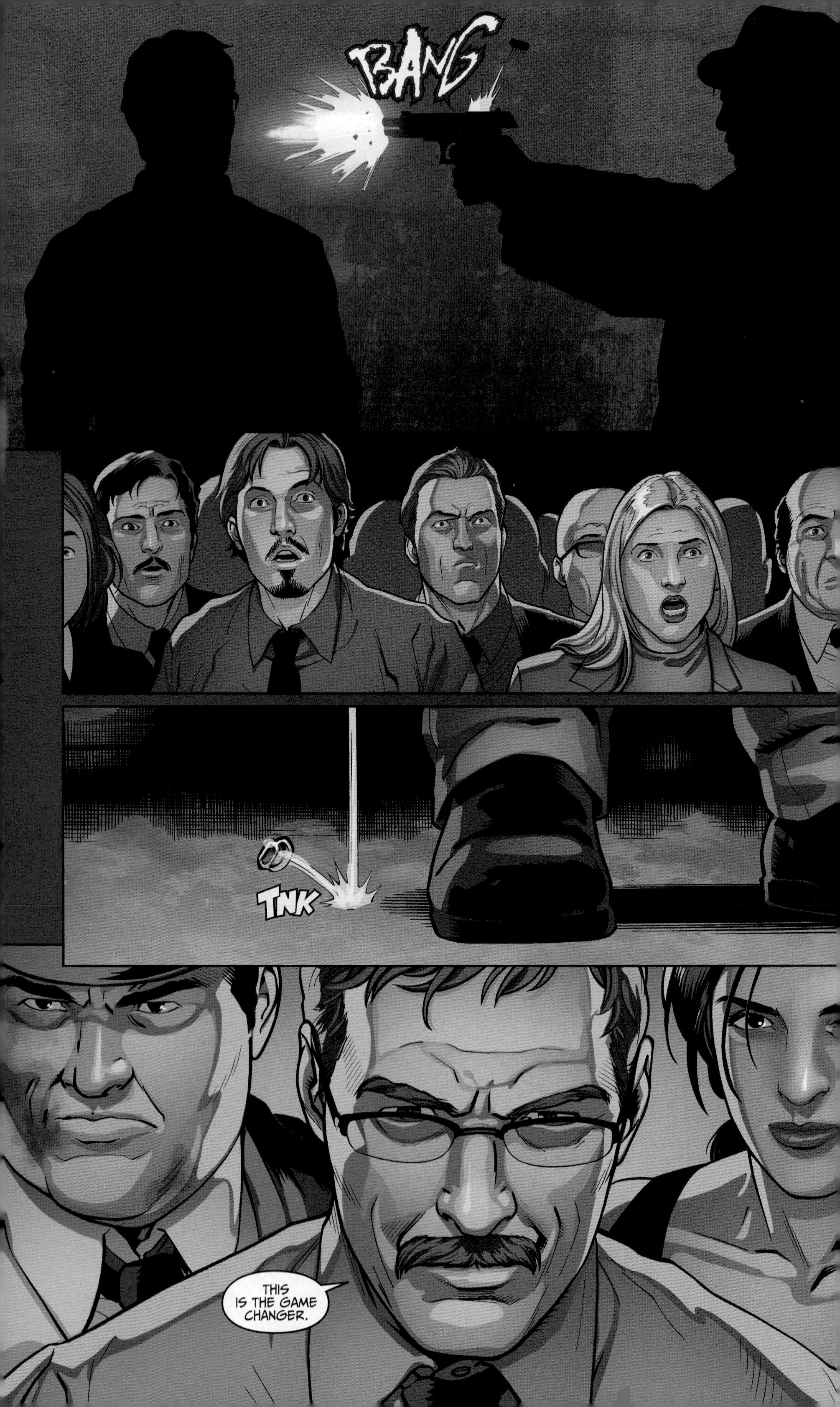
BANG
TNK
THIS IS THE GAME CHANGER.

Injustice Year Two #2 DC Collectibles Variant Cover

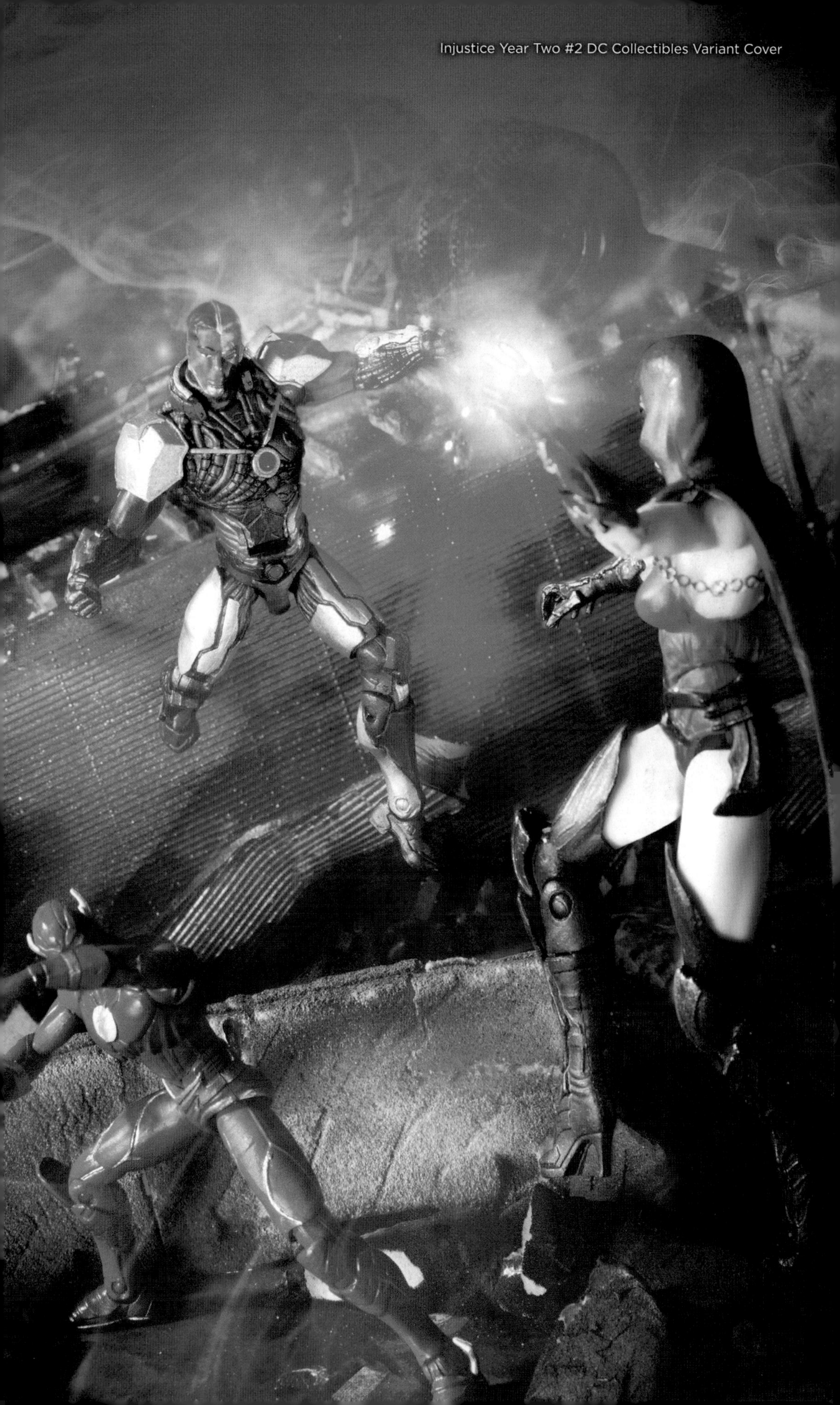

Pencils from Injustice: Year Two #4 by Bruno Redondo

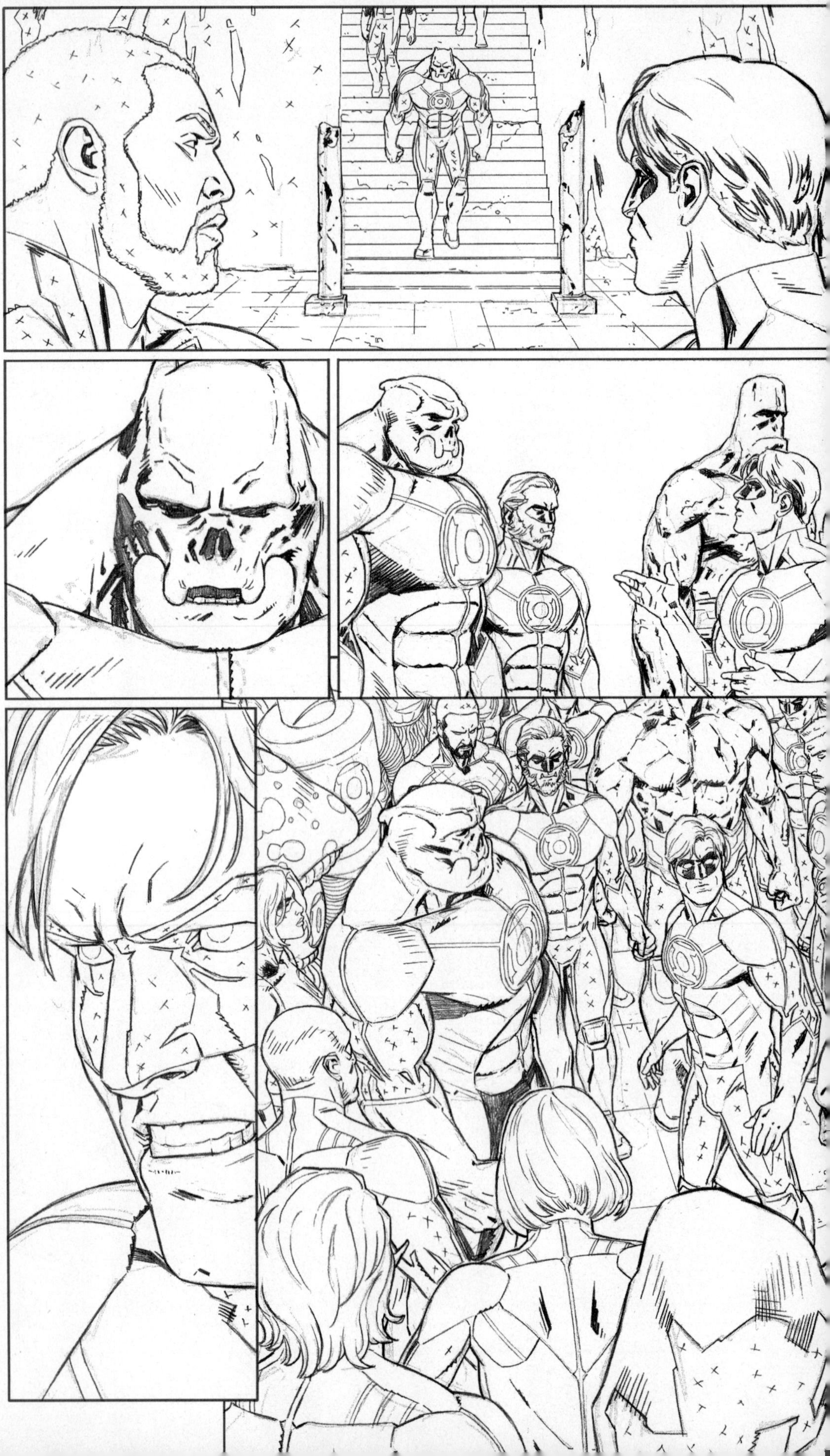

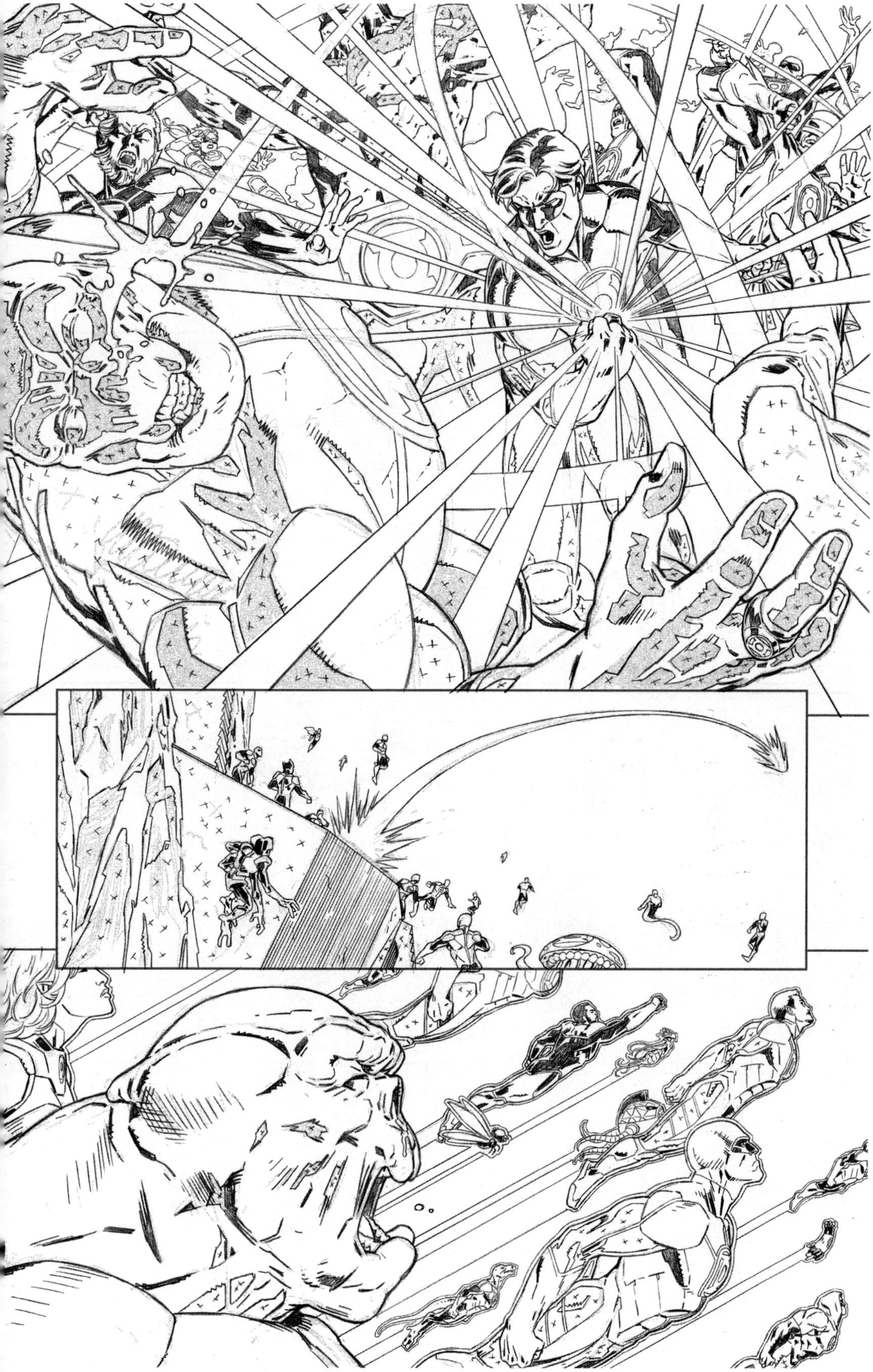

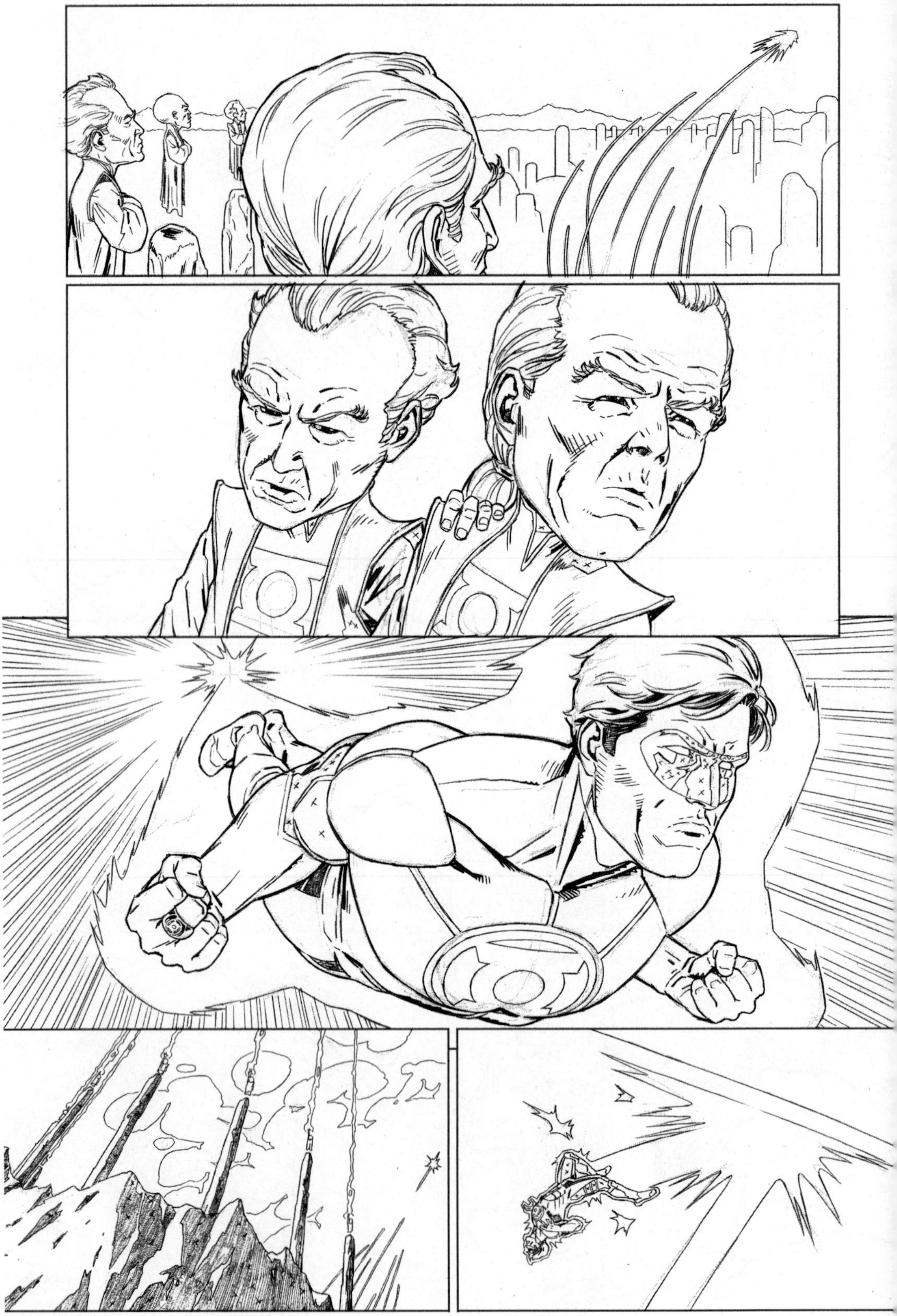

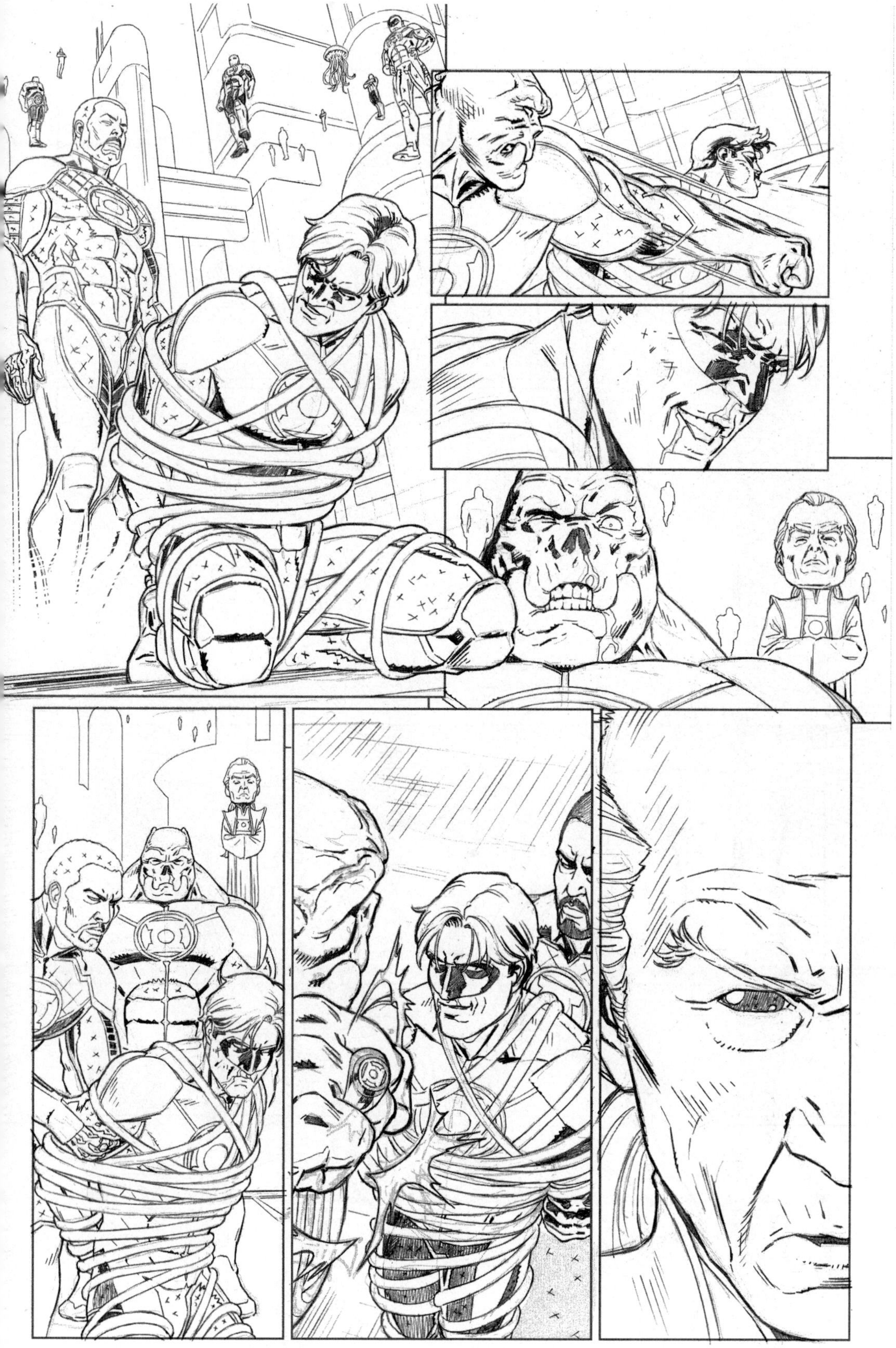

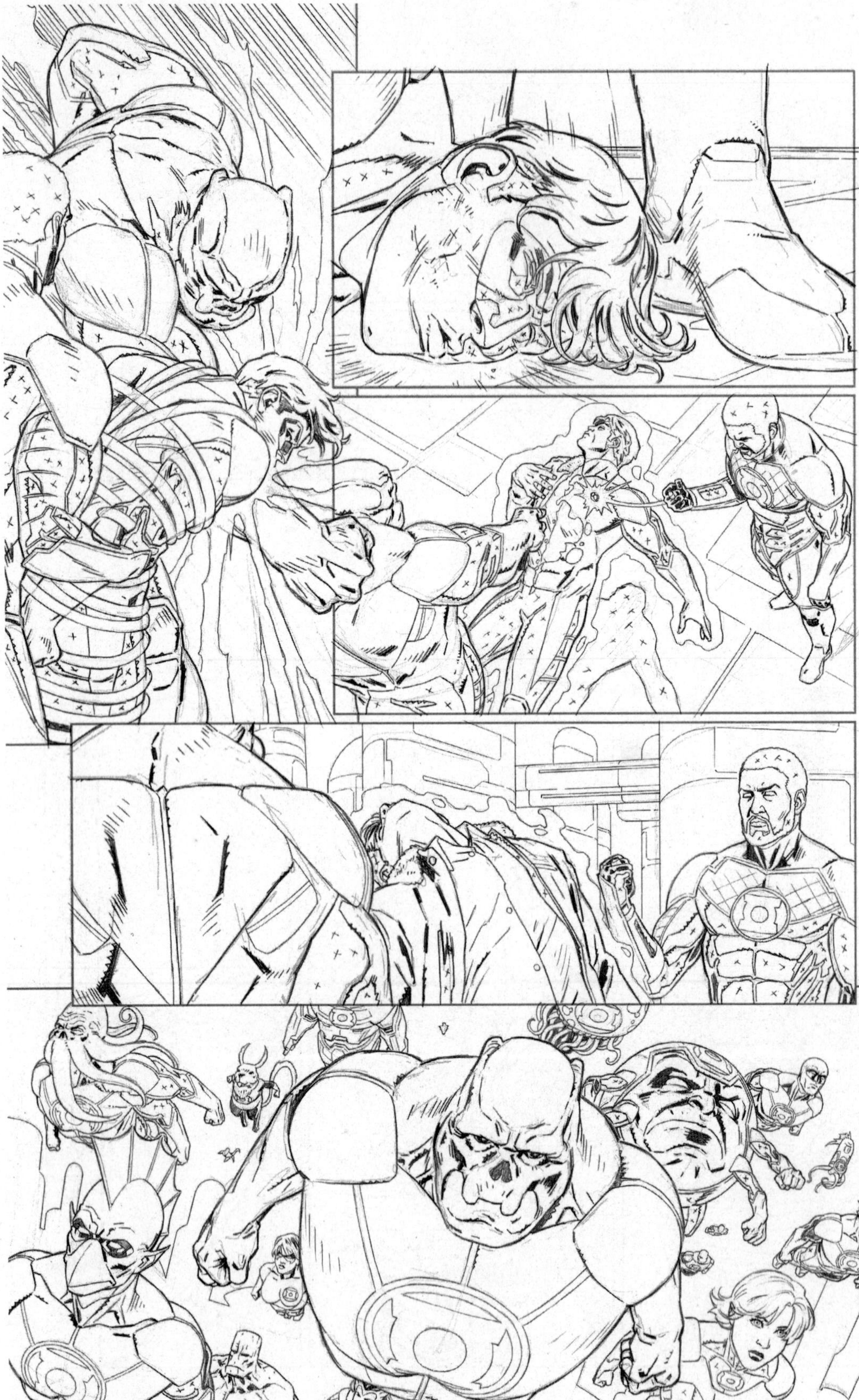